The Interactional Architecture of the Language Classroom: A Conversation Analysis Perspective

Blackwell Publishing

Language Learning Monograph Series

Richard Young, Editor
Alexander Z. Guiora, General Editor

The Interactional Architecture of the Language Classroom:
A Conversation Analysis Perspective

Paul Seedhouse
University of Newcastle upon Tyne

Blackwell
Publishing

Blackwell Publishing, Inc.
350 Main Street
Malden, MA 02148
USA

Blackwell Publishing, Ltd.
9600 Garsington Road
Oxford OX4 2DQ
United Kingdom

Library of Congress Cataloging-in-Publication Data

Seedhouse, Paul.
    The interactional architecture of the language classroom: a conversation analysis perspective / Paul Seedhouse.
        p. cm. – (Language learning. Monograph series)
    Includes bibliographical references and index.
    ISBN 1-4051-2009-6 (alk. paper)
    1. Conversation analysis. 2. Discourse analysis. 3. Oral communication.
4. Language arts. 5. Interaction analysis in education. 6. Second language acquisition. I. Title. II. Series.

P95.45.S44 2004
302.3'46–dc22   2004052898

Contents

Series Editor's Foreword

Like most human activity, learning a second language (L2) happens in a social context. Two questions about social context have occupied the attention of second language acquisition (SLA) researchers over the years. First, is it necessary to study the social context of learning in order to understand SLA? And second, if it is necessary, how does social context influence the process of second language acquisition? Until recently, many SLA scholars have taken the position that the context of acquisition is minimally relevant, and they have framed the development of second language knowledge as a cognitive process located in the mind-brain of an individual learner. The role of social context in this theory is simply to provide input to cognition, but more interesting for these researchers is the way that knowledge of a second language develops.

Scholars who admit the importance of social context in SLA recognize that the vast majority of learners acquire a second language in a unique social context that is recognized throughout the world as a classroom. For many years, educationists have described the unique social properties of classrooms, and in the past few decades linguists have begun to describe the characteristics of the talk that happens in classrooms—talk that provides a critical context for language learning. For many second language scholars, however, classroom talk is still of relatively minor relevance. Some recent SLA textbooks, for instance, limit their treatment of the role of formal instruction to a single chapter. This apparent lack of attention to the social and linguistic context of classrooms is at first sight surprising given that the classroom context is so pervasive and also that classroom researchers have for many years had available to them systematic methods for coding and describing talk in the classroom. Despite this, classroom researchers have so far made little progress in answering the essential cognitive question of how a learner's knowledge of a second language develops.

Perhaps the reason why research into the social and linguistic context of the classroom has had so little influence on cognitive theories of second language learning is that the traditional focus in SLA has been on the acquisition of the linguistic system. Such a view of what is learned in second language acquisition is not, however, without its critics. The question of whether classroom learning involves the acquisition of abstract knowledge or, instead, the relevant object of study is learners' increasing participation in relevant discursive practices was debated a decade ago in *Educational Researcher*. In that debate, Anna Sfard described these two different ways of conceptualizing learning as the "acquisition metaphor" and the "participation metaphor." The name of the field of SLA is itself an indication that scholars of second language acquisition have considered L2 learning to be just that: the acquisition of abstract linguistic knowledge.

The notion of learning as increasing participation in social activity is clearly a very different view of second language development from the cognitive one, but if we adopt the participation metaphor for learning, the relevance of social context becomes clear, and the central question in SLA becomes understanding the organization of talk—direct interaction between persons—as the primordial site of sociality. Conversation analysis (CA), as theorized and practiced by Harvey Sacks, Emanuel Schegloff, and their many students and collaborators, has developed into a highly effective means for recording and transcribing naturally occurring talk in interaction. The aim of conversation analysis is to understand the organization of talk and persons' experience of it. Because participants' *experience* of talk is at the heart of ethnomethodological conversation analysis, CA is not simply a means for linguists to understand the organization of turn-taking, sequence, and repair of talk in general, but instead CA aims to understand what this organization means in a particular conversation for particular participants.

And yet, not every conversation or combination of participants is a world unto itself. Conversations in classrooms between a teacher and students or among students are ways in which participants create and recognize the social institution of a classroom. Although such conversations are "natural" in the sense that they are unscripted, they are also ways in which one participant (usually the teacher) achieves certain institutional goals. Three goals can be recognized in a second language classroom: a focus on the students' accurate production of linguistic forms, the active production of meaningful talk with a view to improving students' fluency in the second language, and a focus on students' achievement of success in a particular task whose outcome may not be linguistic. These diverse instructional goals provide contexts in which participants adopt different understandings of the organization of talk. The organization of conversational repair in a form-and-accuracy context, for instance, often takes a different shape from repair in a task-oriented context, and participants experience the repairs differently. The detailed explication of the ecological relation between pedagogy and talk in second language classrooms is one of Paul Seedhouse's highly original contributions in this volume.

There have been other book-length treatments of second language classroom discourse from the perspective of conversation analysis, but these other books have focused on a small number of lessons or on a small number of classes. A second original contribution of the present volume is that Seedhouse recognizes the tremendous diversity of second language classrooms: Learners differ in their first language(s), whether they speak the same first language or multiple languages, their age, their geographical location, the cultural context of instruction, and so forth. And there are just as many relevant teacher variables. Seedhouse recognizes that diversity by incorporating seven distinct databases of classroom conversations in this study. By comparing talk across many classroom contexts he is able to show that irrespective of that diversity, the reflexive relationship between the pedagogical focus of the lesson and the organization of turn-taking, sequence, and repair holds.

Paul Seedhouse's *The Interactional Architecture of the Language Classroom: A Conversation Analysis Perspective* is the fourth volume in the *Language Learning Monograph Series*. The volumes in this series review recent findings and current theoretical positions, present new data and interpretations, and sketch interdisciplinary research programs. Volumes are authoritative statements by scholars who have led in the development of a particular line of interdisciplinary research and are intended to serve as a benchmark for interdisciplinary research in the years to come. The value of Seedhouse's interdisciplinary focus in the present volume is clear. He synthesizes research from SLA, applied linguistics, and conversation analysis and helps us to see connections among language pedagogy, classroom talk, and the structures of social action.

Richard Young
University of Wisconsin–Madison

Acknowledgments

This book is dedicated to my parents, Kenneth and June, and to my daughters, Alexandra and Francesca.

Enormous thanks are due to Richard Young for incisive and creative editing and advice as well as constant encouragement. I would also like to thank the following people for discussions and advice: Ron Boyle, Paul Drew, Maria Egbert, Graham Low, Numa Markee, Antony Peck, Keith Richards, Peter Roe, Li Wei, and David Westgate. I have also received valuable advice from a number of anonymous referees.

I would like to thank a great number of people (far too great to be listed here) for generously allowing me to record and transcribe their language lessons or for giving me access to their recordings and transcripts. In some cases they are acknowledged in the extracts or in Section 2.4.

I would also like to thank the Universities of York and Newcastle upon Tyne for travel grants and research leave.

Paul Seedhouse
paul.seedhouse@ncl.ac.uk

CHAPTER ONE

Conversation Analysis Methodology

In this chapter I will illustrate the basic principles of conversation analysis (CA) using extracts mostly from ordinary conversation; data will not be presented from the language classroom[1] (second language [L2] classroom) until later chapters, so that I am able to highlight similarities and differences. Ordinary conversation has a "baseline" status in CA (Sacks, Schegloff, & Jefferson, 1974), and L2 classroom interaction will be portrayed in Chapters 2 to 5 as a variety of institutional discourse. It is essential to specify explicitly the principles which underlie ordinary conversation in order to have a firm foundation on which to analyze talk in the institutional setting of L2 classrooms around the world.

This chapter explains the relationship between ethnomethodology and CA, outlining five fundamental principles which underlie ethnomethodology and hence CA. After outlining the aims and principles of CA, I introduce the interactional organizations of sequence (adjacency pairs), preference, turn taking and repair. I then explain the typical analytical procedures followed in CA and introduce the CA perspective on context. The chapter concludes with the argument that a "linguistic" version of CA has diverged from ethnomethodological CA.

1.1 History and Development of Conversation Analysis

A detailed history of the development of ethnomethodology and CA is not relevant to the discussion and may be found elsewhere (see Heritage, 1984b). Very briefly, however, the

1

principal originator of CA was Harvey Sacks, who worked at the University of California until his accidental death in 1975. It appears that his innovation was the result of the convergence of three factors: first, his acquaintance with Harold Garfinkel, the key figure in ethnomethodology; secondly, Sacks's decision to investigate the organization of social interaction by analyzing naturally occurring mundane talk; and thirdly, the new technology of audio recording, which enabled this analysis to take place. The idea with which Sacks was working was that there is "order at all points" in interaction, that is, that talk in interaction is systematically organized and deeply ordered and methodic. This was an extremely radical idea in the 1960s as audio recording was only just emerging, conversation had not yet been studied, and the dominant linguistic view was the Chomskyan one that "ordinary talk could not be the object of study for linguistics since it is too disordered; it is an essentially degenerate realization of linguistic competence" (Hutchby & Wooffitt, 1998, p. 22).

A recurrent theme in this chapter will be the fundamental differences between CA methodology and approaches typical of linguistics. The seminal texts on CA have been written by sociologists (see, however, Levinson, 1983), and as Heritage (1984b, p. 234) notes, CA studies have been presented in a style which presumes a competent audience, and features of the style make access to their methods and findings difficult. This is doubly the case with writings on ethnomethodology. It needs first to be understood that Sacks began his study of CA with a view of it as a sociological "naturalistic observational discipline that could deal with the details of social action rigorously, empirically and formally" (Schegloff & Sacks, 1973, pp. 289–290).

In the course of this chapter I will try to explicate *why* CA methodology proceeds as it does and why, in spite of some fundamental differences between it and the methodology of linguistics, it is a suitable methodology for applied linguists to use. These differences will be teased out during the course of this chapter. At the start, however, we should be clear that there is a fundamental difference between the "CA mentality" and the "linguistic mentality" in relation to the status of language. CA's primary interest is in the social act, whereas a linguist's primary interest is normally in language:

> CA is only marginally interested in language as such; its actual object of study is the interactional organization of social activities. CA is a radical departure from other forms of linguistically oriented analysis in that the production of utterances, and more particularly the sense they obtain, is seen not in terms of the structure of language, but first and foremost as a practical social accomplishment. That is, words used in talk are not studied as semantic units, but as products or objects which are designed and used in terms of the activities being negotiated in the talk. (Hutchby & Wooffitt, 1998, p. 14)

1.2 Ethnomethodology

The basic relationship between ethnomethodology and CA is that the first subsumes the second. Ethnomethodology studies the principles on which people base their social actions, whereas CA focuses more narrowly on the principles which people use to interact with each other by means of language. Ethnomethodology is not well known outside the field; the writings of ethnomethodologists tend to be difficult to access, and Boyle (1997, p. 29) notes that Garfinkel "established a standard of obscurity that most ethnomethodologists seem compelled to follow." Nonetheless, it is especially important for linguists to understand the fundamental principles of ethnomethodology since, as we have already noted, ethnomethodology and CA[2] are in many ways very different from approaches typically used in linguistics. What is ethnomethodology and why should it be used as the basis of the study of human interaction when it is not a linguistic discipline? One way to understand the project of ethnomethodology and CA is to imagine that an alien has been sent from a civilization which is totally different from ours and does not have the concept of language as we know it; the alien may communicate in images through telepathy, for example, and find language puzzlingly indirect, ambiguous, and primitive. The alien's brief is to understand and describe the basis of human behavior and communication. Our project is to explain to the alien the principles according to which people act and use language to interact.

According to Heritage (1984b),

> The term "ethnomethodology" refers to the study of ... the body of common-sense knowledge and the range of procedures and considerations by means of which the ordinary members of society make sense of, find their way about in, and act on the circumstances in which they find themselves. (p. 4)

Ethno methods can be seen as the interpretative procedures used by social actors in situ. Garfinkel's work can be seen as a reaction to the previously dominant top-down Parsonian sociology (Parsons, 1937), which assumed the superiority of the sociologist's knowledge over that of members of society, who were seen as cultural and psychological "dopes" who unthinkingly acted out the macro rules of society as explicated by the sociologist. Garfinkel, however, rejected analytical frameworks which assume the superiority of social science knowledge over the lay social actor's knowledge and sought an answer to the question "How do social actors come to know, and know in common, what they are doing and the circumstances in which they are doing it?" (Heritage, 1984b, p. 76). This can be understood as a rejection of an *etic* or external analyst's perspective on human behavior in favor of an *emic* or participant's perspective. Since the emic/etic distinction is vital to this monograph, it needs to be defined at this point. According to Pike (1967),

> The etic viewpoint studies behavior as from outside of a particular system, and as an essential initial approach to an alien system. The emic viewpoint results from studying

> behavior as from inside the system.... Descriptions or
> analyses from the etic standpoint are "alien" in view, with
> criteria external to the system. Emic descriptions provide
> an internal view, with criteria chosen from within the
> system. (p. 37)

Garfinkel's assumption was that people must make normative use of a number of principles in order to display their actions to each other and allow others to make sense of them. However, these principles are used on a constant basis in everyday life and have become automatized to the extent that they have a taken-for-granted or *seen-but-unnoticed* status which "entitles persons to conduct their common conversational affairs without interference" (Garfinkel, 1967, p. 42). Garfinkel was, then, trying to make explicit and visible those principles to which we orient in everyday life and of which we have implicit knowledge. The basic problem which Garfinkel faced was that of uncovering and identifying these normative practices: Because they are seen but unnoticed, they are not easily perceptible when the norms are being followed. However, he noticed that the norms did become more identifiable when they were being breached. In an uncharacteristically comprehensible sentence, Garfinkel (1967) notes that "for these background expectancies to come into view one must either be a stranger to the 'life as usual' character of everyday scenes, or become estranged from them" (p. 37). This point explains CA's interest in deviant-case analysis, which will be discussed later. Garfinkel therefore devised a series of famous "breaching experiments" which are described in detail in Garfinkel (1967). In a counseling experiment, for example, participants asked 10 questions for advice on personal problems to a "counselor" hidden behind a screen; they were then given yes/no answers without any further explanation. Five *yes* answers and five *no* answers were allocated on a completely random basis, unknown to the participants. In spite of this, participants were determined to make sense of the answers.

Garfinkel designed experiments like these to breach the norms, to undermine the participants' belief in reciprocity of perspectives in which the conversational partner is cooperating in a shared reality or intersubjectivity. However, Garfinkel found, as in the case above, that this was extremely difficult to accomplish, as participants constantly made adjustments and found ways to maintain their belief in a shared reality in which both participants were orienting to the same norms. As Heritage (1984b) puts it, "At every possible point, the participants seemed to be willing to give the 'underlying pattern' the benefit of the doubt. They assumed it was operative despite appearances to the contrary and... they waited for the pattern to reassert itself in new evidences which would enable them to discount any prior discrepancies" (p. 96). Taken as a whole, these breaching experiments demonstrated that utterances in conversation are not treated literally but are understood by reference to context and assumptions about the other party, as part of an emerging sequence and with both retrospective and prospective significance, so that the significance of a question may emerge subsequently.

So in view of the vagueness and indexicality of conversational utterances, intersubjectivity between interactants can only be maintained if the interactants agree to fill in all of the contextual detail and cooperate; this is similar to Grice's (1975) cooperative principle. Therefore victims of breaching experiments (e.g., Garfinkel, 1967, p. 43) tend to react with "moral" outrage because the failure to cooperate "threatens the very possibility of mutual understanding and, with it, the existence of a shared world" (Heritage, 1984b, p. 95). Breaches of the ethnomethodological principles in conversation are therefore said to be "morally sanctionable." Garfinkel (1967) reports that many of the students who undertook his breaching experiments experienced upsetting and very hostile reactions from friends and family as a result.

1.3 The Principles of Ethnomethodology

I will now introduce five fundamental and interlocked principles which underlie ethnomethodology[3] and also CA, although they are rarely referred to explicitly in published accounts of CA methodology: indexicality, documentary method of interpretation, reciprocality of perspectives, normative accountability, and reflexivity.

1.3.1 Indexicality

Of the ethnomethodological principles reviewed here, indexicality or context-boundedness may be the most familiar. Interactants generally do not make every single aspect of their intended meaning explicit, relying on mutually understood features of the background context to supply additional information. According to Boyle (2000b, p. 31) ethnomethodology's unique contribution to the discussion of indexicality is that indexical knowledge is not just something in the environment, but also something talked into being by interactants. In other words, they display through their utterances which aspects of context they are orienting to at any given time, and there is a reflexive relationship between talk and context. *This provides an analytical resource and underlies CA's insistence that we invoke contextual features in analysis only when it is evident in the details of the interaction that the participants themselves are orienting to such features.* There is also a clear link between indexicality and Garfinkel's breaching experiments. People cannot elaborate all aspects of what they are talking about because it is too time-consuming and difficult, so "indexicality allows utterances to represent vastly more than is said and thereby makes mundane conversation possible" (Boyle, 2000b, pp. 32–33).

1.3.2 The Documentary Method of Interpretation

The documentary method of interpretation is central to ethnomethodology. It treats any actual real-world action as a "document" or an example of a previously known pattern. There are similarities here with schema theory.[4] So in practical terms if anyone greets us by saying "Hi," we treat that action as a document and relate it to previously known patterns, normally identify it as a greeting, and respond accordingly. Importantly, the claim is not only that this is the method of interpretation which interactants use, but also that this is the fundamental method which analysts must use in analyzing social interaction, as it is an emic methodology. It should also be noted that there is a reflexive relationship between the patterns and the individual actions so that if, for example, we encounter a new form of greeting, our underlying pattern or schema of forms of greeting is updated. In order to exemplify the documentary method of interpretation in practice, we will consider the following extract from a staff room discussion among three teachers of English to speakers of other languages (ESOL) in a language school in the United Kingdom. ESOL teachers commonly use nationality to index various characteristics of students, with southern Europeans thought to be talkative and East Asians thought to be quiet in class. Ed enters the staff room:[5]

(1.1)

```
1 Ed:      my: God it's quiet in there.
2 Harry:   hhhh
3 Ed:      it's like working in a library in there.
4 Harry:   anyway (0.5) you've ( )
5 Ed:      I can't get anything out of them. (1.0) it's—there are three
6          Japanese students and
7 Keith:   oh right.
```

(Richards, 1996, p. 258)

Up to Line 5 the listeners know only that the learners are quiet. On receipt of Line 6, however, using the documentary method of interpretation, Keith is able to match the quietness to a previously known pattern or schema and reach a new understanding of the situation, so his interruptive "oh" in Line 7 marks a change of information state (Heritage, 1984a). When the documentary method of interpretation is applied to sequential interaction, its explanatory power becomes extremely significant. *Any turn at talk (such as Line 7) becomes a document or display of a cognitive, emotional, and attitudinal state, an analysis of context and of the previous turn(s) in the sequence and a social action which renews the context.*

1.3.3 The Reciprocity of Perspectives

Another principle which social actors use involves a willingness to adopt a reciprocity of perspectives, that is, to agree that we are following the same norms, to show affiliation with the other person's perspective, and to try to achieve intersubjectivity. This is closely linked to indexicality, which cannot function unless all parties can agree to index their interaction in the same way. This is demonstrated by Garfinkel's breaching experiments, which are simultaneously breaching indexicality and reciprocity of perspectives. Recipients of the breaching react strongly because the breaches challenge the entire basis of intersubjectivity, in which indexical expressions can be used without elaboration. This principle does *not* mean that people actually succeed in reaching the same perspective on everything all of the time; this is obviously not the case. Rather, to follow the principle means to agree that we are following the same norms in interaction, including a structural bias toward cooperation. In many ways this is similar to Grice's (1975) cooperative principle.

This principle also functions as a constitutive norm and template for interpretation, so we are able to recognize, in the case of a failure of intersubjectivity, that the failure has occurred by reference to the normal expectation of willingness to adopt reciprocity of perspectives. This principle is also closely linked to preference organization in CA, which can be seen as a structural bias toward affiliation and reciprocity of perspectives. The preferred action is seen but unnoticed and promotes affiliation and reciprocity of perspectives, whereas the dispreferred action is noticeable and accountable, may be sanctionable, and works against affiliation and reciprocity of perspectives.

1.3.4 Normative Accountability

The principle of the normative accountability of actions is perhaps the key to understanding the ethnomethodological basis of CA and also the one which is the furthest removed from linguistic concepts. At this point, we should clarify the position on norms in ethnomethodology, which should be clearly differentiated from the descriptivist "rules and units" approach typical of linguistics. Norms are understood in ethnomethodology as constitutive of action rather than regulative. It is by reference to norms that interactants can design their own social actions and interpret those of others.

For example, when one social actor greets another, a greeting response is the norm or has *seen but unnoticed* status. Failure to respond in this case, however, may be noticeable, accountable, and sanctionable. Here we use a norm of behavior as a point of reference or action template for interpretation rather than a rule. An actor may decide to return a greeting, but "the actor who is determined to declare or continue a quarrel can do so by visibly refusing to return a greeting and leaving the other to draw the conclusion" (Heritage, 1984b, p. 118). The norms are constitutive in that they constitute the setting in which the actions may be performed and interpreted. The seen-but-unnoticed route is that which is overwhelmingly used to accomplish everyday actions. We will see later in the chapter that the same situation applies to CA with respect to norms. CA states norms (or action templates) of conduct with respect to organizations of turn taking, sequence, repair, and preference. This does not mean that interactants have to slavishly follow these norms, but rather that these are points of reference through which we can design and perform our social actions, analyze and evaluate the conduct of another, draw conclusions, and hold the other accountable. So, for example, interactants can and do deviate from the norms, interrupt others, or fail to provide the second part to an adjacency pair, and fellow interactants can evaluate these actions as noticeable and accountable *by reference to the norms*.

The four other ethnomethodological principles can be seen to constitute interlocking norms or background expectancies of behavior, adherence to which enables social actors to carry on everyday action and interaction in a seen-but-unnoticed or normal way. The principle of normative accountability is the "moral force" which holds all the other principles together by providing a basis for interpretation and social action.

1.3.5 Reflexivity

The term *reflexivity* is widely used in the social sciences, but it has a very specific meaning in ethnomethodology. The principle of reflexivity states that the same set of methods or procedures are responsible for both the production of actions/utterances and their interpretation. This principle underlies the CA mechanism of the adjacency pair. Staying with the greeting-greeting adjacency pair, the principle would be manifested as follows. If two acquaintances approach each other along a corridor for the first time one morning and one issues a greeting, then he or she has performed the first part of an adjacency pair. From the perspective of reflexivity, the greeter has not only performed an action but also created a context for its interpretation. If the other person responds with a greeting, that person not only has performed an action but has also displayed an interpretation of the first action as a greeting. We can see the other ethnomethodological principles manifest in this example as well. By returning greetings, both interactants demonstrate that they are using the documentary method of interpretation, or that they are both orienting to the same schemata. They further orient to indexicality in that they display understanding that the context requires a greeting to be performed. Reciprocity of perspectives is achieved in that both interactants have displayed a similar understanding of context. The principle of normative accountability of actions is manifest here in that failure to return a greeting will be noticeable, accountable, and sanctionable.[6]

This concentration of fundamental principles into a very short and simple pair of actions perhaps explains why we become perplexed or annoyed if we greet other people and they fail to return the greeting. Such a failure is potentially sanctionable in that we may decide to retaliate, for example, by snubbing that person in turn in the future. There is also a semiotic sense in which an exchange of greetings is an initial declaration of mutual orientation to ethnomethodological principles. Failure to do so may be a semiotic indicator of social trouble looming. It should be stressed that these norms are *not* prescriptive and restrictive rules, but rather the means or points of reference by which we can express social actions and others can interpret them. We are not obliged to follow the seen-but-unnoticed route and be affiliative. Indeed, we may sometimes decide that we want to display a total lack of affiliation to someone and demonstrate that we do not reciprocate any perspectives with them. In this case it is precisely by reference to the norms that we display our attitude to that person, namely, by deliberately going against the norms. For example, on receipt of an invitation to the person's house, we may proclaim "What? Go to your house? I'd rather die!" In the same way, (using the principle of reflexivity) recipients interpret our display by reference to the norms.

1.4 Aims of Conversation Analysis

From one perspective, CA is the result of applying ethnomethodological principles to naturally occurring talk. *Talk in interaction* has become the accepted superordinate term to refer to the object of CA research (Drew & Heritage, 1992b, p. 4). According to Psathas (1995), CA studies the organization and order of social action in interaction. This organization and order is one produced by the interactants in situ and oriented to by them. The analyst's task is to develop an emic perspective, to uncover and describe this organization and order; the main interest is in uncovering the underlying *machinery* which enables interactants to achieve this organization and order:

> Our aim is...to get into a position to transform...our
> view of what happened here as some interaction that
> could be treated as the thing we're studying, to inter-
> actions being spewed out by a machinery, the machinery
> being what we're trying to find; where, in order to find
> it we've got to get a whole bunch of its products. (Sacks,
> 1992, vol. 2, p. 169)

So one principal aim of CA is to characterize the organization of the interaction by abstracting from exemplars of speci-
mens of interaction and to uncover the emic logic underlying the
organization. A common misconception is that CA is obsessed
with micro detail and has nothing to say about interactional
organization on a larger scale. This monograph, however, portrays the interactional architecture of the L2 classroom.

Another principal aim of CA is to trace the development of
intersubjectivity in an action sequence. This does *not* mean that
CA provides access to participants' cognitive or psychological states.[7]
Rather, it means that analysts trace how participants analyze and
interpret each other's actions and develop a shared understanding
of the progress of the interaction. So CA practitioners aim "to
discover how participants understand and respond to one another
in their turns at talk, with a central focus on how sequences of
action are generated" (Hutchby & Wooffitt, 1998, p. 14).

1.5 Principles of Conversation Analysis

We previously reviewed the basic principles underlying
ethnomethodology. These are generic principles which may be
used to study any kind of human action; CA focuses solely on
human actions which are manifested through talk.[8] Therefore,
CA has developed its own subset of principles and procedures,
which will now be discussed; their links back to ethnomethodological principles will be traced where appropriate. As with other
forms of qualitative research, the principles are not to be considered a formula or to be applied in a mechanistic fashion. It is
essential to adopt a conversation-analytic mentality which

"involves more a cast of mind, or a way of seeing, than a static and prescriptive set of instructions which analysts bring to bear on the data" (Hutchby & Wooffitt, 1998, p. 94).

The first principle of CA, that there is order at all points in interaction, is Sacks's most original idea, according to Hutchby and Wooffitt (1998). This can be traced back to Garfinkel's view of people as rational actors who make active decisions rather than being passive "dopes." As already noted, this was an extremely radical idea in the 1960s, as the dominant linguistic view was that conversation was too disordered to be studied. This idea leads to the concept of rational design in interaction, which is that talk in interaction is systematically organized, deeply ordered, and methodic. When we speak of the rational organization of interaction, this does not in any way imply that everything a speaker says seems rational or logical to everyone else, but rather that interaction is structurally organized. The principle of rational organization (explored in Chapter 5) is vital to an understanding of institutional discourse. Different institutions have different institutional aims and organizations of the interaction appropriate to those aims.

The second principle of CA is that contributions to interaction are *context-shaped* and *context-renewing*. Contributions are context-shaped in that they cannot be adequately understood except by reference to the sequential environment in which they occur and in which the participants design them to occur. Contributions are context-renewing in that they inevitably form part of the sequential environment in which a next contribution will occur. As Heritage (1984b) puts it, "The context of a next action is repeatedly renewed with every current action" (p. 242) and is transformable at any moment. This principle can be traced to Garfinkel's principles of indexicality, reflexivity, and the documentary method of interpretation; see Section 1.3.

The third principle is that no order of detail can be dismissed a priori as disorderly, accidental, or irrelevant (Heritage 1984b, p. 241). This principle follows from the first two and can be seen to underlie the development of the highly detailed CA transcription system, its minute analysis of the detail of naturally occurring data, and its highly empirical orientation. There is a great deal to be said on the matter of transcription, and there are inevitably some differences between linguists (particularly phonologists) and CA practitioners here. However, since these issues are not of central relevance to the argument of this monograph, the reader is referred to the detailed discussions in ten Have (1999), Hutchby and Wooffitt (1998), and Markee (2000). For illustrations of the benefits of CA transcription, see Wei (2002) and Hutchby and Wooffitt (1998). For present purposes we need note only the following:

- CA practitioners regard the recordings of naturally occurring interaction as the primary data.
- Transcripts are designed to make the primary data available for intensive analytic consideration by the analyst and other readers.
- Transcripts are inevitably incomplete, selective renderings of the primary data which invariably involve a trade-off between readability and comprehensiveness.

The fourth principle of CA, which follows from this, is that analysis is bottom-up and data driven; we should not approach the data with any prior theoretical assumptions or assume that any background or contextual details are relevant. So in CA it is not relevant to invoke power, gender, race, or any other contextual factor unless and until there is evidence in the details of the interaction that the participants themselves are orienting to it. This relates to the ethnomethodological principle of reflexivity. In Seedhouse (1998a), for example, I examined interaction in German between a female Greek immigrant to Germany (non-native speaker [NNS]) and a German shop worker (native speaker [NS]) who was delivering soft drinks to her flat. At one point the NS says, "Achsoo, Vater kommen, ja," which may be roughly translated as "Oh well, father come, yes." I argued that the NS is orienting to the NNS's trouble with the L2 by producing minimalized, pidginized interlanguage forms himself, which is a form of modified speech or accommodation. From the CA perspective, it now *and only now* becomes valid to discuss the identities of NS and NNS or to speak of a cross-cultural encounter, because there is now evidence that the participants are orienting to such constructs in the details of their talk. So it is incorrect to say that CA does not consider background or contextual details; the point is that it does so only if and when close analysis reveals participants' orientation to such details (see Sections 1.8 and 2.6 for further discussion).

Another way of presenting the principles of CA is in relation to the questions which CA asks. The essential question which we must ask at all stages of CA of data is "Why that, in that way, right now?" This encapsulates the perspective of interaction as action (why that) which is expressed by means of linguistic forms (in that way) in a developing sequence (right now). Hutchby and Wooffitt (1998) suggest that there are "two core analytic questions in CA: What interactional business is being mediated or accomplished through the use of a sequential pattern? How do participants demonstrate their active orientation to this business?" (p. 99). Alternatively, ten Have (1999, p. 15) proposes that CA's basic analytic strategy is to consider any point in the data and try to find out the kind of problem for which doing this social action might be a solution. This strategy emphasizes the social action orientation of CA and considers what the interactants are trying to achieve in terms of social actions. Sacks's early lectures were often labeled to express this, for example, "How to avoid giving help without refusing to give it (treat the circumstance as a joke)."

1.6 Types of Interactional Organization

We will now look at four different but related types of interactional organization which were uncovered by Sacks and associates by grappling with their data and can now be employed in analysis by CA practitioners. I will attempt to relate these to the principles of ethnomethodology, where appropriate. First I should clarify that these organizations are *definitely not* the same as "units of analysis" in the linguistic sense. Rather, they should be understood as interactional organizations which inter-actants use normatively and reflexively both as an action template for the production of their social actions and as a point of reference for the interpretation of their actions. We as analysts should use them in the same way. The organizations are part of the context-free machinery which we make use of to orient ourselves in indexical interaction; that is, we employ them in a context-sensitive way. Similarly, we are able to interpret the context-sensitive social actions of others only because there is a context-free machinery by reference to which we can make sense of them.

1.6.1 Adjacency Pairs

The concept of the adjacency pair is one which (if considered purely as a structural phenomenon) may appear to be so obvious and superficial that it is hardly worth mentioning. However, the action sequence or sequence organization is the essential key to understanding how CA works and its links to its ethnomethod-ological roots.[9] Therefore we will need to spend some time con-sidering the adjacency pair as the most common and prevalent manifestation of the concept of linked actions in an action sequence. Adjacency pairs are, as Heritage (1984b) puts it, "the basic building-blocks of intersubjectivity" (p. 256). There are of course a number of other possible sequence organizations, which cannot be dealt with here for reasons of space. Adjacency pairs are paired utterances such that on production of the first part of the pair (e.g., question) the second part of the pair (answer) becomes *conditionally relevant*. If, however, the second part is not immediately produced, it may nonetheless remain relevant and accountable and appear later, or its absence may be accounted for:

(1.2)

```
1 A: can I have a bottle of Mich?   Q1
2 B: are you over twenty-one?       Q2
3 A: no.                            A2
4 B: no                             A1
```

(Levinson, 1983, p. 304)

Extract 1.2 is from a conversation in a liquor store. A is not old enough to buy beer, and one question-and-answer adjacency pair (Lines 2 and 3) is embedded in another (Lines 1 and 4). What this sequence also demonstrates is that action sequences do not necessarily unroll in a linear fashion (Q1-A1, Q2-A2) and hence that serial order is not necessarily the same thing as sequential order. When this is the case, the different types of interactional organization (here, adjacency pair and turn taking) combine in a mutually reinforcing fashion to provide normative points of reference which enable interactants (and analysts) to orient themselves. Furthermore, the adjacency pair concept does not claim that second parts are always provided for first parts. Rather, it is a *normative* frame of reference which provides a framework for understanding actions and providing account-ability. So if we ask a question to someone who does not then provide an answer, we may draw conclusions about that person. Deviant-case analysis is used in CA to confirm the normative character of identified organizations. In the case of adjacency pairs, we can demonstrate this by examining the following cases:

(1.3)

```
1 A: is there something bothering you or not?
     (1.0)
2 A: yes or no
     (1.5)
3 A: eh?
4 B: no.
```

(1.4)

```
1 Child:   have to cut the:se Mummy.
           (1.3)
2 Child:   won't we Mummy
           (1.5)
3 Child:   won't we
4 Mother:  yes.
```

(Atkinson and Drew, 1979, p. 52)

Extracts 1.3 and 1.4 illustrate deviant cases because an answer has become conditionally relevant after the question, but no answer has been received, nor has the lack of an answer been accounted for. The second part is therefore noticeably absent and accountable. That this is also A's and the child's analysis in Extracts 1.3 and 1.4, respectively, is demonstrated by their repetition and re-repetition of their questions. The longer the second part remains absent, the more accountable and sanctionable it becomes.[10] This is evidenced by the increasingly short and curt linguistic forms which are used to express the first and second repetitions of their questions. This is an example of conversation analysts' interest in linguistic forms: The interest is not in the linguistic forms themselves, but rather in the way in which they are used to embody and express subtle differences in social actions. We encountered in Section 1.5 the fundamental CA question "Why this, in this way, right now?" If we look at Line 3 in Extracts 1.3 and 1.4 we can obtain clear answers to this question. The questioner in both cases is insisting on receiving an answer to a previously posed question, using increasingly curt linguistic forms, and at this point in the action sequence because the two previous questions have not received the relevant second part. The extracts also demonstrate that questioners orient to their questions' having a normative force with sequential implications which prompt the recipient to provide a second part or alternatively to account for its absence, as in Extract 1.5:

(1.5)

C: yes can you tell me please if air ukay three ni:nety is coming in
   at fifteen twenty five still
A: I'm sorry we're british airways (we) don't handle air ukay

(Hutchby & Wooffitt, 1998, p. 249)

It now needs to be understood that the principles which underlie this straightforward analysis of adjacency pairs are the same ones which are used in much larger and more complex sequences; we will see in Chapter 5 that they underlie the analysis of interaction in the L2 classroom as well. The principles are as follows. A first action is analyzed as projecting the production of a relevant next action by the next speaker. If the relevant next action occurs in the next turn, it is treated in a seen-but-unnoticed fashion by the first speaker, as norms have been adhered to. The relevant action may not occur in the next turn, but its noticeable absence may be accounted for (as in Extract 1.5) by the next speaker. However, if the relevant next action is not produced by the next speaker and no account is provided of why it is not produced, this absence can be treated as noticeable, accountable, and sanctionable by the next speaker. The longer it is absent, the more sanctionable it becomes. So in Extracts 1.3 and 1.4, any further silences on the parts of B and Mother, respectively, might, for example, result in the throwing of an object (in the case of A) or a tantrum (in the case of Child). It is perfectly possible for speakers to deviate from norms, but listeners may negatively evaluate these observable behaviors and impose sanctions against them.

Following a first turn, the interaction continues sequentially, with the second speaker's action creating expectations for subsequent speakers and so on. Moving on to the third turn, this displays an analysis of the second speaker's turn, so the second speaker is able to determine how his or her turn has been interpreted. So the essence of CA is the concept of action sequences or sequence organization, which has been exemplified by the adjacency pair. However, interaction clearly does not consist of an endless succession of adjacency pairs. The point being made is nevertheless that interaction *is* always an action sequence in which "a turn's talk will be heard as directed to a prior turn's talk, unless special techniques are used to locate some other talk to which it is directed" (Sacks et al., 1974, p. 728).

The adjacency pair has been used as an example of a generic phenomenon, namely, next-positioning and linked actions within sequence organization. The adjacency pair is not only an action template with normative force, it is also a template for interpretation. Extrapolating from this, any first action in interaction is an action template which creates a normative expectation for a next action and a template for interpreting it. The second action displays an interpretation of the first action and itself creates an action and interpretational template for subsequent actions, and so on. This can also be termed the *next-turn proof procedure* (Sacks et al., 1974, p. 729), which is the basic tool which analysts can use to develop an emic perspective. The next turn, then, documents an analysis of the previous turn and displays this analysis not only to the other interactants, but also to us as analysts, providing us with a proof criterion and search procedure. This procedure can be traced back to the ethnomethodological principle of reflexivity, which states that the same set of methods or procedures are responsible for both the production of linguistic action and its interpretation.

We can now see that this is reflexive on further levels. Sequence organization is the mechanism by which interactants are able to make their utterances comprehensible and by which cointeractants are able to interpret them. However, it is also the mechanism by which analysts are able to analyze the course of the interaction, using data which are publicly available. This does not mean, however, that we gain a direct window into what interactants "really mean" or their cognitive state.[11] We are rather gaining a direct window into how social actors perform a series of related social actions via the medium of language and into the progress of their *intersubjectivity*. Intersubjectivity is mutual understanding or interpersonal alignment, and one of the key objectives of CA is to explicate how we are able to achieve a shared understanding of each other's actions. The CA perspective is that we are able to orient ourselves by normative reference to interactional organizations. Adjacency pairs (and sequence organization) are therefore called the building blocks of intersubjectivity, because interactants use them to display to one another their understanding of each other's turns, and this permits analysts to follow the progress of their intersubjectivity.

The production of a first turn provides an interpretative basis for the first speaker to interpret the next speaker's actions. In Extract 1.6, the second part is interpreted as a tentative answer to A's question rather than an unconnected observation:

(1.6)

1 A: where's Bill?
2 J: there's a yellow VW outside Sue's house

(Levinson, 1983, p. 102)

However, it can be interpreted in this way solely by virtue of its sequential location after the first part of an adjacency pair. Perhaps CA's major contribution to pragmatics is that in CA, utterances derive much of their pragmatic force from their sequential location and through their relationship to the interactional organizations uncovered by CA. A typical "linguistic" misunderstanding of adjacency pairs is that they are part of a descriptivist system of units and rules which are etically specifiable. For example, Burns (2001) suggests that "a weakness of CA resides in the fact that we still do not have precise ways of recognizing adjacency pairs" (p. 134).

1.6.2 Preference Organization

At this point I will introduce the notion of preference, which issues from the organization of the adjacency pair. The concept has been frequently misunderstood, as Boyle (2000a) demonstrates. It should be clear to readers who have followed the argument so far that this is *not* related to the notion of liking or wanting to do something, but rather involves issues of affiliation and disaffiliation, of seeing, noticeability, accountability, and sanctionability in relation to social actions, and hence the concept derives directly from ethnomethodological principles. From this perspective, interaction should be understood as a business primarily of social actors aiming to achieve social goals (rather than engaged in the production of language) with the interaction rationally organized to help actors to achieve those goals. Next-positioning is the major means by which speakers can exert influence over the actions of their interactional partners, and the institutionalized norm is for interaction to be affiliative, so as to achieve reciprocity of perspectives and to enable social actors to achieve their goals.

As Heritage (1984b) puts it, "there is a 'bias' intrinsic to many aspects of the organization of talk which is generally favorable to the maintenance of bonds of solidarity between actors and which promotes the avoidance of conflict" (p. 265). This is similar in concept to Grice's (1975) cooperative principle. This should be no surprise in terms of the "rational" design of interaction, in that the underlying ethnomethodological principles, such as reflexivity, reciprocity of perspectives, and the documentary method of interpretation, are strongly affiliative. This structural bias manifests itself in preference organization. For many adjacency pairs there are alternative second parts, so an invitation may be answered by an acceptance (preferred action) or a rejection (dispreferred action). These two options are performed in different ways (Pomerantz, 1984). Preferred actions are normally delivered without hesitation or delay at the start of the response turn, as in Extract 1.7:

(1.7)

1 Child: could you .hh could you put on the light for my .hh room
2 Father: yep

(Levinson, 1983, p. 307)

Dispreferred responses are generally accompanied by hesitation and delay and are often prefaced by markers such as *well* and *uh* as well as by positive comments and appreciations such as "You're very kind." They are frequently mitigated in some way and accounted for by an explanation or excuse of some kind. A's turn in Extract 1.8 exemplifies all of these phenomena:

(1.8)

```
1 B:   uh if you'd care to come over and visit a little while this morning
2      I'll give you a cup of coffee.
3 A:   hehh well that's awfully sweet of you, I don't think I can make it
4      this morning. hh uhm I'm running an ad in the paper and—and uh I
5      have to stay near the phone.
```

(Atkinson & Drew, 1979, p. 58)

As Heritage (1984b, p. 269) demonstrates, preferred responses to actions are *affiliative* and conducive to social solidarity, whereas dispreferred responses are *disaffiliative*. This does not mean that the function of agreement is always preferred. In the case of self-deprecating first turns (e.g., "God I'm stupid"), the preferred response is disagreement. At this point we need to refer to our previous discussion of ethnomethodology. The preferred response is the one which follows the established norms, is socially affiliative, and promotes reciprocity of perspectives. So an acceptance of an invitation follows the norms, is the default way of behaving, is socially affiliative, and hence is seen but unnoticed. The seen-but-unnoticed route is that which is overwhelmingly used to accomplish everyday actions. A refusal of an invitation is disaffiliative, does not follow the norms, and hence is dispreferred. This means that it is noticeable and accountable, which is the reason why dispreferred actions are so frequently accompanied by accounts and excuses. However, if the dispreferred action is packaged so as to minimize the degree of disaffiliation and conflict (see the discussion of invitation rejections later in the chapter), then it is not normally sanctionable. By contrast, providing an immediate, bald, and unmitigated *no* as a reply to an invitation will be treated as sanctionable because it fails to provide an account and makes no attempt to minimize the degree of disaffiliation. The basic organization of preference is summarized in Figure 1.1.

So with the preferred pathway (acceptance in this case), no account is necessary, as the norms are being followed. With the noticeable and accountable but not sanctionable pathway (rejection with mitigation and an account in this case), an account is provided, and so affiliation is not threatened and sanctions are unnecessary. With the noticeable, accountable, and sanctionable pathway (immediate, bald, unmitigated rejection), the dispreferred action has been performed without an account, so disaffiliation has occurred, and sanctions or reprisals become relevant: "No more invitations for him!"

We are now in a position to move on to the rational design of preferred and dispreferred second pair parts and attempt to explain why it is that the two types of turn are designed in different ways, with accounts and delays built into dispreferred turns. A preferred second pair part is the seen-but-unnoticed or default response and is performed immediately, as there is nothing to hold the interaction up, and the actors can move on to the next action. As Heritage (1984b, pp. 270–273) notes, invitations are overwhelmingly rejected on the basis of inability (e.g., prior engagement) rather than unwillingness. An inability

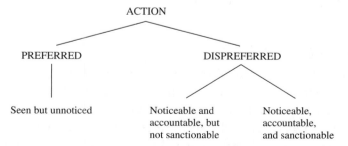

Figure 1.1. The structure of preference. From "Whatever Happened to Preference Organisation?" by R. Boyle, 2000, *Journal of Pragmatics, 32*, p. 590. Copyright 2000 by Elsevier. Reprinted with permission.

account has a "no-fault" quality which is affiliative, does not threaten face,[12] and therefore minimizes the degree of disaffiliation inherent in carrying out a dispreferred action. As far as the use of delays and markers such as *well* and *uh* are concerned, they are rationally linked to the production of accounts in that they allow time for recipients to think of accounts and excuses to mitigate the dispreferred action. Moreover, they allow time for the first speaker to perform two affiliative actions which could minimize the disaffiliation or loss of face caused by a rejection. The first of these is to modify the invitation into a more acceptable form, as in Line 5 of Extract 1.9:

(1.9)

```
1 A:   oh I was gonna sa:y if you wanted to:,=.hh you could meet me
2      at UCB and I could show you some of the other things on
3      the compu:ter
4      (.)
5 A:→maybe even teach you how to program Ba:sic or something. .hh
```

(Davidson, 1984, p. 108)

The second affiliative action is for the first speaker to "help" with the production of the rejection in some way, as in Extract 1.10, which invites the production of an account or excuse:

(1.10)

```
E:   wanna come down have a bite of lunch with me?= I've got some beer and
     stuff
     (0.3)
N:   well you're real sweet hon uhm
     (0.1)
E:→  or do you have something else
```

(Atkinson & Drew, 1979, p. 253)

Delay, then, provides time for both interactants to take further measures to minimize the degree of disaffiliation caused by a dispreferred second turn. I will briefly mention presequences, which are closely linked to the concepts of the adjacency pair and preference. Line 1 in Extract 1.11 can be seen as a preliminary sequence which determines whether B is in principle amenable to an invitation:

(1.11)

1 A: whatcha doin?
2 B: nothin'
3 A: wanna drink?

(Atkinson & Drew, 1979, p. 253)

From the point of view of preference, such a preliminary sequence minimizes the likelihood that a dispreferred rejection will be produced on receipt of an invitation and is therefore affiliative. Presequences are pairs which function as preparation for a future pair, such as preclosings, preannouncements, prequestions, and prerequests. They often function in the way illustrated in Extract 1.11, to preempt the need for the production of a dispreferred action.

So far I have focused on the organization of sequence, introducing the adjacency pair as an example of sequence organization. Preference organization explains the structural bias manifest in the alternative second parts of adjacency pairs. The next section explains how turn taking is organized within sequences.

1.6.3 Turn Taking

The exchange of turns is obviously characteristic of ordinary conversation; what is not so obvious is how it is accomplished so efficiently. Less than 5% of speech (in most contexts) is delivered with overlap, and gaps between speakers are generally measured in tenths of a second. Nonverbal communication cannot explain this, since telephone conversations are actually accomplished with more precise timing than face-to-face conversation (Levinson, 1983, p. 296). The system for turn taking must be extremely robust, since it works however many people are speaking and whatever the length or topic of the conversation. The following is a simplified version of Sacks et al.'s (1974) seminal account of the organization of turn taking. There is a mechanism governing turn taking which is termed a local management system; this means that decisions can be made by the participants, rather than having the turns allocated in advance (preallocated), as is the case in a courtroom.

There is a set of norms with options which the participants can select. The bases of the system are *turn-constructional units* (TCUs), which can be sentences, clauses, or words. I will discuss the nature of TCUs in detail below. Listeners project, then, when a speaker is going to finish a turn, and the point at which speaker change may occur is known as the *transition relevance place* (TRP). At a TRP the norms governing transition of speakers come into play; the speakers may change at that point, but they do not necessarily do so. The following norms apply at the first TRP of any turn:

- If the current speaker selects the next speaker in the current turn, then the current speaker must stop speaking and the next speaker must speak.
- If the current speaker does not select a next speaker, then any other participant may select himself or herself as the next speaker: The first person to speak at the TRP gains rights to the next turn.
- If the current speaker has not selected a next speaker, and if no other participant self-selects as in the second point, then the current speaker may (but need not) continue. The procedure then loops or recycles until the end of the conversation, for which there are of course further norms.

Schegloff (2000a) discusses the organization of overlap and introduces an overlap resolution device as a component of the organization of turn taking. Overlap occurs for a number of reasons and in a number of ways. As we saw with sequence organization, the system of turn taking is normative, so speakers may choose to perform specific social actions "by reference to one-party-at-a-time, even though they are realized through designedly simultaneous talk" (Schegloff, 2000a, p. 48).

It is quite common for preferred, affiliative second turns such as acceptance of an invitation or agreement (as in Extract 1.12) to be undertaken in overlap before the transition relevance point:

(1.12)

A: why don't you come up and <u>see</u> me some[times
B: [I would like to

(Atkinson & Drew, 1979, p. 58)

In these cases it is precisely by normative reference to the norms of turn taking and the TRP that interactants index their degree of enthusiasm for the proposal and affiliation to their partner.

In Extract 1.13, F begins his or her turn in the middle of "reasonable":

(1.13)

C: we:ll I wrote what I thought was a a—a
   rea:son[able explan<u>atio</u>:n
F: [I: think it was a <u>very</u> rude le:tter.

(Levinson, 1983, p. 299)

This cannot be considered a TRP, so it must be an interruption. This is confirmed by the disaffiliative social action embodied in F's turn, which directly contradicts the first speaker, and the bald linguistic formatting, with no attempt at mitigation. Extract 1.13 illustrates that the norms of turn taking can be broken, and that doing so has consequences for the progress of the interaction and social relations. Overlap, then, may be designedly used to intensify the affiliative or disaffiliative nature of particular social actions. However, it is also common to find overlap occurring at TRPs in accordance with the norms of turn taking:

(1.14)

D: he's got to <u>talk</u> to someone (very sor) supp<u>or</u>tive way
   towards you (.)
A: [Greg's (got wha—)]
G: [think you   sh—] think you should have <u>one</u> to: hold him

(Atkinson & Drew, 1979, p. 44)

In Extract 1.14 A and G make a competing first start at the TRP, following the norms. A leaves the floor to G, who then repeats the start of his or her turn ("think you") as the other participants may not have heard it during the period of overlap.

(1.15)

B: I ordered some paint from you uh a couple
      of weeks ago some vermilion
A: yuh
B: and I wanted to order some more the name's Boyd
A: yes[how many tubes would you like sir
B:→   [an—

(Levinson, 1983, p. 305)

In Extract 1.15, B starts a turn at a possible TRP, in that A's "yes" is a complete TCU and the turn could end at this point. When the overlap indicates that the current speaker is in fact continuing, B follows the norms by ceding the turn.

We will now return to the phenomenon which perhaps best exemplifies the differing attitudes of CA and linguistics to language, namely, that of the TCU. It is common for readers from a linguistics background to find characterizations of the TCU in the sociological literature (Hutchby & Wooffitt, 1998; Sacks et al., 1974; Schegloff, 1996; ten Have, 1999) rather perplexing because they are phrased in semilinguistic terms but do not appear to fit in with any linguistic system. In this section, therefore, we will emphasize the difference between CA and linguistics. A TCU can be understood as a single social action performed in a turn or sequence, and the projectable end of a TCU is a TRP. A single social action can be manifested in a wide variety of language forms, from a single word or discourse marker or a clause to a sentence, as we can see in the next two extracts. A TCU can also be performed nonverbally (ten Have, 1999, p. 112). A TCU is essentially a social concept rather than a linguistic one and cannot therefore be delimited in linguistic terms. Since it is an emic or participant's concept, it cannot be specified in etic terms. Extracts 1.16 and 1.17 and the subsequent discussion are intended to illustrate these points.

(1.16)

```
1 A:    it would bum you out to kiss me then, [hunh
2 B:                                          [yeah well we all
3       know where that's at.
4       ((pause))
5 A:    [(   )
6 B:    [I mean you went—you went through a—a long rap on that
7       one.=
8 A:→  =yeah, so I say that would bum you out then, hunh
```

(Sacks et al., 1974, p. 722)

According to Sacks et al. (1974), any turn performs three kinds of sequential work, which can be thought of in terms of past, present, and future. A turn shows how it fits into the sequence so far (past), performs its own social action or contribution to the sequence (present), and thus provides a context for the next turn by another interactant (future). In Extract 1.16, A's single turn in Line 8 consists of three TCUs. "Yeah" relates in the past to B's turn in Lines 6 and 7. "So I say that would bum you out then" performs a social action which contributes to the sequence. "Hunh" looks forward and hands the turn back to B. So these three kinds of sequential work are separated into three separate TCUs which are quite heterogeneous in linguistic terms and are contained in a single turn.

However, in Line 3 of Extract 1.17, we can see that Tony's turn consists of a single TCU of a single word:

(1.17)

```
1 Marsha:  en Ilene is going to meet im:. becuz the to:p wz ripped
2          off'v iz car which is tih say someb'ddy helped th'mselfs.
3 Tony:→  stolen.
4          (0.4)
5 Marsha:  stolen. =right out in front of my house.
6 Tony:    oh: f'r crying out loud,
```

(Schegloff, 1996, p. 75)

Yet not only does this single word constitute an entire turn, but it also performs three kinds of sequential work in the past, present, and future. This is possible because interactants orient to a normative sequential framework, a holistic framework consisting of the interlocking organizations of turn taking, sequence, preference, and repair. Since the normative expectation is that a turn will perform these three kinds of sequential work, Tony can design his turn so that a single word is capable of doing so, and Marsha can interpret it as doing so. *This is the principle of reflexivity in action.* The evidence that the participants are actually orienting to the system described is in the next-turn proof procedure. Marsha analyzes Tony's turn as commenting retrospectively on what happened to her car, as performing a new social action of confirming understanding of Marsha's news by summarizing the content in a new linguistic format and as providing a context for her to take the sequence further. She displays her understanding of the work performed by his turn in her subsequent turn (Line 5) by repeating his turn with the same intonation and adding further information on the theft.

What is clear from the above discussion, then, is that TCUs are only analyzable emically as social actions. They are quite heterogeneous in terms of linguistic form and do not correspond in any way to single linguistic categories. However they are packaged in terms of linguistic form, the point is that social actors are able to recognize them in interaction as complete social actions (as we can see in Line 5 of Extract 1.17) and hence are able to project when they are likely to end. According to Ford and Thompson (1996), the features of a turn which enable a speaker to project the end of a prior turn "must include not only syntactic cues but also intonational features as well as some notion of pragmatic or action completion... these three types of cues converge to a great extent to define transition relevance places in conversations, places to which conversationalists orient in sequencing their turns" (p. 171).

So we can see that CA is not a system of etically specifiable units and rules to be followed in a regulative sense, like, for example, rules for the construction of a grammatically correct sentence. Much confusion may have arisen because Sacks et al.'s early works used the terms *unit* and *rule* without explicating the difference between the CA and linguistic understandings of such terms. This may then have led to the belief that CA organizations were systems of units and rules in the descriptivist linguistic sense. However, CA does not have an etically specifiable unit of analysis in the sense in which this is understood in linguistics; it would be preferable to say that CA has an emic analytical focus on the sequence. In descriptivist linguistics it makes perfect sense to analyze a word or sentence in isolation. In CA, by contrast, it does not make any sense to analyze the turn *stolen* in Extract 1.17 in isolation. Trying to identify the TCU or the turn as a unit of analysis misses the point; *stolen* is a social action embedded in a sequential environment. So in CA we are dealing with a holistic system of analysis, and this is the case because the interactants are using the same holistic system of analysis themselves, as is made clear by Hutchby and Wooffitt (1998):

> It is important to realize that it is not part of the conversation analyst's aim to define...what a turn-construction unit is, as a linguist for instance may want to define what a sentence is. Conversation analysts cannot take a prescriptive stance on this question, because what a turn-construction unit consists of in any situated stretch of talk is a members' problem. That is, such a unit is essentially anything out of which a legitimate turn has recognizably—for the participants—been built. (p. 48)

This is clearly an approach to describing and analyzing language that is very different from the approaches used in linguistics. So the fundamental difference is that linguists attempt etic specifications of aspects of language itself, whereas CA practitioners attempt emic analysis of how social actions are carried out by means of language. Nonetheless, participants in conversation clearly do not have great difficulty in identifying TCUs and projecting TRPs (i.e., in designing and recognizing social actions) since, as already noted, exchange of turns is generally accomplished very efficiently.

The organization of the adjacency pair, preference, and turn taking constitutes the structural organization of talk. However, the fourth element, repair, comes into play whenever there are problems in the accomplishment of talk.

1.6.4 Repair

Repair may be defined as the treatment of trouble occurring in interactive language use. Trouble is anything which the participants judge is impeding their communication, and a repairable item is one which constitutes trouble for the participants. Schegloff, Jefferson, and Sacks (1977) point out that "nothing is, in principle, excludable from the class 'repairable'" (p. 363). From the ethnomethodological perspective, repair is a vital mechanism for the maintenance of reciprocity of perspectives and intersubjectivity. It is of particular importance for L2 learners and teachers to understand how breakdowns in communication and misunderstandings are repaired, and we will see in Chapter 4 that repair in the L2 classroom tends to carry a heavier load than in other settings. It is important to distinguish self-initiated repair (I prompt repair of my own mistake) from other-initiated repair (somebody else notices my mistake and initiates repair). Self-repair (I correct myself) must also be distinguished from other-repair (somebody corrects my mistake). There are therefore normally four repair trajectories:

(1.18) Self-initiated self-repair

A: had to put new gaskets on the oil pan to strop—stop the leak

(Levinson, 1983, p. 360)

(1.19) Self-initiated other-repair

B: he had dis uh Mistuh W—m whatever k—I can't think of his first name,
   Watts on, the one that wrote [that piece
A: [Dan Watts

(Schegloff et al., 1977, p. 364)

(1.20) Other-initiated self-repair

A: hey the first time they stopped me from selling cigarettes was this
    morning.
    (1.0)

B:→ from <u>selling</u> cigarettes?
A:→ from <u>buying</u> cigarettes.

(Schegloff et al., 1977, p. 370)

(1.21) Other-initiated other-repair

C: erm I'm just checking is that (.) right you know (0.5) I d—I don't know
    his flight number and [I'm not sure
A: [(whi—)
C: whether he's coming in to channel four eh:
    (.)
A:→ terminal four
C: yeah

(Hutchby & Wooffitt, 1998, p. 63)

There is a clear preference structure in the organization of repair which corresponds with the above listing: Self-initiated self-repair is most preferred, and other-initiated other-repair least preferred. This order also corresponds with frequency of usage in normal conversation, with other-initiated other-repair being rare.[13] There are two kinds of evidence for the preference for self-repair. The first is the inherent structural bias, with the first two opportunities located in the speaker's own turn— during the same TCU and at the next TRP. According to Hutchby and Wooffitt (1998), "There are various ways in which turns are designed to facilitate self-repair, or display the speaker's sensitivity to the appropriateness of self-repair and the (possible) impropriety of other-repair" (p. 66). In Extracts 1.22 and 1.23, we can see interactants making very different normative usage of the preference system for repair with very different outcomes:

(1.22)

1 L: but y'know single <u>beds</u>'r <u>awfully</u> <u>thin</u> to <u>sleep</u> on.
2 S: what?
3 L: single beds. [they're—

4 E: [y'mean narrow?
5 L: they're awfully <u>n</u>arrow yeah.

(Schegloff et al., 1977, p. 378)

In Extract 1.22 we can see the other speakers (S and E) moving down the preference structure in an attempt to repair the problem, which is that L has used a lexical item ("thin") which does not collocate with "bed." Since L does not appear to have noticed this problem in that there is no attempt at self-repair, in Line 2 S uses the next-preferred option, namely, other-initiation of self-repair. However, S uses an "open" (Drew, 1997) next-turn repair initiator ("what?"), which means that L does not appear to be able to locate the precise problem and seems in Line 3 to be starting to repeat the whole of the initial utterance. Therefore, the other speakers are entitled to move further down the preference organization and use other-initiated other-repair in Line 4. However, note that the repair form is mitigated and shows affiliation, as it is designed as a question. Framing a correction as a question or confirmation check and offering an alternative is a useful strategy as it in effect gives the first speaker the opportunity to self-repair in the next turn. It is an affiliative action in that it portrays the second speaker as orienting to and attempting to help the first speaker. This mitigation of repair occurs in the L2 classroom as well as in ordinary conversations. Other means of mitigation may include the use of jokes and markers such as *I think*. Since S and E have moved gradually down the preference organization and mitigated the other-initiated other-repair, L accepts and confirms uptake of the repair in Line 5.

By contrast, in Line 3 of Extract 1.23, R immediately conducts other-initiated other-repair (i.e., the least preferred option) without any attempt to start higher up the preference organization:

(1.23)

1 A: had to put new gaskets on the oil pan to strop—stop the
2   leak, an' then I put— and then—

3 R: that was a gas leak.
4 A: it was an oil leak buddy.
5 B: 't's a <u>gas</u> leak.
6 A: it's an oil leak.
   ((dispute continues for many turns))

(Levinson, 1983, p. 360)

Also note that there is no attempt at all at mitigation in the linguistic design (i.e., a bald statement), and in terms of a social action it is a flat contradiction. In Line 4 we can see that A interprets this as a face-threatening, disaffiliative action in that A conducts unmitigated other-initiated other-repair on R's turn; it is hence no surprise to find the dispute continuing for many turns. What we can see in the analysis of Extracts 1.22 and 1.23 is that preference organization must not be seen as a system of "rules" which must be followed. Clearly in Extract 1.23 the norms are not being followed. However, the point is that the normative preference system acts as an action template or point of reference which enables participants to display their level of affiliation to each other and to interpret each other's actions. In Line 3 of Extract 1.23, R displays a lack of affiliation with A's perspective precisely by going directly to the least preferred option. A's response in Line 4 demonstrates that A has interpreted this action, by reference to the preference organization, as a display of complete disaffiliation and has therefore "retaliated" through a similar display of disaffiliation.

In Section 1.6 I have characterized the different types of interactional organization which work together in complementary fashion to create an architecture of intersubjectivity (Heritage, 1984b, p. 254). They function as action templates or points of reference which interactants may use to orient themselves in the pursuit of mutual understanding. A vital point is that these interactional organizations are *not* to be understood as rules, units, or coding schemes in the sense in which these would be understood in a descriptivist linguistic paradigm. Rather, they are a set of normative resources which interactants make use of to display the meaning of their social actions to their partners and to interpret their partners' actions:

> In its first phase CA's conceptual apparatus was developed in its originators' struggle with the data, while in its second phase this apparatus is generally available as an established repertoire.... The danger in this situation is that less talented, insightful, or sensitive practitioners may be tempted to "apply" the established concepts in a mechanistic fashion, as "coding instruments."... In other words, the temptation is to use CA's previously established concepts and findings as law-like or even "causal" rules, whereas one should...see them as descriptions of possible normative orientations of participants, available for various usages as they see fit. (ten Have, 1999, p. 41)

Topic is a central concept in the analysis of talk and is coconstructed by participants during the course of the talk. However, it is not an interactional organization and is not part of the context-free architecture of talk. Unlike the organizations of adjacency pairs and turn taking, topic is not oriented to normatively. Topic is not treated at all in recent introductions to CA such as ten Have (1999) or Hutchby and Wooffitt (1998). However, it is extensively discussed by Sacks (1992).

1.7 Conversation Analysis Procedures

Having reviewed the basic components of interactional organization, I will now explicate how these are used in the procedures of CA. The first stage of CA has been described as *unmotivated looking* or being open to discovering patterns or phenomena. Psathas (1995) describes the term *unmotivated looking* as a paradox "since looking is motivated or there would be no looking being done in the first place" (pp. 24–25). So what is really meant is being open to discovering new phenomena rather than searching the data with preconceptions or hypotheses. For example, in my research in L2 classrooms (reported in

Section 4.6), the identification of teachers' avoidance of bald and unmitigated *no* in form-and-accuracy contexts emerged as a phenomenon from unmotivated looking rather than from a preconception that this was an issue which I should focus on. Once a candidate phenomenon has been identified, the next phase is normally an inductive search through a database to establish a collection of instances of the phenomenon. However, single-case analysis can also be undertaken (Hutchby & Wooffitt, 1998, pp. 120–130).

After an inductive database search has been carried out, the next step is to establish regularities and patterns in relation to occurrences of the phenomenon and to show that these regularities are methodically produced and oriented to by the participants as normative organizations of action (Heritage, 1988, p. 131). In order to explicate the emic logic or rational organization of the pattern uncovered, the next step is detailed analysis of single instances of the phenomenon. Deviant cases are seen to be particularly revealing since, as Heritage (1995, p. 399) puts it, they often serve to demonstrate the normativity of practices. Finally, a more generalized account is produced of how the phenomenon relates to the broader matrix of interaction. For reasons of space I will not be illustrating inductive search procedures here, but in Section 6.5 I briefly review an example from Schegloff (1968). Further examples may be found in Drew (1987), Heritage (1984a), and Hutchby and Wooffitt (1998).

At this point is important to understand that what CA practitioners identify as a phenomenon is primarily an example of social action and that they are not interested in it as a linguistic object as such. The phenomenon may indeed be a "superficially linguistic" item such as the marker *oh* (Heritage, 1984a) or a syntactical construction such as the "you say X . . . what about Y" pattern (Hutchby & Wooffitt, 1998, pp. 104–109). However, there may be social actions identifiable by sequential placement, such as Drew's (1987) study of po-faced reactions to teases. The point to be made is that it is perfectly possible for researchers who are interested only in linguistic items to attempt to use CA to investigate such a "superficially linguistic" phenomenon in interaction. However, such an attempt would tend to reveal a lack of a conversation-analytic mentality and would therefore tend to produce superficial results. There are a number of accounts of the procedures to be followed in CA: Drew (1994), Psathas (1995), and ten Have (1999). The following account is a synthesis of these accounts. It is an account of procedures for a single-case analysis (see Hutchby & Wooffitt, 1998, pp. 120–130) focusing on a single data extract. I start the account after recording, transcription, and unmotivated looking have taken place and after a single extract to focus on has been identified:

1. Locate an action sequence or sequences.

2. Characterize the actions in the sequence or sequences. An action sequence can be as short as an adjacency pair or last for hours. We are looking for a first speaker to initiate an action which is responded to in some way by a second speaker. This ends when the speakers move to perform a different action or series of actions. The idea of characterizing the actions in the sequence may be termed form-function matching, speech act analysis, or discourse analysis (DA), in Levinson's (1983) terms. So we may, for example, identify a sequence in which an offer is made and then rejected or a complex sequence of embedded question-and-answer adjacency pairs (e.g., Levinson, 1983, p. 305). It should be noted here that form-function analysis has always been an integral part of CA (even in Sacks's first lecture) and that DA is in effect an integral part of CA (see Section 2.1). However, a major difference is that CA reveals and portrays the fact that utterances often perform several actions simultaneously and are specifically designed to do so (Levinson, 1983, p. 311), so a CA will portray the multiplicity of actions performed by an utterance whereas a DA normally "translates" an utterance into a single function.

3. Examine the action sequence(s) in terms of the organization of turn taking, focusing especially on any disturbances in the working of the system.

4. Examine the action sequence(s) in terms of sequence organization. Here we are looking at adjacency pairs and preference organization but more widely at any action undertaken in response to other actions.

5. Examine the action sequence(s) in terms of the organization of repair.

6. Examine how the speakers package their actions in terms of the actual linguistic forms which they select from the alternatives available and consider the significance of · these. We are in effect returning here to form-function analysis, but this time we are focusing on the forms which are used to manifest the functions. Going back to Extracts 1.3 and 1.4, for example, we noted in our discussion of those extracts that actors repeated questions in increasingly short and curt forms and that this displayed a change in orientation.

7. Uncover any roles, identities, or relationships which emerge in the details of the interaction. As noted in Section 1.5, CA normally tries to avoid making (premature) reference to background information such as institutional setting and personal details (age, gender, etc.) until after the initial analysis. This is so that it can be established which particulars are demonstrably relevant to the actors in the interaction, so that these particulars are manifest *in some way* in the details of the interaction. This may take many different forms; see Section 1.8. Stages 1–7 would be followed whether one were analyzing ordinary conversation or institutional interaction. In the case of institutional interaction, one would move from Stage 7 on to other issues, as will be seen in Section 2.8.

8. Having completed a preliminary analysis which portrays the interactional organization and the participants' orientations, attempt to locate this particular sequence within a bigger picture. Of course, how this is done depends on what has been uncovered in the analysis. However, we are looking for a rational specification of the sequence which can uncover its emic logic and the machinery which produced it and which places it in a wider matrix of interaction; an example of this is provided in Chapter 5. What we see in CA methodology is constant, reflexive interaction between the specific instance and the underlying machinery. So specific episodes are analyzed by reference to types of interactional organization (adjacency pairs, etc.) whereas particular instances help us to further elaborate the underlying machinery.

1.8 Attitude Toward Context

CA has a dynamic, complex, highly empirical perspective on context.[14] The basic aim is to establish an emic perspective, that is, to determine which elements of context are relevant to the interactants at any point in the interaction. The perspective is also an active one in which participants talk a context into being. The perspective is dynamic in that, as Heritage (1984b, p. 242) puts it, "The context of a next action is repeatedly renewed with every current action" and is transformable at any moment. As noted earlier in the chapter, a basic assumption of CA is that contributions to interaction are context-shaped and context-renewing. This view can be traced back to the ethnomethodological principle of reflexivity. The principle of indexicality of utterances is clearly incorporated in the CA view of context, and utterances clearly document the participants' understanding of context.

CA sees the underlying machinery which generates interaction as being both context-free and context-sensitive. The structural organizations (e.g., turn taking) can be seen as context-free resources in that their organization can be specified as a series of norms in isolation from any specific instance of interaction. Nonetheless, the application of these organizations is context-sensitive in that interactants use the organization of (for example) turn taking to display their understanding of context. So professionals and lay clients may talk an institutional context into being through the professionals' taking control of the turn-taking system; we understand this by reference to context-free norms. By tracing how context-free resources are employed and manifested locally in a context-sensitive manner, we are able to uncover the underlying machinery. As Hutchby and Wooffitt (1998) put it, "The aim of conversation analysis ... is to explicate the structural organization of talk in interaction at this interface between context-free resources and their context-sensitive applications" (p. 360). (Extract 1.26, presented in the next section, exemplifies how this is undertaken.)

CA employs a highly empirical, bottom-up approach to the specification of context. According to Schegloff (1987), much CA work "can be seen as an extended effort to elaborate just what a context is and what its explication or description might entail" (p. 221). Evidence for the characterization of a context has to derive primarily from the orientations of the participants as documented in the details of the interactional data rather than from a description of the physical setting or the participants. The key to understanding why CA insists on being so tightly empirical is that the aim is to develop an emic perspective on how the participants display to each other their understanding of the context. Clearly this cannot be achieved by analysts' etically deciding which aspects of context *they* think are relevant, particularly as there are an infinite number of potentially relevant contextual details which could be invoked. We can see an example of how contextual features can become relevant in Extract 1.24:

(1.24)

```
407 L10: oh I see (.) I see the chinese is uh (.) sanku
408        (0.6–0.9)
409 L11: unh?
410 L10: sanku
411        (.)
412 L9:   what
413 L10: c [ orals
414 L11:    [ corals
415 L9:    corals oh okay
```

(Markee, 2000, p. 27)

In this case L10's and L11's ethnic and linguistic identities as Chinese NSs (L9 is from a different ethnic and linguistic background) become available and relevant to CA, since this is made relevant in the details of the interaction through L10's producing the Chinese translation of "corals" and L10 and L11's then translating it back into English.

The final aspect of the complex CA perspective on context is that sequences of actions are seen as a major part of what we mean by context and that "modes of interactional organization might themselves be treated as contexts" (Schegloff, 1987, p. 221). This point will be illustrated in the discussion of Extract 1.25, with which we conclude this section on context by demonstrating how all of these different elements cohere. Whereas static and monolithic approaches to discourse regard institutional context as something given, fixed, and located in the background, CA adopts a dynamic view of context as endogenous to the talk, "showing that the participants build the context of their talk in and through their talk" (Heritage, 1997, p. 164).

(1.25)

```
11 Dr. F:  doctor Hollmann told me something like
12         you were running across the street not so
13         completely dressed or something like that,
14 Ms. B:  (h)yes: that's:—I am a child of God;=
15         I am his child;
16         (.)
17 Ms. B:  does a—does—=
18         =do you have children doctor Fisch[er?
```

```
19 Dr. F:                                        [yes:
20 Ms. B:  yes what age,
21 Dr. F:  uh around s–seven eight [ and eleven
22 Ms. B:                          [ yes and when they
23         were small these children,
24 Dr. F:  yes [ :,
25 Ms. B:      [ didn't they sometimes run around naked
26            [ because they don't yet—because they
27 Dr. F:      [ t(hh) u(h)
28 Ms. B:  don't (.) know that they must not do that. yes and in the same way:
29         you have to see that in my relationship to God
```

(Bergmann, 1992, p. 149. Translated from German.)

Extract 1.25 demonstrates why such a complex approach to context is necessary. A static, top-down, etic approach to context would work from the background contextual information regarding the psychiatrist, the patient, and the institutional setting (mental hospital). However, the extract demonstrates the need for a dynamic, empirical, emic, bottom-up approach rooted in the details of the interaction. Although the interaction starts off in Lines 11–13 with the professional questioning the patient, the "context" is immediately transformed as the patient poses a number of questions to the professional (who answers them) in order to lead the professional (in a Socratic manner) to a new insight in Lines 28 and 29. It is the interactional organization which has fundamentally changed during the course of the dialogue and hence is a significant element of the "context," even though the background factors remain constant. This is why CA proposes that organizations of the interaction can be treated as contexts and that the participants "talk contexts into being." Ms. B's contributions beginning in Line 18 are context-shaped in that they have to be understood in the context of the psychiatrist's previous turn, but they are context-renewing in that they talk a different context into being. The turn taking and adjacency pairs which organize the interaction are context-free resources and function as norms. It is by reference to these norms that we can understand that Ms. B is subverting the previously established context through her use of the organization of turn taking and adjacency pairs in a context-sensitive way.

1.9 Ethnomethodological Conversation Analysis and "Linguistic" Conversation Analysis

As a generalization, CA methodology has often been misunderstood by linguists and the reasons for this are quite easy to trace. First, sociologists have rarely tried to explain the ethnomethodological principles on which CA is based in terms which are comprehensible to linguists, or indeed to anyone outside sociology. By contrast, the interactional organizations of turn taking, adjacency pairs, preference organization, and repair are readily comprehensible and very useful to linguists. So it is in a sense quite natural that introductory texts on DA for linguists (e.g., Burns, 2001; Cameron, 2001; Cook, 1989; McCarthy, 1991)[15] should have introduced the above types of interactional organization without explication of the ethnomethodological principles which revealed them.

Linguists reading such accounts of the organizations might legitimately assume by default that they were a system of units and rules in the linguistic sense and that they were the methodology of CA. By contrast, a brief introduction for social scientists (Bryman, 2001) starts with the principles of reflexivity and indexicality and introduces interactional organizations as "tools for research." It should be noted that Sacks et al. (1974) presented their model of turn taking in a linguistics journal without explicating the ethnomethodological principles on which their work was based or the ways in which it differed from linguistics. It is again easy to understand how the confusion has arisen. In any case, there is now a common misconception among linguists that doing CA is a matter of transcribing talk and then identifying or coding patterns of turn taking, adjacency pairs, preference organization, and repair with the ethnomethodological principles and the dimension of social action entirely absent. Cameron's (2001) introduction to CA demonstrates how serious this misconception has become among linguists. Having introduced the CA model of turn taking, in Extract 1.26, Cameron presents data in which friends speak simultaneously:

(1.26)

```
A:  and she didn't she didn't like Katie she didn't ge[t on with Katie at all      ]
B:                                                     [no she didn't get on with ]
    Katie
```

(Cameron, 2001, p. 92)

Cameron reinforces this by reference to similar observations in two other publications and concludes that

> the simplest systematics model assumes that "one at a time" is both normal and fundamental: there is no obvious place in the model for simultaneous speech which is neither an error nor a violation, but merely a normal feature of certain kinds of talk. The question this raises is whether Sacks and colleagues make assumptions about talk-in-general which are not, in fact, universally valid ... if the analyst's claim is that "one speaker speaks at a time," one would expect participants in talk to display their orientation to that pattern by treating instances of simultaneous speech as problems requiring repair.... But in ... the conversation ... reproduced above [Extract 1.26], there is no display of orientation to the "one speaker speaks at a time" pattern, and this is what motivates speculation that some other system of floor organization may be operative. (Cameron, 2001, p. 93)

Readers who have followed the argument in this chapter, however, will realize that we need to see the turn-taking model as a constitutive norm which interactants make use of to display the meaning of their social actions to their partners and to interpret their partners' actions. First of all I will treat Cameron's point in general terms. It is indeed common for close friends, family, and associates to use overlap and simultaneous speech, and this may be significant social action, although this would have to be explicated on a case-by-case basis. As Schegloff (2000a) puts it, "Specific action ... outcomes are co-constructed by reference to one-party-at-a-time, even though they are realized through designedly simultaneous talk" (p. 48). It is quite common for preferred second turns such as acceptance of an invitation or agreement (as in Extract 1.26 and also Extract 1.27) to be undertaken in overlap before the TRP:

(1.27)

A: why don't you come up and <u>see</u> me some[times
B: [I would like to

(Atkinson & Drew, 1979, p. 58)

The point is that it may be precisely by reference to the TRP and the norms of turn taking that close friends and family index their degree of agreement and affiliation and talk a relationship of intimacy and a context of informality into being. In some cases it may be that the earlier one delivers a preferred action, the greater one's display of unquestioning support for and affiliation to one's partner. Similarly, it may be precisely by reference to the norms of turn taking and to the TRP that we display disaffiliation and prefigure a dispreferred action (for example, if B in Extract 1.27 had left a very long silence before answering A).

However, the point of CA is to analyze data, so we will apply the fundamental CA questions to Cameron's data: Why does overlap occur in Extract 1.26 in exactly the way it does (i.e., in those linguistic forms) at exactly the point where it does? The first thing we notice is that A extends her turn after the first TRP (the first mention of Katie) and repeats the same basic social action. She twice presents an opinion about the relationship between the unnamed "she" and Katie, or proffers this as topic in Schegloff's (1996) terms: "It is a recurrent feature of such sequences that two tries or proffers are put forward, each of which can be taken up and embraced or declined by its recipient" (p. 58). The next thing that we note is that it is not an exact repetition. The first opinion, "she didn't like Katie," is unidirectional and rather stronger than the second opinion, "she didn't get on with Katie," which presents the lack of social harmony as more of a two-way problem. At the first TRP (the first mention of

Katie), B could have performed some kind of agreement. However, as this is not forthcoming at that point, A extends the turn and repackages the same basic point in order to downgrade the degree of social disharmony implied. This creates an additional opportunity for B to give an affiliative response.

As Ford and Thompson (1996) explain, "Turn extensions in our data are regularly geared towards...creating or modifying relevance for another speaker's response. In pursuing recipient responses, speakers may...soften some claim...thus revising the context for agreement or disagreement" (p. 167). Note that B's action of agreement in Extract 1.26 starts in overlap at precisely the earliest possible moment at which B can recognize what A is about to say and recognize that it is a downgrade and therefore an assessment which she can agree with the second time around. We know that B has recognized what A was going to say at that moment because of the next-turn proof procedure. That is, B actually produces the same grammatical structure as A, even though they are talking in overlap. By withholding agreement at the first TRP, B has created a slight disaffiliation between herself and A. A then makes an affiliative action by modifying her opinion and creates a fresh opportunity for B to agree. As soon as B can recognize this, she displays the degree of her enthusiasm for agreeing with the modified opinion and hence for restoring her affiliation with A precisely by delivering the action at the earliest possible point in overlap. Why does B use exactly those linguistic forms? The *no* documents agreement. By adopting exactly the same linguistic forms as A, B again displays the degree of her agreement with A. This also points to another motivation for the overlap's starting at that exact point. According to Lerner (2002),

> At times participants may speak in a fashion that reveals that they are aiming to simultaneously co-produce part or all of a turn-constructional unit more or less in unison with another participant, by recognizably attempting to do such things as match the words, voicing, and tempo of the other speaker.... Choral co-production can be

> employed by an addressed recipient of a turn to demon-
> strate agreement with what is being said. (pp. 226, 237)

Choral coproduction, then, can be a powerful means of displaying the degree of one's empathy with another and in this case could be accomplished only by B's starting her turn in overlap as early as possible. Extract 1.26 is also rather intriguing as it demonstrates how the interactants negotiate their degree of affiliation to each other at the same time as they are negotiating as topic the state of affiliation between two acquaintances.

The stated aim of Cameron's (2001) introduction to CA is to provide "a grounding in the practical techniques of [CA (among other approaches)] and how to apply them to real data" (back cover). It is therefore disappointing that Cameron fails to ana-lyze her data using a CA methodology and instead presents them as having "no obvious place in the model" (p. 93) of turn taking. The degree of B's agreement is indexed by and documented by the timing of the overlap as well as by its linguistic formatting. In other words, the interactants perform their social actions *precisely by normative reference to the model of turn taking.* The interactional organizations themselves are context-free, but the vital point is that participants employ these context-free organizations in a context-sensitive way to display their social actions. It is because the participants (and we as analysts) are able to identify the gap between the context-free model and its context-sensitive implementation that they (and we as analysts) are able to understand the social significance of the context-sensitive implementation. Cameron (2001) is represen-tative of several short introductions to linguistic CA[16] and demonstrates how wide the gulf has now become between *linguistic CA* and ethnomethodological CA. Taking Cameron (2001) as the archetype, the typical features of introductions to linguistic CA are as follows:

- No representative examples of actual CA are provided.
- There is no mention of any of the ethnomethodological principles which are the fundamentals of CA methodology.

- The reader is likely to form the impression that interactional organizations are the methodology of CA and are a system of units and rules to be applied etically in the same way as in a descriptivist linguistics approach.
- There is no indication that participants employ these context-free interactional organizations in a normative, context-sensitive way to display their social actions.
- Hence the reflexive connection between social action and language is entirely absent.

It is therefore no surprise that many students of linguistics now believe *doing* CA means producing a detailed transcription and then merely identifying instances of turn taking, adjacency pairs, preference, and repair; there is description of superficial linguistic features rather than an analysis of social action. Linguistic CA is basically CA minus the methodology: a kind of coding scheme. Metaphorically, it presents the reader with a Porsche which has had a lawn mower engine installed in it. It may have the same name, badge, and bodywork as a normal Porsche and crawl forward in the same direction after a fashion, but the power is no longer there.

We should consider whether there is any fundamental objection to having two alternative versions of CA. In my view there is no crucial problem, provided that the two versions are separated, defined, and named differently. Some linguists will no doubt continue to find it useful to etically employ the interactional organizations as a coding scheme in a descriptivist linguistic paradigm. Provided that it is recognized that this is linguistic CA and is different from doing CA, I cannot see any fundamental objection. This separation and renaming would avoid the current problem which does seem to me to be very serious: the current blurring between the two versions which gives the impression to many linguists that ethnomethodological CA is also an underpowered, etic coding scheme. So, for example, we saw above that Cameron's introduction to CA suggests that CA is unable to handle straightforward data, whereas the ethnomethodological version is perfectly capable of doing so. The term *conversation analysis* should be reserved for the original ethnomethodological version and *linguistic conversation analysis* for the linguistic version. A further problem caused by the current blurred situation is that sociological CA practitioners occasionally express a degree of frustration with a common belief among linguists that these linguists understand CA when what they have actually encountered is the linguistic version. It is therefore possible that formalizing a separation between the two versions would lead to greater clarity and understanding among all parties involved.

1.10 Chapter Summary

In this chapter I have introduced the fundamentals of CA methodology in relation to ordinary conversation. In Chapter 2, I introduce CA methodology in relation to institutional discourse in general, and in Chapters 3–5, CA is applied to L2 classroom interaction in particular. In Chapter 6, we will revisit CA as a social science research methodology in relation to issues such as validity, reliability, generalizability, quantification, and triangulation.

A number of typical criticisms of CA are that it refuses to use available theories of human conduct, is unwilling to invoke "obvious" background contextual features, and is obsessed with "trivial" detail. The "units of analysis" are alleged to be unclear and unreliable, and it is said that interactants often do not follow the "rules" specified by CA. It is hoped that this chapter has clarified the CA position in relation to all of these issues and has explained the coherent rationale underlying CA methodology.

In this chapter I have illustrated the basic principles of CA using extracts from ordinary conversation. The chapter explained the relationship between ethnomethodology and CA, outlining five fundamental principles which underlie ethnomethodology and hence CA. After outlining the aims and principles of CA, I introduced the interactional organizations of sequence (adjacency pairs), preference, turn taking, and repair. I then explained the typical analytical procedures followed in CA and introduced the CA perspective on context. The chapter concluded with the argument that a "linguistic" version of CA has diverged from ethnomethodological CA.

Notes

[1]The terms *language classroom* and *L2 classroom* refer to any classrooms in which a language other than the mother tongue of the students is taught.

[2]The discussion is based on Heritage (1984b), Boyle (1997), Hutchby and Wooffitt (1998), and ten Have (1999).

[3]These principles originate in Boyle (1997), Garfinkel (1967), and Heritage (1984b).

[4]A schema is a hypothetical mental framework for portraying memorized generic concepts. See Cook (1989, p. 69). See Section 6.3 for the CA perspective on socially distributed cognition. It is important to note that CA does not "psychologize" about participants' cognitive states or discuss structures such as schemata; here I am merely pointing to a similarity.

[5]In Section 1.8 we note that ethnographic or contextual information can be invoked in the analysis only if it is evident in the details of the interaction that the participants are orienting to it. However, many extracts in this monograph start with ethnographic or contextual information. Indeed, this is common practice in relation to institutional discourse, with the majority of chapters in Drew and Heritage (1992a) starting with some kind of contextual information. The apparent contradiction can be explained by the difference between process and product. The process is that described in Section 1.8. However, in order to turn technical conversation analyses into publishable work, the analyses need to be made readable and to follow standard academic conventions. Therefore, it is almost always necessary for the published work "product" to start by supplying information necessary to the reader and to employ terms in the transcript such as "teacher" and "judge."

[6]Imposing sanctions means expressing righteous hostility on a social level, for example, by snubbing someone.

[7]See Section 6.3 for a discussion of the CA perspective on socially distributed cognition.

[8]Although gaze and nonverbal communication can also be included in the analysis.

[9]Indeed, Schegloff and Sacks (1973) published on adjacency pairs before turn taking and repair.

[10]Extract 1.4 shows Child sanctioning Mother, which demonstrates why social categories cannot be accepted a priori as immutable constructs.

[11]See Heritage (1984b, p. 260) for further discussion.

[12]See Note 14 of Chapter 4 in relation to face and politeness.

[13]This finding is based on American English and may not apply to all cultures or languages.

[14]The discussion is intended as an introduction for nonpractitioners. Within CA, the treatment of context is one of the most controversial topics, and a variety of conceptions are expressed. Since one of the aims of this monograph is to emphasize elements of compatibility with other research methodologies, my conception of context is more broadly conceived. The interested reader is referred to Duranti and Goodwin (1992) and Sarangi and Roberts (1999).

[15]McCarthy does not claim to be introducing CA.

[16]This is not to imply that all introductions to CA written by linguists constitute linguistic CA. Levinson (1983) and Markee (2000) are linguists but base their accounts on ethnomethodological principles.

CHAPTER TWO

Different Perspectives on Language Classroom Interaction

This chapter reviews several approaches which have been employed over the last 30 years to analyze L2 classroom interaction. Although the review is critical in some respects in order to prepare the ground for a CA perspective on institutional discourse, it nonetheless tries to uncover elements of compatibility between CA and the approaches reviewed and to integrate them wherever possible. The first approach reviewed is DA, which has been the basis for numerous coding schemes in language teaching. I then consider the perspective of the communicative approach on interaction in the language classroom. Next, I show that there has been strong recent research interest in developing dynamic and variable approaches to classroom interaction. This is followed by a discussion of issues relating to databases underlying such research and a specification of the database underlying this study. I then consider the relationship between CA and ethnography and conclude by introducing the CA perspective on institutional discourse on which this study is based.

2.1 Discourse Analysis Approaches

According to Levinson (1983, p. 286) there are two major approaches to the study of naturally occurring interaction: DA and CA. The majority of previous approaches to L2 classroom interaction have implicitly or explicitly adopted what is fundamentally a DA approach. In this section I review the DA approach critically, but this is not in an attempt to discredit it or suggest that it is worthless. Any current attempt at analysis of L2 classroom interaction is very much built on the foundations of what has been achieved through the DA approach. Furthermore, we will see (as mentioned in Chapter 1) that DA is actually used in practice as one integral component of CA and that integration would in effect enable DA to function in a much broader sociolinguistic context and create a link to the pedagogical level. So in the following section I make explicit the limitations of the DA approach when it is used in isolation and argue strongly for it to be integrated into a CA approach. DA uses principles and methodology typical of linguistics to analyze classroom discourse in structural-functional linguistic terms (Chaudron, 1988, p. 14). For example, "Could I borrow your pencil?" could be mapped as *request*. Once sequences of speech acts or moves have been plotted, a set of rules can be written which show how the units fit together to form coherent discourse. Then, hierarchical systems which depict the overall organization of classroom discourse can be developed.

The outstanding study of (first language [L1]) classroom interaction which takes this DA approach is Sinclair and Coulthard (1975). Probably their most significant finding as far as the teaching profession is concerned is their identification of the three-part sequence typical of classroom interaction. This sequence is generally known as teacher initiation, learner response, and teacher follow-up or feedback (IRF) in the British school, and initiation, response and evaluation (IRE) in the American school.[1] I will refer to it as the *IRF/IRE cycle* in this study. It should be noted that a full-scale and explicit DA model of the organization of *L2* classroom interaction has never been published. The DA system of analyzing classroom interaction has proved highly appealing to the language-teaching profession (particularly as it uses a linguistic approach) to the extent that the majority of studies of classroom interaction have been based more or less explicitly on it. This includes the many coding schemes which have been developed specifically for the L2 classroom. All coding schemes for L2 classroom interaction are implicitly based on a DA paradigm and embody "the assumption that those features of the interaction of teacher and taught which are relevant to the researcher's purposes are evident 'beneath' or 'within' the words exchanged" (Edwards & Westgate, 1994, p. 61).

The basis of the DA approach and of classroom coding schemes is that an interactant makes one move on one level at a time. The move the teacher makes can be specified and coded as a pedagogic move, for example, *initiates* or *replies*. This *one-pedagogic-move-on-one-level-at-a-time* coding approach is the basis of the following coding systems developed especially for the L2 classroom: the Communicative Orientation of Language Teaching (COLT) instrument (Froehlich, Spada, & Allen, 1985), Target Language Observation Scheme (TALOS; Ullman & Geva, 1984), and Foreign Language Interaction (FLINT; Moskowitz, 1976); a list of observation instruments is available in Chaudron (1988, p. 18). Some of the above coding systems involve coding on different dimensions of analysis, such as content, type of activity, skill focus, and language used (see Chaudron, 1988, p. 22, for a summary). But the assumption is still that on each of these separate coding dimensions, the teacher makes one pedagogical move at a time, and the coder has to make a choice as to which slot the pedagogical move should be coded into. The DA approach has been subject to considerable criticism on a theoretical level, most notably by Levinson (1983, p. 289), who suggests that there are strong reasons to believe that DA models are fundamentally inappropriate to the subject matter and thus irremediably inadequate. The following is a simplified summary of Levinson's (1983, pp. 287–294) discussion of the main problems inherent in a DA approach:

- A single utterance can perform multiple speech acts at a time, but DA translates a single utterance into a single speech act.

- Responses can be addressed not only to the illocutionary force of utterances, but also to their perlocutionary force; perlocutions are in principle unlimited in kind and number.
- It is impossible to specify in advance what kinds of behavioral units will carry out interactional acts; laughter and silence can function as responses, for example.
- There is no straightforward correlation between form and function.
- Sequential context and extralinguistic context can play a role in determining utterance function.
- It is not possible to specify a set of rules which show how the units fit together to form coherent discourse, as it is in syntax; cases of impossible or ill-formed discourses are hard, if not impossible, to find.
- The textual analyses produced by a DA approach are quite superficial and disappointing, involving an intuitive mapping of unmotivated categories onto a restricted range of data.

It may be argued that such theoretical problems do not mean that the DA approach is fundamentally unsuitable in practical terms for the analysis of L2 classroom interaction, given that the DA approach has proved popular with the L2 teaching profession. I therefore propose to analyze extracts from L2 lessons in an attempt to reveal the fundamental practical limitations of the DA approach in isolation and in order to demonstrate that it tends to homogenize and oversimplify the interaction. A focus on the IRF/IRE cycle (and on other pedagogic moves) appears attractive at first, in that all an analyst need do is identify cycles within the interaction, and the DA is virtually complete. The following two extracts both demonstrate teacher-led IRF/IRE sequences:

(2.1)

1 T: after they have put up their tent, what did the boys do?
2 L: they cooking food.
3 T: no, not they cooking food, pay attention.

4 L: they cook their meal.
5 T: right, they cook their meal over an open fire.

(Tsui, 1995, p. 52)

The focus in Extract 2.1 is on the accurate production of a string of linguistic forms by the learners. So although no one would have any problem in understanding the gist of the learner's first utterance, it is not accepted by the teacher, and the interaction continues until the correct forms are produced. The initiation slot of the IRF/IRE cycle prompts the learner to produce a specific sequence of linguistic forms; the response slot is the learner's attempt to produce that sequence; the follow-up slot is, in Line 3, negative evaluation and a prompt for the repeated attempt at the production of a specific sequence of linguistic forms; in Line 5 it is positive evaluation plus repetition of the correct sequence of forms. The type of repair used is *exposed correction* (Jefferson, 1987) in which correction becomes the interactional business and the flow of the interaction is put on hold while the trouble is corrected.

(2.2)

1 T: Vin, have you ever been to the movies? what's your favorite movie?
2 L: big.
3 T: big, OK, that's a good movie, that was about a little boy inside a big man, wasn't it?
4 L: yeah, boy get surprise all the time.
5 T: yes, he was surprised, wasn't he? Usually little boys don't do the things that men do, do they?
6 L: no, little boy no drink.
7 T: that's right, little boys don't drink.

(Johnson, 1995, p. 23)

Taking first of all a conventional DA approach, Extract 2.2 can also be analyzed quite straightforwardly. What we have is a sequence of consecutive IRF/IRE cycles which can be coded as follows: Line 1: initiation; Line 2: reply; Line 3: follow-up and initiation; Line 4: reply; Line 5: follow-up and initiation; Line 6: reply; Line 7: follow-up. The analysis is simple and complete, and we can confirm that this is therefore traditional, lockstep classroom interaction of the type often criticized by the communicative approach (Dinsmore, 1985; Nunan, 1987) because it is teacher-dominated and different from genuine interaction. Using the DA approach, then, the analyses are quick, straightforward and complete; we have an impression of homogeneity, and there are no fundamental differences between Extract 2.1 and Extract 2.2.

I will now reanalyze Extract 2.2 using a CA methodology and suggest that in fact this is a very complex, fluid, and dynamic piece of interaction indeed and that there are huge differences between Extracts 2.1 and 2.2. If we analyze turn taking, sequence organization, repair, and topic[2] at the same time, we can see that the learner in Extract 2.2 is able to develop a subtopic and is allowed interactional space. In Line 1 T introduces the carrier topic (movies) and constrains L's turn in Line 2, which is a minimum response appropriate to the turn. In Line 3 T shifts the topic slightly from the carrier topic (movies) to the subtopic of the specific movie *Big*, which has been nominated by L. In doing so T validates and approves L's subtopic by calling it a good movie. This particular comedy movie involves a "magical" swap in which a young boy and a man have their minds transferred into each other's bodies. T constrains L's next turn by making a general statement summarizing the plot of the movie ("that was about a little boy inside a big man") together with a tag question. This allocates a turn to L, constrains the topic of L's turn (the plot of the movie *Big*), and simultaneously provides the other students in the class (who may not know the movie) with sufficient information to be able to follow the evolving dialogue. The tag question effectively requires L to confirm the accuracy of T's summary of the movie's plot but also allows L the interactional space to develop the subtopic (if L wishes). L does confirm T's summary of the subtopic and then chooses to contribute new information which develops the subtopic (the plot of the movie), namely, in Line 4 ("boy get surprise all the time"). This utterance is linguistically incorrect, although the propositional content is clear to T. Since L is introducing "new" information, L is effectively developing the subtopic, to which T could respond in his or her next turn. At this point T could choose (a) to correct the learner's utterance, (b) to continue to develop the subtopic, or (c) to decline to adopt L's subtopic and change the course of the interaction: T has superior interactional rights (Mehan, 1979) and is not obliged to adopt the direction in which L is pushing the interaction. T effectively chooses to combine choices (a) and (b) in Line 5: "Yes, he was surprised, wasn't he?" There is positive evaluation of the propositional content of the learner utterance followed by an expansion of the learner utterance into a correct sequence of linguistic forms. The type of repair used is embedded correction (Jefferson, 1987, p. 95), that is, a correction done as a by-the-way occurrence in the context of a social action, which in this case is an action of agreement and confirmation.[3]

This form of correction and expansion is highly reminiscent of adult-child conversation (see, for example, adult-child conversation transcripts in Harris and Coltheart, 1986, p. 50; Painter, 1989, p. 38; and Peccei, 1994, p. 83), and the technique being used by the teacher here is often termed *scaffolding* (Johnson, 1995, p. 75). Further, in Line 5, T then accepts L's invitation to develop the subtopic, and T's statement "usually little boys don't do the things that men do" also simultaneously provides the other students in the class with an explanation as to why the boy was surprised all the time, thus enabling them to continue to follow the evolving dialogue. The tag question (Line 5) again allocates a turn to L and effectively allots to him the interactional space to continue to develop the subtopic should he wish to do so. L uses "no" in Line 6 to agree with the negative tag question and chooses to develop the subtopic by providing an example from the movie to illustrate T's previous generalized statement: "little boy no drink." Again his utterance is linguistically incorrect, although the propositional content is clear. Since L is again introducing "new" information, L effectively invites T to respond to this elaboration of the subtopic in T's next turn. T's response in Line 7 is similar to Line 5 in that T performs an action of agreement, simultaneously corrects L's utterance (using embedded correction), and displays a correct version for the other students.

What is clear from the reanalysis of Extract 2.2 is that, although it could at first sight be mistaken for a rigid, plodding, lockstep IRF/IRE cycle sequence in which everything is planned and predictable, the interaction is in fact dynamic, fluid, and locally managed on a turn-by-turn basis to a considerable extent. There is some degree of planning in that the teacher has an overall idea of what is to be achieved in the interaction and in that it is the teacher who introduces the carrier topic of films and has overall control of the speech exchange system. However, the question in Line 1 is an open or referential one—the teacher does not know how L will respond[4]—and L is able to nominate and develop a subtopic.

I would now like to demonstrate that the teacher is balancing multiple and sometimes conflicting demands. As Edmondson (1985, p. 162) puts it, "The complexity of the classroom is such that several things may be going on publicly through talk at the same time." The teacher is orienting to five separate (though related) concerns simultaneously:

1. The teacher's pedagogical focus (Johnson, 1995) is "to allow the students to share their ideas and possibly generate some new vocabulary words within the context of the discussion" (p. 23). This implies that the teacher needs to control the overall topic while allowing the learners some interactional space to develop their own subtopics. The teacher has to orient, then, to an overall pedagogical plan.

2. The teacher also has to respond to the ideas and personal meanings which the learner chooses to share and does so successfully in that he or she develops the subtopic introduced by the learner. So in Lines 5 and 7 the teacher responds to the learner's utterance with a conversational action of agreement which validates the propositional

content of the utterance as well as the introduction of the subtopic.

3. The teacher also responds to linguistic incorrectness in the individual learner's utterances and conducts embedded repair on them. The linguistic repair is performed in a mitigated way, because it is prefaced by an action of agreement and approval and because this type of embedded correction can be treated as a by-the-way matter.

4. The teacher must also orient to the other learners in the class. One problem faced by teachers is that individual learners often produce responses which are inaudible or incomprehensible to the other students in the class. So in Lines 5 and 7 the teacher is simultaneously displaying approved versions of learner utterances, so that the other learners are able to follow the propositional content of the interaction and are also able to receive correctly formed linguistic input.

5. One of the most difficult feats in L2 teaching is to maintain a simultaneous dual focus on both form and meaning (Seedhouse, 1997b). The teacher in Extract 2.2 is skillfully managing to maintain elements of a simultaneous dual focus on both form and meaning. There is a focus on form in that the teacher upgrades and expands the learners' utterances on a linguistic level, which means that the learners have a linguistically correct utterance which can function as both model and input. The focus is simultaneously also on meaning in that the learner is able to contribute "new" information concerning his or her personal experiences and to develop a subtopic.

Now the CA of Extract 2.2 does not dispute that the extract consists of IRF/IRE cycles; the DA is certainly right to point this out. However, the point which is missed in the DA approach is that *the IRF/IRE cycles perform different interactional and pedagogical work according to the context in which they are operating*. This is clear if we contrast the interactional work the IRF/IRE cycle is doing in Extract 2.1 with that which it is doing in Extract 2.2. Some studies of L2 classroom interaction (Dinsmore, 1985; Nunan, 1987) suggest that it is the IRF/IRE cycle which is primarily responsible for traditional patterns of interaction. However, the analysis of Extract 2.2 shows that the interaction is not necessarily completely closed with the IRF/IRE cycle. A variable approach to context is therefore necessary for a valid and adequate description of L2 classroom interaction. A focus on superficially isolable, identifiable, and quantifiable features such as the IRF/IRE cycle and display questions will inevitably result in monolithic and acontextual overgeneralizations. From the analysis of Extracts 2.1 and 2.2 we may conclude the following: The identification of the IRF/IRE cycle (or any other quasi-syntactic DA category) in isolation does not elucidate the nature, interest, or orientation of the interaction. The DA approach is inherently acontextual and is unable to portray the different contexts and the different focuses of the interaction. The analysis reveals the need for a variable conception of context, which is discussed further in Sections 2.3 and 5.6. A basic problem with the DA approach is that it portrays teachers as making one pedagogical action on one level at a time. The analysis of Extract 2.2 shows that teachers may be simultaneously orienting to multiple separate pedagogical concerns and that classroom interaction may be operating simultaneously on multiple levels.

The focus and context of an interaction may switch with great fluidity. Halliday (1985) suggests that "the context of spoken language is in a constant state of flux, and the language has to be mobile and alert. . . . The complexity of spoken language is more like that of a dance; it is not static and dense but mobile and intricate" (p. xxxiv). I have tried to show that DA cannot portray the flow of an interaction because it is essentially a static approach which portrays interaction as consisting of fixed and unidimensional coordinates on a conceptual map. Since the DA approach was developed for L1 classrooms and transferred for use in L2 classrooms, it has difficulty in portraying the extra dimension which distinguishes L2 classroom interaction from L1 classroom interaction. As J. Willis (1992) puts it, "language is used for two purposes; it serves both as the subject matter of the lesson, and as the medium of instruction. It is precisely this dual role that makes language lessons difficult to describe" (p. 162).

Some coding schemes have tried to adapt the DA approach to the L2 classroom. In order to try to make the DA approach cope with two different levels of language use, J. Willis (1992) proposes coding on either an inner or an outer level: "The 'Outer' structure is a mechanism for controlling and stimulating utterances in the 'Inner' structure which gives formal practice in the foreign language" (p. 163). However, this still implies that an utterance is being used either on one level or the other, whereas I have demonstrated in my analysis of Extract 2.2 that utterances often operate on both levels simultaneously.

The DA approach massively oversimplifies the interaction in Extract 2.2, and I would argue that it must in general do so in order to make the DA system work. The microinteraction has to be coded as a single instructional sequence (Mehan, 1979) or as a single move (Sinclair & Coulthard, 1975) so that it can be fitted into the hierarchy. In contrast to the DA of Extract 2.2, the CA of that extract was better able to capture the dynamic, fluid, complex interplay and dialectic between the different levels on which the L2 classroom operates and hence portray the complexity of the teacher's interactional work. Because the focus in DA is on fitting the microinteraction into a system, whereas the focus in CA is on portraying the participants' interactional concerns, DA tends to conceal the complexity of the interaction and homogenize it, whereas CA tends to reveal its complexity, fluidity, and dynamism.

It was suggested in the analysis of Extract 2.2 that, by virtue of language's being the object as well as the vehicle of instruction, L2 teachers are doing very complex interactional work compared with "content" teachers and compared with professionals in other institutional settings. Unfortunately, the DA methodology and coding schemes which have been predominantly employed to represent their work tend to portray them as plodding from one monotonous IRF/IRE cycle to the next and as working on a single level. So I feel that the DA approach we have predominantly used up until now to portray what we do in the classroom has not done sufficient justice to the complexity of the interactional work language teachers are engaged in, and that it has therefore not done sufficient justice to the profession (Seedhouse, 1998b).

So the position reached at the end of this section is that if DA is used as an isolated system, it has a great number of problems and limitations for the reasons given. However, the basis of DA—form-function mapping—forms an integral part of CA, namely the "why that?" part of the question "why that, in that way, right now?" We can see how this integration of DA into CA would work in the CA of Extract 2.2. Form-function mapping or speech move DA is certainly undertaken, but it forms only a part of a much broader perspective which concentrates on the relationship between pedagogical focus and the organization of the interaction, in particular the organization of turns, sequence, repair, and topic. So a CA institutional-discourse approach to L2 classroom interaction is very much founded on and compatible with the many studies of L2 classrooms under-taken in a DA paradigm. The CA approach is, however, able to take the exploration much further and create more connections with social and institutional context. Most importantly, CA is able to portray the reflexive relationship between pedagogy and interaction, whereas DA is not.

2.2 The Communicative Approach to Second Language Classroom Interaction

In the previous section, DA was reviewed as an example of an interactional approach to L2 classroom interaction. In this section, I review the communicative approach as an example of a pedagogical approach to L2 classroom interaction. Although one might have expected the communicative approach to have adopted a complex and sophisticated perspective on communication in the

L2 classroom, in this section I argue that in fact the communicative approach has, most surprisingly, adopted a monolithic, static, and invariant perspective on classroom interaction. Moreover, the communicative perspective on L2 classroom interaction is not based on any communication or sociolinguistic theory, but rather on a single, invariant pedagogical concept. However, it should be pointed out at the outset that there is no intended criticism of the value of the communicative approach to language teaching as such, but rather of its perspective on classroom interaction and the analyses produced. I would first like to examine the elements which constitute the communicative position on L2 classroom interaction and then review communicative analyses of L2 classroom interaction.

In the late 1980s a communicative tradition developed which saw much traditional L2 classroom communication as undesirable in comparison to "genuine" or "natural" communication. Nunan (1987), for example, examined five exemplary communicative language lessons and found that they resembled traditional patterns of classroom interaction rather than genuine interaction. Nunan sums up the results of the research up to that point:

> There is a growing body of classroom-based research which supports the conclusion drawn here, that there are comparatively few opportunities for genuine communicative language use in second-language classrooms.... A disconfirming study is yet to be documented. (p. 141)

Kumaravadivelu (1993) confirms that this tradition was still prevalent in the 1990s: "Research studies ... show that even teachers who are committed to communicative language teaching can fail to create opportunities for genuine interaction in the language classroom" (p. 12). The main assumptions of this tradition can be summarized as follows:

1. There is such a thing as genuine or natural communication (Kramsch, 1981, p. 8; Kumaravadivelu, 1993, p. 12; Nunan, 1987, p. 137).

2. It is possible for L2 teachers to replicate genuine or natural communication in the classroom, but most teachers fail to do so (Kramsch, 1981, p. 18; Kumaravadivelu, 1993, p. 12; Legutke & Thomas, 1991, p. 8; Nunan, 1987, p. 144).

3. Most teachers instead produce interaction which features display questions and examples of the IRF/IRE cycle, which are typical of traditional classroom interaction and rarely occur in genuine interaction (Dinsmore, 1985, pp. 226–227; Long & Sato, 1983, p. 284; Nunan, 1987, p. 141; 1988, p. 139).

4. Teachers can be trained to replicate genuine or natural communication in the classroom (Kumaravadivelu, 1993, p. 18; Nunan, 1987, p. 144).

I will now examine each element of this tradition and attempt to reveal the problems inherent in the underlying assumptions.

Assumption 1. There is such a thing as "genuine" or "natural" communication.

The terms *genuine communication* and *natural communication*, as used by the communicative tradition, are not precise sociolinguistic or discoursal terms. Many writers have used the terms *genuine* or *natural* in regard to communication without attempting to define or characterize them. Nunan (1987), however, does provide a characterization of genuine communication. He suggests that

> genuine communication is characterized by the uneven distribution of information, the negotiation of meaning (through, for example, clarification requests and confirmation checks), topic nomination and negotiation by more than one speaker, and the right of interlocutors to decide whether to contribute to an interaction or not. In other words, in genuine communication, decisions about who says what to whom and when are up for grabs. (p. 137)

Although Nunan does not actually say that he is characterizing ordinary conversation, the quotation is a short characterization of ordinary conversation within the CA paradigm. In CA terms, his last sentence clearly implies 100% local allocational means, which can only mean conversation rather than any other speech exchange system, all of which use greater preallocation (Sacks et al., 1974, p. 729). Other authors reinforce the point that what is actually meant by genuine or natural discourse is in fact conversation. Kramsch (1981, p. 17) explicitly equates natural discourse with conversation, and Ellis (1992, p. 38) equates naturalistic discourse with conversation. The communicative tradition, then, equates genuine or natural communication with ordinary conversation, which is a CA term (as well as a lay term). I will use only the term *ordinary conversation* from now on. The clear implication in the communicative tradition is that it is possible for conversation to be produced within the setting of an L2 classroom lesson, and indeed this looks perfectly reasonable at first sight. However, CA sees conversation as a benchmark against which institutional varieties can be described and recognized (Drew & Heritage, 1992b, p. 19).

Conversation, then, is clearly differentiated from the numerous varieties of institutional discourse. If we rephrase the implication in sociolinguistic terms, it begins to look unreasonable; the clear implication in the communicative tradition is that it is possible for conversation (a noninstitutional form of discourse) to be produced within the setting of an L2 classroom lesson (an institutional form of discourse). We should also note at this point that there is no basis in communication or sociolinguistic theory for characterizing one variety of discourse as more genuine or natural than another, with the exception of scripted interaction typical of films and television programs. The concept of interaction in the classroom being not genuine or natural and that outside the classroom being genuine and natural is a purely pedagogical one.

Assumption 2. It is possible for L2 teachers to replicate conversation in the classroom, but most teachers fail to do so.

I will now argue that it is, in theory, not possible for L2 teachers to replicate conversation (in its CA sense) in the L2 classroom as part of a lesson. Warren (1993)[5] is based on a corpus of 40 recordings of ordinary conversation (totaling 25,000 words) in natural settings. Warren develops a precise and consensual definition of conversation which distinguishes it from other discourse types: "a speech event *outside of an institutionalized setting* [italics added] involving at least two participants who share responsibility for the progress and outcome of an impromptu and unmarked verbal encounter consisting of more than a ritualized exchange" (p. 8).

For L2 classroom interaction to be equivalent to ordinary conversation, the following features of naturalness in conversation (paraphrasing Warren) would have to be met: The setting must not be an institutional one; turn taking and participation rights in conversation must be unrestricted; and responsibility for managing and monitoring the progress of the discourse must be shared by all participants (see also Edwards & Westgate, 1994, p. 116). Conversations are open-ended, and participants jointly negotiate the topic and the language/dialect in which the conversation is conducted. The only way, therefore, in which an L2 lesson could become identical to conversation would be for the learners to regard the teacher as a fellow conversationalist of equal status rather than as a teacher, for the teacher not to direct the discourse in any way at all, and for the setting to be noninstitutional. No institutional purposes could shape the discourse, in other words.

The stated purpose of L2 institutions is to teach the L2 to foreigners. As soon as the teacher instructs the learners to have a conversation in the L2, the institutional context is talked into being (see Section 5.4), and the interaction could not be conversation as defined here. In order to replicate conversation, the L2 lesson would therefore have to cease to be an L2 lesson in any understood sense of the term (van Lier, 1988b, p. 267) and become a conversation which did not have any underlying pedagogical purpose, which was not about the L2 or even, in most situations, *in* the L2. Van Lier underlines the point that the communicative approach would in effect like L2 classrooms to stop being L2 classrooms.

It is not suggested that it is impossible for ordinary conversation in the CA sense to take place in the physical setting of an L2 classroom, but rather that it cannot occur as part of an L2 lesson. In the vast majority of L2 classrooms around the world, the learners share the same L1. The only conceivable way in which conversation could occur in these monolingual L2 classrooms would be for the learners to converse in their L1. In multilingual English Language Teaching (ELT) classrooms, which are frequently found in the United Kingdom and the United States, it would be quite natural for learners to use English (their L2) to have a conversation. (See Markee [in press] for an example of students switching between a private conversation and L2 classroom business.) In order for it to be a conversation, however, the teacher would not be able to suggest the topic of the discourse or direct it in any way. Such a conversation might just as well take place in a coffee bar as in the L2 classroom. It is therefore impossible, in theory, for L2 teachers to produce conversation (in the CA sense) in the classroom as part of a lesson. I will attempt to demonstrate that this is also impossible in practice during the discussion of Assumption 4.

Assumption 3. Most teachers instead produce interaction which features display questions and examples of the IRF/IRE cycle, which are typical of traditional classroom interaction and are rarely found in conversation.

Both Nunan (1987, p. 137) and Dinsmore (1985, p. 226) give the presence of the IRF/IRE cycle as their initial reason for asserting that there was little genuine communication in the L2 classrooms which they observed. Dinsmore claims that the prevalence of the IRF/IRE cycle and the unequal power distribution "hardly seems compatible with a 'communicative' language teaching methodology" (p. 227). Nunan writes that

on the surface, the lessons appeared to conform to the sorts of communicative principles advocated in the literature. However, when the patterns of interaction were examined more closely, they resembled traditional patterns of classroom interaction rather than genuine interaction. Thus, the most commonly occurring pattern of interaction was [IRF]. (p. 137)

I made the point in the analysis of Extract 2.2 that interaction featuring the IRF/IRE cycle can be dynamic and fluid and offer the learner some interactional space, but that DA methodology cannot reveal this. The problem is that a focus on identifying IRF/IRE cycles tends to be self-fulfilling and limiting and to blind analysts to other aspects of the interaction. Dinsmore (1985) actually decided to search for this exchange structure before examining his data: "I had predicted that the basic exchange structure...would not be so prevalent in the adult EFL [English as a foreign language] classes I observed" (p. 226). I would now like to suggest that there is a fundamental problem with the communicative approach's assumption that, because the IRF/IRE cycle is normally noticeably absent from adult-adult conversation, it is therefore unnatural and should not occur in the L2 classroom either. It is important to note that the IRF/IRE cycle is very noticeably present in a particular discourse setting outside the classroom, namely, in the home in parent-child interaction.[6] Examples of the IRF/IRE cycle are to be found in virtually every published collection of transcripts of parent-child conversation, for example, Maclure and French (1981, p. 211), Painter (1989, p. 38), and Peccei (1994, p. 83). The interactional structure cannot be differentiated from that which takes place in the L2 classroom, for example:

(2.3)

(Mother and Kevin look at pictures)
Mother: and what are those?
Kevin: shells.
Mother: shells, yes.
         you've got some shells, haven't you?
         what's that?
Kevin: milk.

(Harris & Coltheart, 1986, p. 50)

It appears that critics of the IRF/IRE cycle in L2 learning contexts have failed to notice the significant role it plays in L1 learning in a home environment. Ellis (1992, p. 37) reports that much second language acquisition (SLA) research is based on the assumption that classroom SLA will be most successful if opportunities are created for learners to engage in interactions of the kind experienced by children acquiring their L1. Given the prominence of the IRF/IRE cycle in parent-child interaction, one might therefore have expected communicative theorists to be actively promoting the use of the IRF/IRE cycle rather than attempting to banish it. A CA institutional-discourse approach (Drew & Heritage, 1992b, p. 41) would attempt to account for the fact that the IRF/IRE cycle is prevalent in the classroom and in parent-child interaction but rare in conversation in the following way: In the classroom and in parent-child interaction, the core goal is learning or education, and the IRF/IRE cycle is an interactional feature which is well suited to this core goal (see Section 5.1). The business of learning is accomplished through this interactional feature.

Display questions have come in for the same type of criticism from the communicative approach as the IRF/IRE cycle. Nunan (1988, p. 139) states that one of the characteristics of genuine communication is the use of referential questions and that one of the reasons the patterns of interaction in the lessons he observed are noncommunicative is that the questions are almost exclusively of the display type. Nunan's (1987) conclusion was that "increasing the use of referential questions over display questions is likely to stimulate a greater quantity of genuine classroom interaction" (p. 142). Research within a broad SLA/communicative paradigm by Long and Sato (1983), Pica and Long (1986), Brock (1986), and Kramsch (1985) also suggests that an increased use of referential rather than display questions is likely to create more genuine interaction and therefore be more beneficial to SLA:

> ESL [English as a second language] teachers continue to emphasize form over meaning, accuracy over communication.

This is illustrated, for example, by the preference for display over referential questions, and results in classroom NS-NNS conversation which differs greatly from its counterpart outside.... Indeed, on this evidence, NS-NNS conversation during SL [second language] instruction is a greatly distorted version of its equivalent in the real world. (Long & Sato, 1983, pp. 283–284)

As was the case with the analysis of the IRF/IRE cycle, there are many problems with this communicative analysis of display questions. The same arguments which were used previously concerning the IRF/IRE cycle apply equally to the use of display questions. As with the IRF/IRE cycle, display questions "are also very common in adult-child talk in the pre-school years" (Maclure & French, 1981, p. 211). Display questions are very common in virtually every collection of transcripts of parent-child conversation, as in Extract 2.4:

(2.4)

(Mother and Hal, age 19 months, are reading)
Mother: what's this Hal?
Hal: bunny
Mother: yes. bunny's sleeping.

(Painter, 1989, p. 38)

From a CA institutional-discourse perspective, then, both the IRF/IRE cycle and display questions are interactional features which are appropriate to the core goals of education and learning, whether at home (learning an L1) or in the L2 classroom (learning an L2). The IRF/IRE cycle and display questions seem not to be interactional features which are specific to a particular culture or age; they appear to be universal phenomena in education and learning contexts. The following quotation is from a 4th-century Buddhist scripture and shows an example of the IRF/IRE cycle combined with a display question in a learning context which is identical in interactional terms to examples found in 21st-century classrooms:

The Lord asked Subhuti: What do you think, was there
any dharma which awoke the Tathagata, when he was
with the Tathagata Dipankara to the utmost, right, and
perfect enlightenment?
Subhuti replied: As I understand the meaning of the
Lord's teaching, this was not due to any dharma.
The Lord said: So it is, Subhuti, so it is. (Conze, 1959,
p. 164)

The point to be made in this section of the analysis, then, is that
individual interactional features have to be understood in the
interactional and institutional environment in which they are
embedded.

*Assumption 4. Teachers can be trained to replicate gen-
uine or natural conversation in the L2 classroom.*

I argued in the discussion of Assumption 2 that it is in
theory impossible for L2 teachers to replicate conversation in
the L2 classroom as part of a lesson. It follows that it is not
possible to train teachers to do so. However, I would now like to
examine a classroom extract in which the teacher has succeeded
in replicating interaction which is ostensibly as close to conversation as possible. I will then attempt to demonstrate that it is
not in fact conversation (if we are to use precise sociolinguistic
terms) but L2 classroom discourse. The teacher does not take
part in the interaction, in which teenaged-girl learners (in a
state secondary school in rural Malaysia) are discussing fashion
photographs in a group.

(2.5)

1 L1: I like this fashion because I can wear it for: sleep! not to go anywhere.
2 L2: ooh:!
3 L3: I like this fashion.
4 L2: I like this.
5 L4: why?
6 L5: I like this.
7 L2: because: be [cause:,]
8 L1:   [the girl,]
9 LL: ((laugh))

10 L4: this is good this fashion.
11 L2: this is a beautiful skirt.
12 L1: (.) beautiful, (.) but when I: done it [I put it long: long]
13 L4:   [this one better than] that one.
14 L4: (5.0) who like this one?
15 L1: aah, I like this.

(Warren, 1985, p. 223)

The interaction in this extract seems highly communicative and corresponds neatly (on the surface) to Nunan's characterization of genuine communication or conversation (see the discussion of Assumption 1). The point, however, is that the linguistic forms and patterns the learners produced were directly related to the pedagogical focus which the teacher introduced, even though the teacher did not participate in the interaction. Warren states clearly what his pedagogical focus was with these learners. A collection of women's fashion photographs was selected in order to engage the interest of the students, who were left alone with a tape recorder. Warren devised the activity "to stimulate natural discourse in the classroom" (p. 45), and "the only instruction was that the students should look at the photographs and that anything they might say had to be in English" (p. 47). Warren hoped that the exercise "might lead to the voicing of likes and dislikes" (p. 45). We can clearly see the link between the teacher's pedagogical focus and the linguistic forms and patterns of interaction produced by the learners: The learners speak only in English, discuss the photographs, and express likes and dislikes. The learners are orienting to the teacher's pedagogical focus even in his absence.[7]

Occasionally the way in which learners are orienting to external constraints and the teacher's agenda becomes visible in the linguistic forms which the learners choose. For example, the teacher set up the interaction in Extract 2.5 in hopes that the exercise might lead to the voicing of likes and dislikes. Four out of the first six utterances of Extract 2.5 begin with "I like this," which is more reminiscent of free practice work in the L2 classroom than of ordinary conversation. The details of the interaction, then, demonstrate an orientation to the teacher's pedagogical focus and to the institutional goal. For the interaction to have been conversation, the teacher could not have influenced the topic of conversation in any way or even required the learners to speak in English. My point is, then, that whatever methods the teacher is using—and even if the teacher claims to be relinquishing control of the classroom interaction—the linguistic forms and patterns of interaction which the learners produce will normally and normatively be linked in some way to the pedagogical focus which the teacher introduces into the L2 classroom environment (see Section 5.1.2). So although Extract 2.5 appears superficially to resemble characterizations of conversation, when it is seen in context, it becomes clear that it is an example of institutional interaction. As soon as the teacher gives the learners any instructions (even if the instruction is to have a conversation in the L2), the resultant interaction will be institutional discourse and not conversation.

The foregoing analysis has revealed the fundamental problems and paradoxes inherent in any approach which compares typical L2 classroom discourse unfavorably with conversation or any other variety of discourse. Classroom communication is a variety of institutional discourse like any other and has not been regarded as inferior or less "real" by sociolinguists; quite the opposite.

When Sinclair and Coulthard (1975) wanted to gather data to build a model for DA, they chose to record classroom communication, and one of the reasons which they give is quite revealing: "We also wanted a situation where all participants were genuinely trying to communicate" (p. 6). Hymes (1972) wrote that "studying language in the classroom is not really 'applied' linguistics; it is really basic research. Progress in understanding language in the classroom is progress in linguistic theory" (p. xviii). There is simply no basis or mechanism in sociolinguistics or communication theory for evaluating one variety of discourse as better, more genuine, or more natural than another; the concept is a purely pedagogical one. A very fundamental problem with the communicative tradition is the belief that it is possible to apply concepts derived from pedagogy (*genuine* and *natural*) to interaction.

Having suggested that there are theoretical problems with the communicative approach, I will now attempt to show how these theoretical problems result in practical problems in the analysis of interaction by examining possibly the most influential communicative study of L2 classroom interaction: Nunan (1987, 1988).[8] Again, this will serve as an exemplar of the problems inherent in analyzing interaction on the basis of pedagogy and pedagogical concepts alone. Nunan (1987, p. 137) begins his study by providing a characterization of genuine communication (reproduced earlier in this section). It is against this characterization of genuine communication, a single and invariant criterion, that Nunan compares his recorded classroom interaction data and finds them wanting. Nunan (1987, p. 137) offers the presence of the IRF/IRE cycle as *his initial reason* for asserting that there was little genuine communication in the language classrooms observed. Nunan then examines a transcript of a teacher introducing a class to the information gap activity which comes later in the lesson:

(2.6)

T: today, er, we're going to um, we're going to do something where, we, er, listen to a conversation and we also talk about the subject of the conversation er, in fact, we're not going to listen to one conversation, how many conversations are we going to listen to?

L: three

T: how do you know?

L: because, er, you will need, er, three tapes and three points

T: three?

L: points

T: what?

L: power points

T: power points, if I need three power points and three tape recorders, you correctly assume that I'm going to give you three conversations, and that's true, and all the conversation will be different, but they will all be on the same (.)?

LL: subject, subject

T: the same (.)?
L: subject, subject
T: right, they will all be on the same subject

(Nunan, 1988, p. 139)

Nunan's (1988) main point in relation to Extract 2.6 is that "the teacher is firmly in control of who says what when ... the exchanges are essentially non-communicative, despite the best intentions of the teacher" (p. 140). However, as he says, "The teacher is introducing the class to the information-gap activity" (p. 139). We are in a *procedural context*. The teacher's pedagogical focus at this moment is to give procedural information as well as to set the scene for the main activity. It is *not* on producing genuine communication; that may come in the subsequent information gap. I am suggesting, then, that it is unfair to evaluate the extract as if it had been the teacher's intention to produce genuine communication.

By contrast, in Extract 2.5, it *is* actually the teacher's stated intention to produce genuine communication, and in such cases Nunan's evaluatory criterion would be perfectly applicable. The CA methodology which will be outlined in Section 5.3 suggests that the researcher should analyze and evaluate the extract according to participants' own orientations by matching the pedagogical focus to the resultant patterns of interaction. In the procedural context of Extract 2.6, the teacher is asking display questions instead of transmitting procedural information in a monologue in order to involve and interest the learners in the activity and maximize motivation. He or she is maximizing the potential for interaction in that particular stage of the lesson. It is not legitimate to compare the transcript of the extract with those of information gaps or ordinary conversation, but it would be legitimate to compare it with other transcripts of procedural contexts. In my database (see Section 2.4), the vast majority of transcripts of procedural contexts show the teacher delivering a monologue (see, for example, Extract 3.12). Therefore, the transcript of Extract 2.6 appears to be maximally communicative and interactive *for the context it is operating in*. The learners appear to validate the interaction by contributing energetically, there is a match between the teacher's pedagogical focus and the resultant patterns of interaction, and the extract should therefore be evaluated very positively on its own terms.

This analysis shows that it is easy for analysts using etic and acontextual approaches to impose their own extraneous concerns onto an interaction; however, the CA methodology outlined in Section 5.3 should help ensure an emic analysis focused on the *participants'* concerns and perspectives. It is essential, then, in order for fair evaluation to take place, that the pedagogical focus be related to the linguistic forms and patterns of interaction which the learners produce.

To put the above criticisms into context, no fundamental objections have been raised in relation to the communicative approach to language teaching. The criticisms relate solely to its perspective on and analyses of classroom interaction. In order to justify the need for a contextual and variable CA approach to L2 classroom interaction which is able to portray the reflexive relationship between pedagogy and interaction, it has first proved necessary to demonstrate the problems inherent in approaches which are based solely on pedagogical concepts. It is also necessary to be clear that the fact that L2 teaching is currently operating within a broadly communicative paradigm does not mean that L2 teaching is based on a sound and sophis-ticated perspective on communication in the L2 classroom. Although we have looked specifically at the communicative approach to L2 classroom interaction in this section, we may consider it an example of a purely pedagogical approach to interaction.

The DA and communicative perspectives reviewed so far are in one sense at opposite ends of a methodological continuum in that DA provides a purely interactional perspective and the communicative approach a purely pedagogical perspective on L2 classroom interaction. In that sense they have been analyzed as exemplars of interactional and pedagogical approaches at different ends of a continuum. From another perspective, however, they are very similar in that they both operate in invariant and acontextual perspectives; they both view all varieties of L2 classroom interaction from the same viewpoint. They both operate from an etic perspective and have no way of portraying the participants' emic perspectives.

2.3 Dynamic and Variable Approaches to Classroom Interaction

By contrast to the acontextual approaches reviewed so far, a number of researchers in both L1 and L2 classrooms have been developing dynamic and variable approaches to classroom interaction which recognize different varieties of classroom interaction. A dynamic and variable approach to context is typical of contemporary sociolinguistics (Heritage, 1984b) and of the ethnography of communication (Gumperz & Hymes, 1986; Saville-Troike, 1989). Research by Judith Green and associates (e.g., Green & Wallat, 1981) has shown that the concept of variable context is applicable to L1 classrooms.

In the L2 classroom, at least five writers have recently proposed that L2 classroom interaction is best understood as divisible into several distinct varieties. This may be seen as a movement toward a variable and contextual perspective on L2 classroom interaction. Van Lier (1982, 1988a) is concerned with establishing a variable and contextual approach, and the overall goal of his studies is an understanding of what goes on in L2 classrooms (van Lier, 1988a, p. 14). He asserts that different varieties of interaction occur in the L2 classroom and that these are a result of a different focus on activity or topic, and he identifies four different types of L2 classroom interaction as follows (p. 156):

> *Interaction type 1.* Less topic orientation, less activity orientation

Interaction type 2. More topic orientation, less activity orientation

Interaction type 3. More topic orientation, more activity orientation

Interaction type 4. Less topic orientation, more activity orientation

Ellis (1984) identifies five different types of L2 classroom interaction:

1. Interaction with medium-centered goals

2. Interaction with message-centered goals

3. Interaction with activity-centered goals

4. Interaction involving framework goals

5. Interaction involving social goals

Tsui (1987, p. 345) identifies three different types of L2 classroom interaction:

1. Negotiating

2. Nonnegotiating: matching

3. Nonnegotiating: direct verbal

Abdesslem (1993) identifies four frames in L2 classroom discourse:

Frame 1. Saying the linguistic form of the foreign language

Frame 2. Talking in the foreign language

Frame 3. Transacting in the foreign language

Frame 4. Interacting in the foreign language

Hasan (1988, p. 136) identifies five types of interaction in and beyond the English as a foreign language (EFL) classroom:

Type 1. Formal interview

Type 2. Formal classroom interaction

Type 3. Informal classroom interaction

Type 4. Informal classroom discussion

Type 5. Informal conversation

There appears to be a reasonable level of consensus at present that different varieties of communication do occur in the L2 classroom. However, we do need to observe that five different writers have looked at the same type of data, namely L2 classroom interaction, and have produced five different descriptive systems. This is not to suggest that there are no points of convergence; there clearly are many similarities among the five systems. However, if we focus on the differences, we find that the names of the varieties are different in every case, the glosses (not reproduced here) are different, and the writers do not agree on how many varieties there are. We saw that the five writers used slightly different terms to denote the different varieties: types of interaction (Hasan), interaction types (van Lier), frames (Abdesslem), types of interaction (Tsui), and interactions (Ellis).

There would be advantages to using the term *L2 classroom context* to denote those subvarieties or types of interaction which occur in L2 classrooms; the concept is developed in Section 5.5. Using the term *context* would enable the research to be connected with the body of sociolinguistic work on context which exists (including Green's), and including *L2 classroom* in the term would both narrow the scope and indicate that we are dealing with an institutional discourse variety. In Section 5.6 there is a presentation of the broader perspective on context adopted in this study, and it should be merely noted here that the adoption of the term *context* in this study will facilitate the development of this broader perspective. The adoption of the term *context* should not be taken to imply that this is the only conception of context relevant to L2 classrooms. We will see as the argument develops that a very complex conception of context is necessary to portray the interaction.

2.4 Database Issues

In general CA studies rarely provide a detailed description of the database on which they are founded. Previous studies of L2 classroom interaction have often provided minimal information on their database. In this monograph, however, such a description is provided for the following reasons. The overall aim is to produce a model and methodology for the analysis of L2 classroom interaction, whatever the setting. However, as van Lier (1988a) puts it, "One of the problems with L2 classroom research is that there is such a tremendous variety of L2 classrooms" (p. 5). The size, nature and variety of the database should also be of interest to researchers, and to L2 teachers in particular in determining the generalizability of the study and its applicability to the reader's own professional context. Elsewhere (Seedhouse, 1995) I have argued that, because of the diversity of L2 classrooms, one should specify the database not only in terms of number of lessons or fragments of lessons, but also in terms of the following background contextual factors, in order that the diversity of the database may be assessed: L1, culture,[9] country of origin, and age of learners, level of learners' proficiency in L2, type of institution, and whether the classes are multilingual or monolingual.[10] In this section a brief description of the database underlying the present study is provided. There then follows a discussion of issues relating to databases in general. Table 2.1 shows that the database on which this study relies is actually made up of seven distinct databases.

2.5 Adequacy of Databases for the Study of Second Language Classroom Interaction

Banbrook and Skehan (1989, p. 147) point out that classroom research has not addressed the issue of how one can justify one's sampling base and suggest that there is an urgent need for guidelines in this area. In this section I address issues relating to databases supporting L2 classroom research in general and

Table 2.1

Databases used in the study

Database number	1	2	3	4	5	6	7
Title of database	Seedhouse's Norway data	Transcript collection	Peck's European data	Seedhouse's U.K. data	Seedhouse's China data	Yazigi's Abu Dhabi data	Ellis, Basturkmen, & Loewen's New Zealand data
Number of lessons or fragments	10 complete lessons	350 lessons or fragments	16 lessons	2 whole lessons	27 whole lessons	18 fragments	1,821 fragments and 3 lessons
L2 taught	English	8 different L2s	English, French, German	French, English	English	English	English
L1 of the learners	Norwegian	Many	French, German, Danish, Spanish	English and a variety of European and Asian languages	Chinese	Mostly Arabic, also Persian, Chinese, English	A variety of Asian and European languages
Multilingual or monolingual classes	Monolingual	Both	Monolingual	Both	Monolingual	Multilingual	Multilingual
Culture	Western European	Many	Western European	Western and Asian	Chinese	Mostly Arabic	Mostly Asian, some Western
Country of origin	Norway	14 different countries	France, Germany, Denmark, Spain	England and a variety of European and Asian countries	China	Mostly Middle Eastern states, also Iran, Argentina, United States, Australia, Senegal, and Algeria	Japan, Korea, China, Switzerland, Taiwan, Thailand; also Western Europe and South America
Age of learners	8–19	Young children to aged adults	Young children to adults	Adult	Primary age range (6–12)	6–8	Adult, generally young
Type of institution	Primary school, lower and upper secondary school	Wide range	State schools, private language schools	University and further education	Primary schools	Primary international school	Private language school
Level of learners' proficiency in L2	Beginners to advanced	Beginners to advanced	Beginners to advanced	Beginners to upper intermediate	Beginners to intermediate	Beginners to intermediate	Preintermediate to upper-intermediate

consider the adequacy of the database on which this study is founded. If one were operating in a quantitative, etic paradigm, one might relate the size of the current database with those of other, similar studies to determine what previous researchers have considered an adequate sample size for their classroom research. It is essential in each case, however, to relate the size and nature of the database to the researcher's stated research aims and methodology.

One of the best-known studies of L1 classroom interaction, Mehan (1979), has as its goal the location of "the organizing machinery of classroom lessons in the interaction" (p. 23). Mehan's goal, then, is fairly similar to that of this study, except that Mehan deals with L1 rather than L2 classrooms. Mehan's study is based on a corpus of nine lessons involving the same teacher, an academic on a sabbatical placement in a school. Mehan uses an ethnographic methodology together with a classic DA system. In relation to the L2 classroom, van Lier's (1982) doctoral dissertation and book (1988a) are based on nine lessons recorded in Great Britain and the United States with Venezuelan, Dutch, and Mexican learners, with data added sporadically from other sources. Van Lier states that his overall aim is an understanding of what goes on in L2 classrooms (1988a, p. 14) and that this aim is not dissimilar to that of the present study. He uses a hybrid ethnographic methodology, although he uses the terminology of CA in Chapters 5–7. The aim of Johnson (1995) in a book length study is to "enable teachers to recognize how the patterns of communication are established and maintained in second language classrooms" (p. 3) and to develop a framework for understanding communication in L2 classrooms. Johnson's goal, then, is reasonably similar to that of this study. Although Johnson includes numerous extracts from L2 classroom transcripts in her book, she does not make explicit the size or nature of her database. Her study is based on a model of communication for L1 classrooms created by Barnes, Britton, and Torbe (1990).

Mitchell's (1986) doctoral dissertation is based on two sets of audio-recorded French lessons from Scottish secondary schools. The first set consists of 13 lessons (p. 129), and the second set consists of a selection from an unspecified number of lessons. The aim of Mitchell's study was to investigate the capacity of foreign language teachers to make the L2 the sole or main means of communicating with pupils. I was not able to find an explicit statement concerning the study's methodology. Hasan (1988, p. 95) states that the corpus for his doctoral dissertation consists of five recordings of interaction lasting 35 min each, comprising audio and video data which were then transcribed. Fifteen Arabic-speaking Algerian postgraduate students at a British university were recorded together with four NSs. The aim of the research was to investigate the discourse variability exhibited by classroom participants (p. 2). Hasan describes his methodology as a "discourse analysis approach which takes both quantitative and qualitative procedures into consideration" (p. 53). Abdesslem's (1987) doctoral dissertation is based on eight English lessons obtained in Tunisian secondary schools. The aim is to discern the regularities in English lesson discourses in Tunisian secondary schools (Abdesslem, 1993, p. 227). The methodology used appears to be an attempt to blend DA and CA approaches (1993, p. 224). Chapters and journal articles have drawn general conclusions about the L2 classroom based on six ESL classrooms (Long & Sato, 1983, p. 273; Pica & Doughty, 1988, p. 47) and five EFL lessons (Nunan, 1987, p. 137).

It seems, then, that recent classroom research into communication in both L1 and L2 classrooms has considered between 5 and 10 lessons a reasonable database from which to generalize and draw conclusions. Indeed, some recent studies have not stipulated the exact size of their underlying database.

Having compared the database underlying this study with those underlying similar studies, the following conclusions can be drawn. The size of the current database is specified in relatively explicit terms and is considerably larger than those on which similar studies have been based. The nature and variety of the current database is also specified in relatively explicit terms, and this database is considerably more varied than those on which similar studies have been based.

It should be noted at this point that I have been diverging from a standard CA approach in this section. CA operates within a qualitative and emic paradigm and proceeds by "case by case analysis of singular exhibits of interactional conduct" (Heritage, 1995, p. 406) and thereby uncovers the underlying machinery or organization of an interaction. The CA perspective, then, is that the validity of a study is primarily related to the quality of the analysis rather than the size of the database. Hence, CA studies typically do not provide detailed information about databases. However, since one aim of this monograph is to link CA research processes to more mainstream social science research methodologies, I have tried to be as explicit about databases and procedures as possible given constraints on space.

My overall aim in conducting this study was to produce a model and methodology which would be able to analyze L2 classroom interaction whatever the variables, including country, L2 taught, age or proficiency of students, and teaching approach. In order to do this, I assembled interactional data eclectically from many sources. Sometimes these data have not been transcribed to CA standards. In some cases it has been possible for me to obtain the original recorded data and retranscribe, and in other cases this has not been possible, which means that some extracts in this monograph are not presented in CA transcription. They are included because they illustrate interesting phenomena and increase the diversity of the data presented. Atkinson and Drew (1979) and Levinson (1992) also include some transcripts obtained elsewhere which for similar reasons are not transcribed to CA standards.

2.6 Ethnography

One mainstream social science research methodology with which CA may create links is ethnography, and this has been another popular approach to the study of L2 classroom inter-action. Both approaches are qualitative and holistic and attempt to develop an emic perspective, although by different means. Recent papers (Auer, 1995; Silverman, 1999) have attempted a rapprochement between these two methodological approaches. Silverman's basic argument is that the two approaches are compatible and may be applied to the same instances of talk provided that the crucial issue of timing is taken into account. An initial CA of *how* participants locally produce context for their interaction can be followed by an ethnographic analysis of *why* questions about institutional and cultural constraints. Auer (1995, p. 427) points out that data collection procedures in ethnography are eclectic by principle and therefore incorporate CA methods.

I concur with Silverman that the two approaches may be applied to the same instances of talk; the relationship should be complementary and sequential. First, the details of the inter-action are analyzed. Interactants reveal through the details of their talk whether they are orienting to particular cultural or social issues; they actively evoke and create a social world and culture in and through their talk. As a consequence, it may then become relevant to invoke social or cultural details which are extraneous to the interaction.

There have been various suggestions as to what an approach combining CA and ethnography would look like, notably Moerman's (1988, 1996) culturally contexted CA. Seed-house (1998a) illustrates CA's ability to analyze cultural issues by evaluating data involving a "cross-cultural" encounter between an NS and NNS of German. It is argued that the issues raised are of particular importance in L2 classrooms, since cross-cultural issues and NS-NSS interaction are characteristic of this institutional setting. Seedhouse suggests that the data provide a clear example of participants actively evoking or talking into being their own culture or cultural frame through the details of their talk. In interaction between NSs and NNSs, the NNSs' difficulty with the L2 is a type of trouble to which participants may

orient in the interaction. Different participants in different contexts find different methods of coping with this trouble and thereby
evoke different cultures. In the case of the data in Seedhouse
(1998a), the NS is orienting to the NNS's trouble with the L2 by
producing minimalized, pidginized interlanguage forms himself.
For example the NS says, "Vater kommen, ja" ("father come, yes,"
using an infinitive form of the verb) instead of "mein Vater ist
gekommen, ja" ("my father came, yes," using the perfective form of
the verb in German). The participants are creating a context of
intercultural communication or *interculture* through the use of
interlanguage in the details of their talk. The important methodological point here is that we initially take the interculture to be
evoked and created through the use of the interlanguage. That is,
we move in our analysis from the detail of the talk to the exploration of the culture (or other social construct), and we take the
culture to be endogenous to the talk. To talk of a cross-cultural
encounter or interculture is relevant only when it is evident that
the participants orient to such a construct in the details of their
talk. As Schegloff (1987) puts it, "in an interaction's moment-to-
moment development, the parties, singly and together, select and
display in their conduct which of the indefinitely many aspects
of context they are making relevant, or are invoking, for the
immediate moment" (p. 219).

So for the purposes of CA we initially take culture and
cultural frames not to be lurking somewhere "out there" in the
background, but to be talked into being by the participants
through the details of their interaction. Of course macro social
structures such as culture do exist independently of talk. However, for the methodological reasons which will be outlined
below, CA has found it necessary to ground the analysis, in the
first instance, in the details of the talk. Seedhouse (1998a) also
finds interactional evidence to support a characterization of a
cross-cultural encounter in the topical development and the
social actions performed. So although the talk of Seedhouse's
participants is ostensibly about the delivery of soft drinks, it is
also, on another level, about cross-cultural trouble, and this is

evident again in the details of the interaction, in the *types of social action* which the participants perform. What a CA of the extract in Seedhouse (1998a) shows us, then, is that this is an interactional sequence in which both linguistic and cultural troubles are oriented to and in which the participants jointly create an interlanguage and interculture through the details of their talk. There is a *reflexive* relationship between interaction and culture here. It is the use of those particular linguistic forms, topics, and types of social actions which talk the interculture into being. From another angle, however, the interculture is evident in the linguistic forms produced, in the topic of the talk, and in the types of social actions performed.

It must be stressed that the CA claim is *not* that macro social structures such as culture or cultural frames do not exist except in the interaction. Talk is reflexively related to context, culture and macro social structures, and talk is certainly shaped by culture. However, the methodological imperatives detailed by Schegloff (1987, 1992) dictate that we ground the analysis in the first instance in the details of the interaction. The basic problem, when trying to link talk and culture, is that there is an indefinite number of external aspects of cultural, social, or personal identity or context which could be potentially relevant to any given instance of talk in interaction. So it might or might not be relevant, for example, that the NS in the data is a heterosexual male, that he has a beard, that he is a socialist, or that he does karate. Any of these characteristics might in principle be relevant to our analysis of the data.

What needs to be shown in an analysis of such data, however, is which of these innumerable, potentially relevant characteristics are *actually* procedurally relevant to the participants at that moment. CA suggests that the only feasible way to do this is to start in the details of the interaction, rather than in the external details of the culture. For example, in Seedhouse (1998a), I showed that one particular characteristic of the interactants' identities is procedurally relevant to and consequential for the interaction. This is their national or cultural identities as German and as

Greek immigrants and their linguistic identities as German NSs and NNSs. Working from the details of the interaction, this was shown to be procedurally relevant to the linguistic forms used, to the topic of the talk, and to the social actions performed. A cultural characteristic is relevant to a CA only if it can be shown to inhabit the details of the talk. I feel that the CA position, as detailed previously, is quite compatible with calls for culturally contexted analysis (Moerman, 1988, 1996). There is, in principle, no limit to the amount of background knowledge of culture or of the number of cultural characteristics which can be brought to bear in CA. As Moerman (1988) puts it, "Contexted conversation analysis is directed towards discovering which of the many culturally available distinctions are active and relevant to the situation, how these distinctions are brought to bear, and what they consist of" (p. 70).

CA, then, can provide a secure warrant for the introduction of relevant ethnographic information and hence a link between the micro and macro levels. The same basic procedures could apply to an approach to the L2 classroom which combined CA with ethnography. A CA could reveal which "cultural" or con-textual aspects the participants were orienting to in the details of their talk. This would then provide a warrant for the ethno-graphic description of cultural or contextual information.

An issue of recent interest (e.g., Arminen, 2000) has been the extent to which conversation analyses of institutional dis-course make use of ethnographic or expert knowledge of the institutional setting. Arminen's argument is that conversation analysts inevitably do make use of such knowledge and indeed that their analyses depend on such knowledge. It follows that it is helpful for conversation analysts to make as transparent as possible the extent to which their analyses derive from the details of the interaction or from use of ethnographic or expert knowledge. In the case of this monograph I explain in Section 5.3 that I use three kinds of evidence. Although I work primarily from the details of the interaction, I supplement this with two kinds of ethnographic evidence (when available) and indicate the source of such evidence. Since I worked as a classroom language teacher for 10 years, I invariably make use of my expert knowledge of the setting during analyses. However, any analytical claims should be based on the orientations of the participants, as evidenced in the details of the interaction.

2.7 The Pedagogical Landing-Ground Perspective

So far in this chapter I have reviewed several explicitly stated, methodologically informed perspectives on L2 classroom interaction. By contrast, the pedagogical landing-ground perspective has, to the best of my knowledge, never been stated explicitly by anyone and has no methodological basis. Nonetheless, I will argue that it is by far the most pervasive perspective and indeed is the implicit or "default" perspective if none other is stated. The pedagogical landing-ground perspective consists of the view that intended pedagogical aims and ideas translate directly into actual classroom practice as if the L2 classroom had no intervening level of interactional organization. In other words, the *task-as-workplan* or intended pedagogy translates directly into the *task-in-process* or actual pedagogy (Breen, 1989). Although no one has ever explicitly expressed such a perspective on L2 classroom interaction, if one opens any L2 teaching magazine or journal or textbook at random, one will most often find that this perspective is implicit, in that there is no consideration of how the proposed pedagogy will interface with the interactional organization of the L2 classroom or of how the task-as-workplan will translate into the task-in-process. In other words, the conceptualization in the literature is overwhelmingly in terms of the task-as-workplan or intended pedagogy. The pedagogical landing-ground perspective, then, is the default perspective if no consideration is given to how pedagogy is translated into interaction.

Why does this matter? The pedagogical vision of the task-as-workplan interacts with the interactional organization of the L2 classroom to produce an L2 classroom context, which is the pedagogical focus as analyzed by the participants in combination with an organization of the interaction appropriate to that focus. To illustrate how this transformation occurs, I will examine Extract 2.7. The task-as-workplan in the extract is for L8 to ask L11 a question using the present perfect followed by a question using the simple past. This sounds fairly unproblematic in terms of task-as-workplan, especially as the teacher has just drilled the learners in the infinitive, simple-past, and past-participle forms of the verbs involved:

(2.7)

```
 1 T:    °have you ever° ((whispers))
 2 L8:   (.) you ever: (.) gone to (.)
 3 T:    gone to?
 4 L8:   er: gone to Sümela Manastir? Sümela attraction?
 5 L11:  (1.0) hmm yes=
 6 T:    =YES   [((laughs))   ]
 7 LL:          [((laughter)) ]
 8 T:    yes okay ask him now when? when?
 9 L1:   when?
10 LL:   ((laughter))
11 T:    ((uses body language)) make a sentence ((laughs))
12 L1:   when uhm—
13 L11:  last summer
14 TLL:  ((laughter))
15 T:    when last summer okay ((laughter)) okay now someone else (.) ask
16       him with who with who
```

(Üstünel, 2003, p. 75)

A problem arises with the task-in-process in this extract precisely because the task-as-workplan interacts with the interactional organization of the L2 classroom to produce a particular sequence organization and because the learners interpret the pedagogical focus in a different way than that intended by the teacher. There is a question-and-answer adjacency pair in the present perfect in Lines 2, 4, and 5. The consequence is that the follow-up question in Lines 9 and 12 needs only the single word "when?" to form a complete TCU precisely by virtue of its sequential location. So, although we can see in Line 11 that T wants a full sentence with the simple past, she accepts the sequence produced (Line 15). The sequence which the learners have produced is a very "natural" and understandable one, and in fact their analysis of the task demonstrates a good understanding of sequential organization. So the mismatch between task-as-workplan and task-in-process, between intended and actual pedagogy, is due to the way in which the pedagogical focus has interacted with the interactional organization of the L2 classroom and the way in which the learners have reinterpreted the task in the light of this.

The perspective I develop in this monograph is intended to replace the pedagogical landing-ground perspective. I argue that L2 classroom interaction has a specifiable organization which transforms task-as-workplan into task-in-process, intended pedagogy into actual pedagogy. Therefore, the main focus of L2 teaching research should be on what actually happens, that is, on the task-in-process, rather than on what is intended to happen, that is, on the task-as-workplan.

2.8 A Conversation Analysis Institutional-Discourse Perspective

In this monograph I adopt a CA institutional-discourse perspective on L2 classroom interaction. In Chapter 1 we looked predominantly at how CA is used to analyze ordinary conversation, which has a benchmark status with respect to other varieties of interaction. Studies of institutional interaction (e.g., Drew & Heritage, 1992a) have focused on how the organization of the interaction is related to the institutional aim and on the ways in which this organization differs from the benchmark of ordinary conversation. Heritage (1997) proposes six basic places to probe the institutionality of interaction:

- Turn-taking organization
- Overall structural organization of the interaction
- Sequence organization

- Turn design
- Lexical choice
- Epistemological and other forms of asymmetry

Heritage also proposes four different kinds of asymmetries in institutional discourse:

- Asymmetries of participation, such as a professional asking questions to the lay client
- Asymmetries of interactional and institutional know-how, such as professionals being used to the type of interaction, agenda, and typical course of an interview in contrast to the lay client
- Epistemological caution and asymmetries of knowledge, such as professionals often avoiding taking a firm position
- Rights of access to knowledge, particularly professional knowledge

We will see many of these issues surfacing in Chapters 3–5. Perhaps the most important analytical consideration is that institutional discourse displays goal orientation and rational organization. In contrast to conversation, participants in institutional interaction orient to some "core goal, task or identity (or set of them) conventionally associated with the institution in question" (Drew & Heritage, 1992b, p. 22). CA institutional-discourse methodology attempts to relate not only the overall organization of the interaction, but also individual interactional devices to the core institutional goal. CA attempts, then, to understand the organization of the interaction as being *rationally* derived from the core institutional goal. Levinson (1992) sees the structural elements of institutional discourse as

> rationally and functionally adapted to the point or goal of the activity in question, that is the function or functions that members of the society see the activity as having. By taking this perspective it seems that in most cases apparently ad hoc and elaborate arrangements and constraints of very various sorts can be seen to follow from a few basic principles, in particular rational organization around a dominant goal. (p. 71)

A related methodological precept is that one should "search for the raison d'être of a particular conversational organization, and the implications that the existence of one device has for the necessity for others" (Levinson, 1983, p. 322). This acts as an antidote to the tendencies of researchers to consider particular interactional devices in isolation and label them desirable or undesirable for pedagogical reasons and without considering the *interactional* consequences of such devices or how a particular device relates to the interactional organization of the L2 classroom as a whole. For example, we will see in Section 4.9 that current pedagogy considers the direct and overt negative evaluation of learner errors to be highly undesirable. However, it is argued that this choice creates serious new problems on the interactional level and may be counterproductive.

In Chapter 1, I described the fundamentals of CA in relation to ordinary conversation. It should be understood that in the case of institutional discourse, all of these fundamentals are in effect reorganized in relation to the institutional goal. The methodology for analysis is transformed into the next-turn proof procedure in relation to the institutional goal, as elaborated in Section 5.3. In Chapter 5 I characterize the interactional architecture of the L2 classroom from this CA institutional-discourse perspective using the principles outlined in the foregoing; therefore I will not go into much detail here. However, I should note at this point that this perspective is very different in many ways from previous perspectives on L2 classroom interaction. Language teachers and researchers have often tended to present their professional setting as a special case, even by comparison with teachers of other subjects, because, as J. Willis (1992) puts it, "language is used for two purposes; it serves both as the subject matter of the lesson, and as the medium of instruction. It is precisely this dual role that makes language lessons difficult to describe" (p. 162). By regarding L2 classroom interaction as a special case, L2 classroom researchers have sometimes produced perspectives on such interaction which have had little or no connection with sociolinguistic and communication theory or education theory.

However, from a CA institutional-discourse perspective, all varieties of institutional discourse have many common features (Drew & Heritage, 1992b). Moreover, all institutional varieties of discourse have a unique and distinctive institutional goal and a peculiar organization of the interaction suited to that goal. Certainly the L2 classroom does have its unique goal, which means that language is both the vehicle and object of instruction. We will see that the entire architecture is constructed around this unique goal; however, the same can be said for other institutional varieties as well. In the following chapters, I apply the CA perspective on institutional discourse to the organization of turn taking and sequence (Chapter 3) and to the organization of repair (Chapter 4).

Besides my own publications (see References), a number of CA studies of interaction involving L2 learners have revealed subtle interactional practices which transform our perceptions of L2 learners and teachers. Olsher (2004) demonstrates how L2 learners in small-group project work may complete sequential actions through gestures or embodied displays. Koshik (2002) reveals how teachers use the pedagogical practice of designedly incomplete utterances in order to initiate self-correction by learners. Carroll (2000, 2004, in press) challenges the general perception of L2 novice learners as incompetent communicators. Carroll uncovers their ability to make creative communicative use of their minimal linguistic resources and employ sophisticated conversational microadjustments. Novice learners can precision-time their entry into interaction, recycle turn beginnings to solicit the gaze or attention of partners, and use vowel marking as a resource for forward-oriented repair. Mori (2002) traces how a task-as-workplan (discussion with NSs) is transformed into a task-in-process resembling a structured interview of question-and-answer exchanges. Markee (in press) demonstrates how learners working in pairs on a task carefully disguise their social talk from the teacher and are able to instantly switch between on-task and off-task talk. Markee (2000) portrays the progress of intersubjectivity during two tasks, one of which results in learner comprehension of the target item whereas the other does not.

2.9 Chapter Summary

This chapter has stressed the importance of providing information in relation to the databases on which studies of L2 classroom interaction are founded and has provided information about the database underlying this study. The chapter introduced the importance of developing a dynamic and variable perspective on L2 classroom interaction and used this as a basis for the critique of other approaches. I argued that CA is compatible with an ethnographic approach in that an initial CA can provide a warrant for the introduction of relevant ethnographic information. I further argued that the DA approach is in effect one integral element of CA methodology. However, the CA perspective is quite incompatible with the communicative approach to L2 classroom interaction. The communicative approach is an example of an entirely pedagogical approach, taking the pedagogical concept of genuine interaction as its basis. At the other extreme the DA approach is an entirely interactional one and has no intrinsic means of creating links between speech moves and pedagogy or the social and institutional levels. As we will see in Chapter 5, the unique and universal feature of the L2 classroom is the way in which pedagogy and interaction are inextricably intertwined in a reflexive relationship. Only a methodology which is able to portray this relationship at all levels of analysis (and indeed which is founded on this relationship) will be able to provide an adequate model and methodology for the analysis of L2 classroom interaction.

Notes

[1]Mehan (1979) employs an ethnographic approach.
[2]See the brief discussion on "topic" in Section 1.6.4.

[3]As we will see in Chapter 6, this type of repair often overlaps with the second language acquisition conception of "recast."

[4]By contrast, a display question is one to which the teacher already knows the answer.

[5]Warren operates within the Birmingham school of DA, rather than within CA.

[6]The data have been predominantly collected from White, middle-class homes.

[7]Here I am employing Type 1 evidence (see Section 5.3) and using an extract to develop an argument, rather than for detailed CA. I use extracts in this way a number of times in the monograph, and there are precedents for such use in CA work, including Levinson (1992).

[8]By contrast to this invariant perspective on interaction, Nunan (1988) provides a complex perspective in relation to the authenticity of materials.

[9]For reasons of space it has not been possible to provide a detailed description of database features. It is acknowledged that some of the "shorthand" descriptors (e.g., "Asian") oversimplify complex cultural, national, and linguistic issues.

[10]I am grateful to an anonymous reviewer for pointing out that accessibility to databases is an important issue. The transcripts of database 1 are available from the author on request, but databases 4 and 5 are not yet fully transcribed. The other databases do not belong to the author, and database 2 consists mainly of published transcripts and/or recorded data.

CHAPTER THREE

The Organization of Turn Taking and Sequence in Language Classrooms

In Chapter 1, I introduced the principles of CA methodology in relation to ordinary conversation, and in Chapter 2 I introduced an institutional-discourse perspective. In this chapter I apply these principles and this perspective to the institutional setting of the L2 classroom and to the organization of turn taking and sequence in particular. The overall argument of this chapter is that there is a reflexive relationship between the pedagogical focus and the organization of turn taking and sequence. As the pedagogical focus varies, so the organization of the interaction varies. It is strongly argued that the data demonstrate that it is not possible to conceive of a single speech exchange system for L2 classroom interaction. As Markee (2002) suggests, "The category of classroom talk in fact subsumes a network of inter-related speech exchange systems, whose number, organizational characteristics and acquisitional functions are as yet little understood" (p. 11). A variable perspective which conceives of multiple subvarieties, or L2 classroom contexts, each with its own basic pedagogical focus and corresponding organization of turn taking and sequence, is therefore necessary.

In the L2 classroom, a particular pedagogical focus is reflexively related to a particular speech exchange system. As the pedagogical focus varies, so the organization of turn and sequence varies. An explanation for this phenomenon is sought

in the rational design of institutional discourse, which is outlined in Chapter 5. As Sacks et al. (1974) put it, "Turn-taking
systems are characterizable as adapting to properties of the
sorts of activities in which they operate" (p. 696). In this chapter
I illustrate the main argument by reference to four different
L2 classroom contexts; characterizations of other contexts
may be found in Seedhouse (1996). I outline the organization
of turn taking and sequence in form-and-accuracy contexts,
meaning-and-fluency contexts, task-oriented contexts, and
procedural contexts,[1] illustrating these with extracts from L2
lessons.

3.1 Turn Taking and Sequence in Form-and-Accuracy Contexts

A pedagogical focus on linguistic form and accuracy
occurs throughout the database and in all previous descriptive
studies of L2 classroom interaction. With this focus, presentation and practice are typically involved; the learners learn
from the teacher how to manipulate linguistic forms accurately. Personal meanings do not normally enter into the
picture. The teacher expects that learners will produce precise
strings of linguistic forms and precise patterns of interaction
which will correspond to the pedagogical focus which he or
she introduces. With this tight pedagogical focus it is
normally essential for the teacher to have tight control of
the turn-taking system. The interaction in Extract 3.1 is
from a Norwegian primary school:

(3.1)
Episode 1

1 T: now I want everybody (.) to listen to me. (1.8) and when I say you are
2   going to say after me, (.) you are going to say what I say. (.) °we can try.°
3 T: I've got a lamp. a lamp. <say after me> I've got a lamp.
4 LL: I've got a lamp.
5 T: (.) I've got a glass, a glass, <say after me> I've got a glass
6 LL: I've got a glass

 7 T: I've got a vase, a vase <say after me> I've got a vase
 8 LL: I've got a vase.

((39 lines omitted))

Episode 2

 9 T: I've got a hammer. what have you got (Tjartan)?
10 L6: I have got a hammer.
11 T: can everybody say <u>I've got</u>.
12 LL: ((whole class)) I've got.
13 T: fine. I've got a belt. what have you got? (1.0) Kjersti?
14 L7: (.) hmm I've got a telephone

((24 lines omitted))

Episode 3

15 T: and listen to me again. (.) and look at what I've written.(.)
16   I've got a hammer, <just listen now> have you got a hammer?
17 L: (1.0) yes
18 T: raise your hand up now Bjorn=
19 L13: =yes
20 T: I've=
21 L13: =I've got a hammer.
22 T: you've got a hammer and then you answer (1.2) yes I have (1.0) yes I
23   have. <I've got a belt>. have you got a belt Vegard?
24 L14: er:: (.) erm no
25 T: (.) you are going to answer only with yes.=
26 L14: =yes=
27 T: =yes
28 L14: (.) I:: (.) I have
29 T: I have. fine. I've got a trumpet. <have you got a trumpet Anna?>
30 L15: ah er erm °yes I have°

(Seedhouse, 1996, pp. 471–473)

The focus in Extract 3.1 is clearly on form and accuracy, in that the accurate production of the modeled sentences is what the teacher requires from the students. This is evident in Lines 9–14. In Line 10, L6 produces an uncontracted form ("I have got") which is linguistically correct and appropriate. However, the teacher is targeting the contracted form "I've got" and initiates repair in Line 11. T has the whole class repeat the contracted form in Line 12. This is to ensure that all students are aware that the contracted form is to be produced, and we can see in Line 14 that L7 is able to produce the contracted form successfully. The teacher makes the nature of the speech exchange system explicit in Lines 1–2. In Extract 3.1 only the teacher is able to direct speakership, and the interaction follows a rigid lockstep sequence. We can see in Lines 23–24 that real-world meaning does not enter into the interaction. It is evident from the video that L14 does not have a belt and therefore answers "no" when asked if he has a belt. However, the teacher requires him (in Line 25) to answer "yes" in order to produce the targeted string of linguistic forms. In Lines 16–22 we also see that the aim is to practice a very specific string of linguistic forms: T insists on the form "yes I have," where "yes" on its own would be perfectly appropriate.

The focus is on the production of linguistic form, but the forms do not carry topic, content, or new information in the same way as in ordinary conversation. So the term *topic* often does not apply to interaction in form-and-accuracy contexts; the participants do not develop a topic in the normal sense. This is why Kasper (1986) terms this type of interaction language-centered as opposed to content-centered. This type of exclusively form-focused or accuracy-focused classroom activity has been subject to extensive attack for decades now. The main criticisms are that there is a lack of correspondence between the forms practiced and any kind of real-world meaning, that there is no scope for fluency development in such a rigid lockstep approach, and that the discourse is "unnatural" in that such sequences do not normally occur outside the classroom. When the pedagogical focus is exclusively on linguistic form, the organization is necessarily formal in the way described by Drew and Heritage (1992b) as being "strongly constrained within quite sharply defined procedures. Departures from these procedures systematically attract overt sanctions" (p. 27).

We can see clear evidence of constraints on contributions. When learners make contributions which would be perfectly acceptable in conversation (Lines 10 and 24) they are not accepted by the teacher. There is extreme asymmetry in terms of interactional rights; the teacher is in total control of who says what and when. The students may speak only when nominated by the teacher. They have no leeway in terms of what they say or even the linguistic forms which they may use. If they deviate even slightly from the production envisaged by the teacher, the teacher may conduct repair, as in Lines 11 and 25. Extract 3.1 also illustrates the point that there is plenty of variation within a single overall L2 classroom context and that the interaction may be further broken down into episodes. In Episode 1 vocabulary revision, structure, and pronunciation practice are achieved through the whole class's repeating the sentences which the teacher produces while pointing to the picture of the object. In Episode 2, T asks a standard question, "What have you got?" of an individual student, who must reply "I've got a ..." and then insert one of the vocabulary items. So Episode 2 is practicing a specific structure, pronunciation, and a "slot and filler" insertion of a vocabulary item with a slight element of choice. Episode 3, by contrast, involves having individual students practice the production of the answer "Yes, I have" as preparation for subsequent pair work. In spite of the variations in very specific pedagogical focus and interactional organization, the extract as a whole can be said to be typical of a form-and-accuracy context.

Extract 3.1 illustrates the very delicate and reflexive relationship between pedagogical focus and the speech exchange system as well as the need to develop a perspective involving multiple layers of context. Every time a teacher introduces a pedagogical focus, in orientation to which learners produce turns in the L2, an L2 classroom context is talked into being. How we choose to characterize Extract 3.1 varies according to the perspective we adopt. If we consider it from the broadest perspective, the extract displays homogeneity. We can observe typical features of institutional interaction, and the extract is instantly recognizable as an instance of the interactional variety "L2 classroom interaction." If we come down to the subvariety perspective, then we can see that the extract shows typical features of the subvariety (or L2 classroom context) "form-and-accuracy context." A fuller discussion of the concept of

L2 classroom contexts is introduced in Section 5.5. Briefly, however, L2 classroom contexts are subvarieties of L2 classroom interaction in which a particular pedagogical aim enters into a reflexive relationship with a particular organization of the inter-action. If we come down to the micro level we can see a great deal of variation in the episodes in terms of specific pedagogical focuses and organizations of the interaction. From this perspective the interaction is unique and heterogeneous. So we need to bear in mind that we are using (at least) three levels of context or ways of representing and characterizing the same instance of discourse. These are not separate or competing characterizations, but rather complementary ones. This three-dimensional perspective on context is developed further in Section 5.6.

As far as sequence organization is concerned, one might expect the IRF/IRE cycle (see Johnson, 1995) to predominate in the formal interaction typical of form-and-accuracy contexts. IRF/IRE cycles certainly do occur but do not predominate in the database for this study. In Extract 3.1, for example, there are only two explicitly verbalized evaluations ("fine" in Lines 13 and 29). So the evaluation action is decidedly optional in the database of the current study. Moreover, as we will see in Section 4.6, positive evaluations are far more common than negative ones in this context.

How do we account for the frequent absence of a verbalized evaluation? Sometimes of course the evaluation may be performed nonverbally, for instance, with a nod. However, in terms of rational organization, I note in Chapter 5 that one key interactional property of L2 classroom interaction is that every-thing the learners say is potentially subject to evaluation by the teacher. So in these data the learner production is always subject to teacher evaluation. If the learner production corresponds to that envisaged by the teacher, the subsequent teacher action may be a different prompt. A positive evaluation may be expressed verbally or nonverbally. If not, however, it is understood, and this understanding becomes routinized so that if repair work is not undertaken, a positive evaluation is understood. If, however, the learner production does not correspond to that targeted by the teacher, repair work will be undertaken, generally without overt negative evaluation. Again this becomes routinized, so that if repair work is undertaken, a negative evaluation is understood.

In the data, then, the predominant sequence organization in form-and-accuracy contexts is an adjacency pair. The first part of the pair can be called *teacher prompt*: The teacher introduces a pedagogical focus which requires the production of a precise string of linguistic forms by the learner nominated. The second part of the adjacency pair can be called *learner production*. In the case of a learner production which coincides with the string targeted by the teacher, there may (or may not) be positive evaluation by the teacher of the learner production. In Extract 3.2 there is no verbally expressed positive evaluation of the learner utterance in Line 2:

(3.2)

```
1 T:    I have. fine. I've got a trumpet. >have you got a trumpet Anna?<
2 L15:  ah er erm °yes I have°
3 T:    I've got a radio. have you got a radio e:r (.) e:r Alvin?
4 L16:  yes I have.
```

(Seedhouse, 1996, p. 473)

A lack of repair work and prompt for another student is understood by all parties as signifying that the learner has produced the targeted string of linguistic forms. In the case of a learner production which does not coincide with the string targeted by the teacher, the teacher will normally initiate repair in order to obtain the targeted string. There may or may not be negative evaluation by the teacher of the learner production, but in Section 4.6, I suggest that the production of direct and overt negative evaluation is dispreferred.

In Extract 3.3 we can see T (in Line 3) initiating repair of L's utterance without negative evaluation:

(3.3)

```
1 T: what are these? ((T holds up two pens.))
2 L: this are a pen.
```

3 T: these are (.)
4 L: are pens.
5 T: what is this? ((T holds up a ruler.))

(Ellis, 1984, p. 103)

L produces the target string in Line 4. T does not produce a positive evaluation in Line 5, but merely continues with the next "teacher prompt." The "evaluation" is therefore generally implicit in the data and is not manifested as an explicitly verbalized action on its own. If the teacher moves on to the next adjacency pair after the learner production, then a positive evaluation is understood, whereas if the teacher initiates repair subsequent to the learner production, then a negative evaluation is understood by all parties. After this interactional route has been completed, the teacher will normally start another adjacency pair with a teacher prompt. The advantage of this description of the sequence (compared to the IRF/IRE cycle description) is that it covers all of the data in the database and fits neatly into the interactional architecture described in Chapter 5.

   I have so far specified the organization of the interaction in terms of teacher control. It is indeed typical of institutional interaction that a professional controls the interaction (Drew & Heritage, 1992a). However, in the L2 classroom the picture can sometimes be rather more complex and subtle, as Extract 3.3 illustrates. When, in form-and-accuracy contexts in the database, there is centralized attention, with the teacher leading whole-class interaction, then the interaction will tend to be "formal" in the way described previously by Drew and Heritage (1992b, p. 27). However, a focus on form and accuracy can also be maintained in group work and pair work from which the teacher is absent, as we can see in Extract 3.4:

(3.4)
((Pair work commences. The following is a recording of a single pair.))

1 L21: I've got a radio. have you got a radio?
2 L22: yes.
3 L21: what?

4 L22: yes I have. I've got a book. have you got a book?
5 L21: yes I have.

(Seedhouse, 1996, p. 473)

I noted in my discussion of Extract 3.1 that the teacher in this Norwegian primary school had prepared the students for pair work by practicing a question-and-answer sequence using vocabulary items as fillers in a structural slot. Now, when the pair work commences the teacher is not taking part in the interaction, and yet we can see that there is a degree of constraint imposed on the interaction by the teacher. The teacher has allocated the adjacency pairs which the learners should use in the interaction (question and answer) and has allocated the precise linguistic forms to be used, with only the name of the object to be transformed: These have already been practiced. Lines 2–4 are very revealing: L22 answers "yes," which would, in normal conversation, be an appropriate answer. However, L21 initiates repair, since the target string of linguistic forms "yes, I have" has not been produced. L21 is in effect substituting for the teacher and assuming the teacher's role in the interaction. L22 demonstrates comprehension of the purpose of the repair initiation by supplying the rest of the targeted string of forms in Line 4. I also noted in my discussion of Extract 3.1 that in Line 22 of that extract, the same teacher corrected "yes" answers until learners supplied "yes, I have."

So in the L2 classroom it is not always sufficient or accurate to say that the teacher personally controls the interaction, even in a formal form-and-accuracy context. There are instances in the data in which the teacher is entirely absent from the classroom when the planned interaction is taking place and yet the interaction orients to the teacher's pedagogical focus (e.g., Extract 5.3). The formulation which does cover all of the data is as follows. A pedagogical focus in relation to linguistic form and accuracy is introduced (normally by the teacher, but in learner-centered approaches the focus may be chosen by learners), and learners produce patterns of interaction which are normatively related in some way to the pedagogical focus. I will note many times in the course of this monograph that the vital and omnipresent factor in L2 classroom interaction is the reflexive relationship between the pedagogical focus and the organization of the interaction; the physical presence and participation of the teacher in the interaction is not always a necessary factor in the data. Extract 3.4 also illustrates that, at primary school level, learners have internalized the architecture of L2 classroom interaction to the extent that they are able to reproduce it accurately in the absence of a teacher and even adopt the teacher's role and repair policy.

This brings us to the complex relationship between spatial configuration of participants and degree of preallocation and hence, according to McHoul (1978), formality. McHoul specifically equates feelings of formality with the degree of preallocation and suggests that

> a commonsense observation would be that formal (as opposed to casual, conversational) talk can be accomplished through the spatial arrangement of the participants to that talk. In particular the configuration of and relative distances between participants might be thought of as significant. (p. 183)

This point may be valid for the L1 classrooms which McHoul examined, but the situation in the L2 classroom is more complex. The vital factor in all L2 classroom interaction is the reflexive relationship between the pedagogical focus and the organization of the interaction. This influences the degree of preallocation and formality of the interaction just as much as (and possibly more than) the spatial configuration. In Extracts 3.1 and 3.4 we see the spatial configuration change from whole-class to pair work, and we should therefore expect the degree of preallocation and formality to decrease. However, as noted previously, this does not happen, because the pedagogical focus and corresponding organization of the interaction have remained similar even though the spatial configuration has changed and the teacher has disappeared.

We have seen in this section that when the pedagogical focus is on linguistic forms, and there is a requirement for learners to produce forms with accuracy, then there is also a formal overall organization of the interaction which is appropriate to this pedagogical focus. This generally involves tight control of turn taking and an adjacency pair consisting of teacher prompt and learner production with optional evaluation and follow-up actions. However, this does not mean that all interaction in this context is identical; on the contrary, we have seen variability and heterogeneity within the context. In the next section I introduce a contrasting L2 classroom context, in which the focus is on meaning and fluency.

3.2 Turn Taking and Sequence in Meaning-and-Fluency Contexts

When the pedagogical focus is on meaning[2] and fluency, the aim is on maximizing the opportunities for interaction presented by the classroom pedagogical environment and the classroom speech community itself. Participants talk about their immediate environment, personal relationships, feelings, and meanings, or the activities they are engaging in. The focus is on the expression of personal meaning rather than on linguistic forms, on promoting fluency rather than accuracy. This context is often contrasted with the form-and-accuracy context; Kasper (1986), for example, contrasts language-centered and content-centered interaction. This major shift in pedagogical focus (by comparison with form-and-accuracy contexts) necessitates a major shift in interactional organization. Because the learners require interactional space to express personal meanings and develop topics, the organization of the interaction will necessarily become less narrow and rigid. A frequent criticism of the form-and-accuracy context is that it does not allow learners to develop interactional skills in the L2 (van Lier, 1988a, p. 106). Often meaning-and-fluency contexts are conducted through pair or group work. When the teacher is not present, the learners may manage the interaction themselves to a greater extent. However, in this section we will see teachers having various degrees of control over the interaction while maintaining a meaning-and-fluency focus. In Extract 3.5, T has asked the learners to bring personal belongings to class, and the pedagogical focus introduced is for the learners to describe their personal possessions and their significance to them:

(3.5)

```
 1 L1: OK. as you see this is a music box, (.) .hh and my mother made it. it's=
 2 L2: =oh, your mother made it?=
 3 L1: =yes, my mother made it. .hh the thing is that when: (.) this is the first
 4     thing she did (.) like this, with .hh painting and everything, .hh so nobody.
 5     nobody thought that it was going to come out like this. [ hahh  ] that's the
       point. that's why
 6 LL:                                                          [ heehee]
 7 L1: this is special because it took her about three weeks to: to make it, .hh and
 8     erm she put erm a really special interest in that and tried to, to make it
 9     the best that, er she could. so, (.) so, that's all. (1.5)
```

((4 lines omitted))

```
10 L3: well. this: this is a record, that for me is really very important. because
11     I've always liked poetry. (.) and one day when I was traveling (.) erm in
12     Can—by Can—in Canada, .hh I saw this record but I—I didn't know that it
13     was written in French (.) and I bought it.  [        ] and ah=
14 LL:                                              [ huhuhu]
15 L2: =did you understand?
16 L3: of course I,—I didn't understand any anything. but er the with this record I
17     made up my mind, and I decided to, erm to take up (.) a course in French,
18     and (.) now I, I (.) understand almost all the poetry and er, (.) all of them
19     are really pretty because some of them are er, written by Baudelaire, (.)
20     and, er they are (.) really good, really good and the voice of this man is
21     excellent. (.) is something really incredible, so for me is, erm (.) well, em
22     (.) a treasure.
23 LL: ( )
24 L4: well, my turn.
```

(British Council, 1985, Volume 4, p. 52)

We can see in Extract 3.5 that the learners manage the interaction locally to a great extent in the absence of the teacher. Now the teacher has in fact specified the nature of the speech exchange system as a monologue, in that the instructions were to "talk about your things now in the same way I did about mine" (p. 51), namely, in a monologue. However, the teacher has also made it clear that the learners can organize the turn taking locally, saying, "Whoever wants to can start" (p. 51). The learners do manage the speech exchange system locally in that L2 interrupts L1's turn (Line 2) and L3's turn (Line 15) with utterances which relate to the content of their previous turns. In Line 24 we can see L4 explicitly managing the turn-taking system. Line 24 also shows an orientation to the idea that the interaction should be organized so that all group members should take a turn at speaking. The learners express personal meanings, and the linguistic errors (as in Lines 9 and 22–23) are ignored. The exception is Line 12 in which L3 conducts self-initiated self-repair.

We can also see that it makes sense in this L2 classroom context to talk of the topic of the interaction, in contrast to form-and-accuracy contexts. This is evident in the details of the interaction. For example, the discourse marker *oh* often occurs in a meaning-and-fluency context as a marker of change of information state (Heritage, 1984a), since new information is being exchanged, and it occurs in Line 2 of Extract 3.5.

Although meaning-and-fluency contexts are often found in small groups of learners, they can also be created and maintained in the presence of the teacher. In Extract 3.6, 2 learners have just given talks on their respective countries (Germany and France) and are now discussing issues relating to their countries:

(3.6)

```
1 L6: at first you said you had a lot of problems in France about the Russian
2      immigrants, and I think it's the same problem now in West Germany with
3      the integration of East German people in the west part of Germany.
4 L2: yes, but I think it's quite different because (.) er it's the same race. I mean
5      (.) er East and West Germany was the same country before so you are
6      near, and in France it's with Arabian people and we don't have the same
7      culture.
8 L6: but (.) er (.) With nearly 40 years difference also mean the last 40 years
9      are so different and (.) er (.)
```

10 L2: yes
11 L6: in both countries that I think it's nearly the same. it's not the same [but
12 L2:   [yes,
13   because religion is a big problem and (.) er I think that between East and
14   West Germany it's the same religion and in France we don't have we have
15   Catholic religion and Arabian people is musulman religion
16 L6: most of the East German people have no religion
17 L2: yes, yes in fact and er the last big problem was with chador. I don't know
18   how we call it in English. it is the thing the woman put on her head?
19 T: in fact it isn't English 'cos it's Arabic, it's the chador. we use the same
20   because it's from the Arabic
21 L2: and er 3 or 4 months ago we had a big problem because some girls want to
22   go to school with this chador
23 L6: or work
24 L2: yes, and the principal of the school don't want that this girl come at school
25 L6: well, I think that it's normal when you go in another country you must
26   accept the rules of this country
27 T: mm. we had the same thing, a curious thing, the same thing happened here
28   and the girls in the school wanted to wear the chador
29 L6: uhu
30 T: and we came to a peculiarly British compromise that, yes, they could wear
31   it but only if it was in the school colour
32 L2: and the other problem is that er a lot of Arabian people are living in the
33   same place so they, their integration is very hard. they can't be integrated.
34   they are together.
35 L6: they have their own areas

(Mathers, 1990, p. 123)

Prior to Extract 3.6 the teacher had introduced a carrier topic, namely, the learners' countries. However, in Extract 3.6, the two learners are able to introduce subtopics of their own choice. So in Line 1, L6 introduces the subtopic of immigrants, which is taken up by L2, and the subtopic shifts in a stepwise movement to religion in Line 13 and to the sub-subtopic of the chador in Line 17. The teacher then takes up in Line 27 the topic nominated by the learners and makes a topical contribution. The teacher has not thereby taken control of the topic, however, because we see L2 regaining control of the topic in Line 32. L2 skip-connects back to the topic which he or she was developing in Line 4: the argument that France has bigger problems with integration than does Germany. So in spite of the presence of the teacher, the learners are able to nominate and negotiate topics themselves.

As far as turn taking is concerned, we see that the learners are able to take turns without reference to the teacher; in Lines 1–17 the teacher is effectively cut out of the speech exchange system as the learners address each other directly. In Line 17, L2 nominates the teacher and constrains the teacher's turn, using a form of self-initiated other-repair which is in effect using the teacher as an interactional resource. In Line 21, L2 continues with his or her own topic. In Line 27, T nominates herself to take a turn, but as this is to make an on-topic contribution, it does not alter the speech exchange system, and the two learners continue to address each other. However, the interaction does not continue like this indefinitely—there are, after all, other learners in the class, and so the teacher subsequently nominates other learners to speak while remaining within the carrier topic.

We have looked at two extracts in which this meaning-and-fluency context has been maintained by learners' having a degree of control over the turn-taking system. As we saw in Extracts 3.5 and 3.6, the learners were able to locally manage the interaction to some extent in that they were able to nominate themselves and each other for turns rather than having the teacher allocate them. However, as we will see in Extract 3.7,[3] it is possible for the teacher to have fairly firm control over the turn-taking system and to allocate turns to learners and yet still maintain a meaning-and-fluency focus. However, this does seem to require some complex interactional work on the part of the teacher. The setting is a primary school in Abu Dhabi, and the activity is *sharing time* (Yazigi, 2001), in which a student comes to the front of the class to share his or her experiences with the rest of the class:

(3.7)

1 L1: before on Wednesday I went to a trip to Dubai because my father's work
2   they gave him a paper that we could go to a free trip to Dubai.
3 T: ah::
4 L1: ya, and on the paper it said we could stay in a hotel for any days you want

5   so I said to my father for two days and when I was going to Dubai Mark
6   called me.
7 T: he called you?
8 L1: ya, and we were talking and then when we finished talking, er:: on
9   Thursday my father took me to Burjuman, ya, there was something like
10   this big just twenty dirhams, ya, I bought it and it..=
11 T: = what is this, something like this, it's big?
12 L1: it's like a penguin but not a penguin. it's a bear, ya, not very big like this.
13 T: uhu::
14 L1: like me, ya. I press a button, it moves like this, and it carries me up like
15   this and puts me down.
16 T: are you serious?
17 L1: and also in the hotel I saw the tallest man in the world and the shortest
18   man in the world.
19 T: really? ha! where do they come from?
20 L1: er:: I don't know. one is from China, I don't know, Japan and one is from
21   here. the tall man he's like this ((extending his right hand up)) bigger than
22   the short man.
23 T: is he the same one that came to school?
24 L1: no, bigger than that one.
25 T: oh really? even taller?
26 L1: ((nods))
27 T: jeez! o.k. thank you Arash for sharing.

(Yazigi, 2001, p. 42)

In Extract 3.7 T initiates the interaction by allocating interactional space to L1. L1 introduces the topic of his trip to
Dubai. T's response in Line 3 ("ah") functions as a marker of
change of information state (Heritage, 1984a) and conveys that
the message is understood and that L1 can proceed. In Line 4, L1
confirms the new information ("ya") and adds further information to clarify the situation. He also introduces a subtopic in
Lines 5–6: "Mark called me." Mark is a student in class, and
the speaker is thereby making a connection between the trip in
the outside world and the classroom speech community. T
responds to the piece of information in Lines 5–6 by rewording
it into a question (Line 7). The purpose is to encourage L1 to
proceed and to show that the point caught her interest. L1
elaborates on the subtopic of speaking to Mark but he soon
drops it and returns to the previous main topic of the trip to
Dubai. In Line 11 T interrupts L1 requiring clarification and

more specific details about what the something is which L1 bought.

Apparently T fears that the meaning and hence interest may get lost on the learners. It should be remembered that L1 was addressing the whole class, and clarification was indeed needed so that the listeners can follow the evolving dialogue. L1 responds to the teacher's initiation and attempts to clarify the point in Line 12. Again in Line 13, the discourse marker ("uhu") occurs as a marker of change of information state and allows the learner to proceed with the topic and offer further information (Line 14). T responds with a question in Line 16 which expresses surprise, allocates a turn to L1 and in effect allots him interactional space to continue to develop the topic further. However, L1 declines and chooses to open up a new subtopic, thus inviting T to respond to his new subtopic. The question posed in Line 19 indicates T's interest in the topic; it also effectively requires L1 to confirm the information shared and asks him to provide further information, which he does in Lines 20–22. T then draws on common background knowledge (Line 23) to make the input more comprehensible to the rest of the class and to enable them to continue to follow the dialogue. She also relates the outside world to the classroom speech community. T finally concludes the sharing episode in Line 27.

The analysis of Extract 3.7 shows the interaction to be locally managed on a turn-by turn basis. T neither initiates the topic of interaction nor is aware of where the interaction may lead. She also does not know how the learner may respond. The focus is on meaning rather than form, on fluency rather than accuracy. This is evident in that enough interactional space was allocated to the learner to enable him to develop topics and subtopics.

The teacher does not attempt at any point to correct minor linguistic errors, as these did not impede communication. The pedagogic focus is on the speaker's expression of personal meaning and on the contribution of new information to the immediate classroom community. The teacher's role is more that of a mediator whose purpose is to ensure that L1's message is conveyed to all of the other students, as well as a collaborator in the dialogue, thereby encouraging a smooth flow to the conversation and nurturing fluency. The teacher's utterances therefore contain markers of change of information state and clarification requests. There is an attempt on both sides, teacher and learner, to connect the real world to the classroom speech community (Lines 5 and 23). The teacher attempts to keep the other learners engaged, focused, and interested.

In terms of sequence organization, the situation in this context is far more varied than was the case in form-and-accuracy contexts examined previously. In Extract 3.5 the teacher is absent, and there are a series of descriptions of objects interspersed with questions about the objects. In Extract 3.6 we have a series of points and counterpoints in a discussion or debate. In Extract 3.7 we see the teacher controlling turn taking and using a set of question-and-answer adjacency pairs. Elsewhere in the data we find a great variety of sequence organizations, which is quite comprehensible in terms of rational organization. If the pedagogical focus is to allow freedom of expression, then it is natural that there will be considerable variety in terms of organizations of the interaction. The common feature is that the learners are developing a topic and the organization is appropriate to the development of the topic.

We have seen that a meaning-and-fluency context can be maintained (a) in the absence of the teacher; (b) in the presence of the teacher, but with the learners managing the turn taking; and (c) with the teacher being present and in overall control of the turn taking. Although the precise pedagogical focus and speech exchange system vary, the crucial point is that sufficient interactional space is allocated to learners to enable them to nominate and develop a topic or subtopic and to contribute new information concerning their immediate classroom speech community and their immediate environment, personal relationships, feelings and meanings, or the activities they are engaging in.

3.3 Turn Taking and Sequence in Task-Oriented Contexts

The concept of task-based learning (TBL) has come to occupy a central position in SLA research, and we now turn our attention to task-oriented interaction. However, it is first necessary to disentangle problems related to intended and actual pedagogical focus. At this point we need to reintroduce a distinction vital to the argument of this monograph, namely, that between *task-as-workplan* and *task-in-process* (Breen, 1989). As discussed in Chapter 2, the task-as-workplan is the intended pedagogy, the plan prior to classroom implementation of what the teachers and learners will do. The task-in-process is the actual pedagogy or what actually happens in the classroom. As we saw in a preliminary way in Chapter 2 and will see again during the course of this monograph, there is often a significant difference between what is supposed to happen and what actually happens. The task-as-workplan is always an etic specification and it has a very weak ontology, comparable to that of an airplane flight plan. Although the task-as-workplan may exist in the physical shape of a lesson plan or textbook unit, the actual event is always the task-in-process. Empirical data in classroom research are gathered from the task-in-process, and this monograph focuses solely on the task-in-process, although it often compares the ethnographic evidence of task-as-workplan with the actual task-in-process.

We should therefore be very clear that in this section we are not necessarily dealing with the concept of *task* as etically specified in terms of task-as-workplan in the TBL literature. Rather, we are dealing with interactions in which we can emically demonstrate in the details of the interaction (task-in-process) that the learners are focused on a task. The characterization *task-oriented* in this monograph therefore derives empirically from the data. The perspectives of the TBL literature and this monograph may coincide, but they do not necessarily do so. There is further discussion of this matter later in the chapter.

In task-oriented contexts, the teacher introduces a pedagogical focus by allocating tasks to the learners and then generally withdraws, allowing the learners to manage the interaction themselves. It appears to be typical in this context, therefore, that the teacher does not play any part in the interaction, although learners do sometimes ask the teacher for help when they are having difficulty with the task. By contrast with the two previous contexts, there is generally no focus on personal meanings or on linguistic forms. The learners must communicate with each other in order to accomplish a task, and *the focus is on the accomplishment of the task rather than on the language used.* In effect, as we will see, it is the nature of the task-in-process as interpreted by the learners which constrains the nature of the speech exchange system which the learners use.

We will now consider three characteristics of task-oriented interaction (Seedhouse, 1999b) by examining extracts from the database. These characteristics are (a) that there is a reflexive relationship between the nature of the task and the turn-taking system, (b) that there is a tendency to minimalization and indexicality, and (c) that tasks tend to generate many instances of clarification requests, confirmation checks, comprehension checks, and self-repetitions.

> *Characteristic 1: There is a reflexive relationship between the nature of the task and the turn-taking system.*

Sacks et al. (1974) suggest that

> since they are used to organize sorts of activities that are quite different from one another, it is of particular interest to see how operating turn-taking systems are character-izable as adapting to properties of the sorts of activities in which they operate. (p. 696)

In order to illustrate how this is operationalized, we will consider the interaction produced by tasks in Warren (1985). I quote here Warren's task-as-workplan, so that it is clear how the nature of the task and the resultant turn-taking system are related:

> The "Maps" task...was based on the "information gap" principle and was carried out by pairs of students separated from each other by a screen. Both students had a map of the same island but one of the maps had certain features missing from it. A key illustrating the missing features was given to each student so that they knew what these features were. In the case of the student with the completed map the key enabled him/her to know what was missing from the other map and in the case of the other participant it showed how the missing features were to be represented on his/her map. The student with the completed map had to tell the other student where missing features had to be drawn. Throughout the activity the teacher was present to ensure that the students did not abuse the presence of the screen. The idea behind having a screen to separate the participants was that they would then be forced to communicate verbally in order to complete the task. (Warren, 1985, p. 56)

Extract 3.8 is typical of the interaction which resulted from this task:

(3.8)

```
 1 L1: the road from the town to the Kampong Kelantan (pause) the coconut =
 2 L2: =again, again.
 3 L1: (.) the: the road, is from the town to Kampong Kelantan (6.5) the
 4     town: is: (.) in the Jason Bay.
 5 L2: (3.5) again. the town (.) where is the town?
 6 L1: the town is: (.) on the Jason Bay.
 7 L2: (1.0) the: road?
 8 L1: the road is from the town to Kampong Kelantan (10.4) OK?
 9 L2: OK
10 L1: (.) the mountain is: behind the beach, and the Jason Bay (8.1) the
11     river is: from the jungle, (.) to the Desaru (9.7) the mou—er the
12     volcano is above on the Kampong Kelantan (7.2) the coconut
13     tree is: (.) along the beach.
```

(Warren, 1985, p. 271)

The progress of the interaction is jointly constructed in Extract 3.8. Turn order, turn size, and turn design are intimately related to the progress of the task. So, for example, in Line 1, L1 provides one item of information to L2 and then proceeds with the second item of information without checking whether L2 has noted the first piece of information (as noted by Warren, because of the screen between them, the two learners cannot see each other). Because L2 has not finished noting the first piece of information, L2 initiates repetition. In Line 2 we see that L2 is able to alter the course of the interaction through a repetition request which requires L1 to backtrack. In other words, because the task has not yet progressed sufficiently, L2 takes a turn to allocate both a turn and a turn type to L1 which will facilitate the progress of the task. In Line 7, L2 asks where the road is. In Line 8, L1 supplies the information, waits for 10 s, then makes a confirmation check ("OK?") to ascertain whether L2 has completed that subsection of the task. L1 appears to be orienting his utterances to L2's difficulty in completing the task in that L1 uses an identical sentence structure each time and leaves pauses between different items of information. We can see these pauses in Lines 3, 8, 10, 11, and 12, and they vary from 6.5 s to 10.4 s in length. Repetition requests are focused on information necessary for the task in Lines 2, 5, and 7. In Line 8 the confirmation check is focused on establishing whether a particular subsection of the task has been accomplished or not.

We can see in Extract 3.8 that the nature of the task, in effect, tends to constrain the organization of turn taking and sequence. In task-oriented interaction, the focus is on the accomplishment of the task. In order to accomplish the task in the extract, the learners must take turns in order to exchange information. The nature of the task here pushes L1 to make statements to which L2 will provide feedback, clarification, repetition requests, or repair initiation. The speech exchange system is thus constrained to some degree. However, the two learners are also to some extent actively developing a turn-taking system which is appropriate to the task and which excludes elements which are superfluous to the accomplishment of the task. So we should clarify that there is a reflexive relationship between the nature of the task as interpreted by the learners (the task-in-process) and the turn-taking system.

I will now examine another instance of interaction within a task-oriented context from Warren (1985) in order to further illustrate the reflexive nature of the relationship between the task focus and the turn-taking system. "Blocks" is another task based on the information gap principle. In this activity the students were in pairs separated by a screen and in front of each student were five wooden building bricks of differing shapes and colors. The teacher arranged the bricks of one of the students into a certain pattern, and it was then the task of that student to explain to his or her partner how to arrange the other set of bricks so that they were laid out according to the pattern. A time limit of 60 s was imposed after which the teacher arranged the other student's bricks into another pattern, and the activity was carried out once more (Warren, 1985, p. 57):

(3.9)

```
 1 L1: ready?
 2 L2: ready
 3 L1: er (.) the blue oblong above the red oblong, eh? the yellow oblong.
 4 L2: (.) alright. (.) >faster, faster.<=
 5 L1: =the: red cylinder (.) beside the (.) blue oblong,
 6 L2: (.) left or right?=
 7 L1: =right.
 8 L2: (.) right yeah ( ) OK.
 9 L1: (1.0) the the red cube (.) was: (1.0)
10 L2: the red cube?
11 L1: (.) the red cube was (.) behind the (.) blue oblong.
12 L2: (.) blue oblong, (.) blue oblong. yeah.
13 L1: and the: (.) red cube was (.) er behind the (.) red oblong.
```

(Warren, 1985, p. 275)

In Extract 3.9 we can see the learners' orientation to the time limit set for completion of the task (1 min), in that L2 says "faster, faster" in Line 4. When we compare this extract with 3.8, we can see that these learners have developed a variant of the turn-taking system apparently in orientation to the time limit.

In Extract 3.9 we see L2 telling L1 when he has finished a particular stage (Lines 4, 8, and 12), and this enables L1 to commence giving the next item of information as soon as L2 has finished noting the previous one. This procedure clearly minimizes gap, as we can see when we compare this extract with 3.8. In Lines 8, 10, and 12, L2 appears to repeat what L1 has said in order to confirm his understanding of L1's utterance, to display the stage that L2 is at in the process of noting the information, and to delay L1 so that he does not begin the next item of information until prompted to do so. In this sense L2's repetition may be functioning in a similar way to a filler or gap avoider in normal conversation (McHoul, 1978). This is particularly evident in Line 12, in which L2 repeats L1's utterance twice before giving confirmation of completion.

The types of turns are constrained by the nature of the task, as are turn order and even turn size, because of the time limit. The basic organization of turn taking and sequence is again that L1 makes statements to which L2 will provide feedback, clarification or repetition requests, or repair initiation. On the one hand, the learners are creatively engaged in developing turn-taking systems which are appropriate to the accomplishment of the task. On the other hand, we can see that the nature of the task constrains the turn-taking system which the learners create. This illustrates very neatly the central argument of this monograph, namely, that the relationship between the pedagogical focus and the organization of the interaction is a reflexive one. We can see in this case that it is not merely that the pedagogical focus and the nature of the task constrain the patterns of interaction produced. From the opposite perspective, no one has told the learners exactly how to conduct the interaction, so by actively creating an organization of the interaction which they see as appropriate to the task, they are modifying and reinterpreting the nature of the pedagogical focus and of the task. The way in which they choose to conduct the interaction transforms the teacher's task-as-workplan into the learners' task-in-process.

Characteristic 2: There is a tendency to minimalization and indexicality.

We now shift our attention from the speech exchange system to the linguistic forms which are used. The nature of the task tends to constrain the kinds of linguistic forms used in the learners' turns, and there is a general tendency to minimizing linguistic forms. This is evident in Extract 3.9. L1 produces utterances from which the verb *be* is missing, with the exception of Lines 9, 11, and 13, where it is used in an inappropriate tense. This is an example of what Duff (1986) calls "topic comment constructions without syntacticized verbal elements" (p. 167), which are quite common in task-oriented interaction. It should also be noted that omission of copulas is a feature of pidgins and creoles (Graddol, Leith, & Swann, 1996, p. 220). There is a general tendency toward ellipsis, toward minimizing the volume of language used, and toward producing only that which is necessary to accomplish the task. Turns tend to be relatively short, with simple syntactic constructions (Duff, 1986, p. 167). What we also often find in practice in task-oriented interaction is a tendency to produce very indexical or context-bound interaction; that is, it is inexplicit and hence obscure to anybody reading the extracts without knowledge of the task in which the participants are engaged. The interaction can be understood only in relation to the task which the learners are engaged in. Interactants in a task seem to produce utterances at the lowest level of explicitness necessary to the successful completion of the task, which is perfectly appropriate, since the focus is on the completion of the task. Indeed, the interactants are displaying their orientation to the task precisely through their use of minimalization and indexicality. However, L2 teachers who are reading the transcripts may tend to find the actual language produced in task-oriented interaction to be impoverished and esoteric. In Extract 3.10, for example, learners are required to complete and label a geometric figure:

(3.10)

L1: what?
L2: stop.
L3: dot?
L4: dot?
L5: point?
L6: dot?
LL: point point, yeah.
L1: point?
L5: small point.
L3: dot.

(T. Lynch, 1989, p. 124)

Task-oriented interaction often seems very unimpressive to L2 teachers when read in a transcript because of these tendencies to indexicality and minimalization. The tendency toward context-boundedness is probably not a serious problem from a pedagogical point of view. The whole point of TBL is that learners should become immersed in the context of a task, and anyway, task-oriented interaction in the world outside the classroom frequently displays precisely this context-bound nature. However, the tendency toward minimalization and ellipsis may be a more significant problem as far as L2 pedagogy is concerned. It could be argued that people engaged in tasks in the world outside the classroom also often display some tendency toward minimalization, although generally not to the extent seen above. However, the point is that L2 teachers want to see in classroom interaction some evidence of the learners' linguistic competence being stretched and challenged and upgraded.[4]

The theory of TBL (derived from an etic consideration of task-as-workplan) is that tasks promote this; for example, Nunan (1988) suggests that two-way tasks "stimulate learners to mobilize all their linguistic resources, and push their linguistic knowledge to the limit" (p. 84). However, what we often find *in practice* in task-oriented interaction is more or less the opposite process, with the learners producing a minimum display of their linguistic competence using minimalized, reduced forms.[5] The learners appear to be so concentrated on completing the task that linguistic forms are treated merely as a vehicle of minor importance. However, this is precisely as the TBL theory says it should be, as in D. Willis's definition of a task (1990): "By a task I mean an activity which involves the use of language but in which the focus is on the outcome of the activity rather than on the language used to achieve that outcome" (p. 127).

Characteristic 3: Tasks tend to generate many instances of clarification requests, confirmation checks, comprehension checks, and self-repetitions.

TBL/SLA approaches have promoted task-based interaction as particularly conducive to SLA. There are two points to be noted here.[6] First, the surprising thing about TBL literature is the lack of evidence in the form of lesson transcripts concerning those benefits which are claimed for tasks. For example, Prabhu (1987) promotes, in a book-length study, the advantages of task-based teaching as opposed to structural teaching. Turning to Prabhu's "transcripts of project lessons" (pp. 123–137), one might therefore expect to find transcripts of impressive task-oriented interaction. In actual fact, one finds *no examples of task-oriented interaction at all*, but rather transcripts of "pre-task stages of a lesson" which contain exclusively teacher-led question-and-answer sequences.

Secondly, proponents of TBL/SLA approaches have tended to use a self-fulfilling methodology which presents task-oriented interaction in the most favorable light. A quantitative, segmental methodology has been used which isolates and counts individual features which tend to be abundant in task-oriented interaction. It is claimed that these individual features are particularly conducive to SLA, from which it follows that TBL approaches are particularly conducive to SLA. According to Long (1985, 1996) and associates, modified interaction or negotiation for meaning is necessary for language acquisition.[7] The relationship may be summarized as follows: Interactional modification makes input comprehensible.

Comprehensible input promotes acquisition. Therefore, interactional modification promotes acquisition. There has been considerable criticism of the interaction hypothesis (summarized in Ellis, 1994, p. 278), much of it targeting the reasoning just cited.

The features of interactions which have generally been selected for quantitative treatment are clarification requests, confirmation checks, comprehension checks, and self-repetitions, which are all characteristic of "modified interaction" or negotiation for meaning. As we have seen in Extracts 3.8 and 3.9, task-oriented interaction may feature numerous clarification requests, confirmation checks, comprehension checks, and self-repetitions (but see Foster, 1998), and indeed interactants may display their orientation to the task by means of these features. Tasks may or may not generate modified interaction; this may or may not be beneficial to SLA. However, from the perspective of this monograph, this subvariety of interaction needs to be evaluated as a whole, and from a holistic perspective, rather than selecting superficially isolable features of the interaction for quantification. The organization of repair in task-oriented contexts is outlined in Section 4.3. It is worth pointing out here, however, that clarification requests, confirmation checks, and comprehension checks are merely the social actions or functions performed by the repair. This constitutes only one small part of the overall organization of repair, which includes trajectories and preference organization (see Section 1.6.4). From the perspective of this monograph, then, SLA research on modified interaction has deprived itself of the analytical power of the CA approach to repair by using in isolation only one small and isolated component of this complex organization (see also Wagner, 1996).

Two potential problems on the pedagogical level with task-oriented interaction which appear in the data are associated with the lack of teacher supervision. This is not to say that learners are always unsupervised, but in a large class the teacher must circulate among groups or pairs. In the Norwegian data, in which I recorded four groups working on tasks simultaneously, there was sometimes evidence of learners going more off-task as the teacher moved away and more on-task as the teacher approached (see also Markee, in press). The problems are that students can produce linguistic errors which go uncorrected and that students can go off-task, including speaking in the L1. In Extract 3.11 we can see learners going considerably off-task, producing untreated errors in the L2 and using the L1. The task-as-workplan was to discuss paintings, but the task-in-process at this point has no connection with this:

(3.11)

L1: *skal vi synge en sang? vi synger den derre Fader Jakob!* ((tr.: Shall we sing a song? Let's sing "Frère Jacques"!))
L2: *hae?* ((tr.: what?))=
L1: =*Fader Jakob* ((tr.: Frère Jacques))=
L3: =NO!=
L2: =on English, I can't sing that song in English,
L1: yes,=
L2: =no.(.)
L1: you can!
L3: how it starts?
L1: are you sleeping, are you sleeping, ↑brother John, brother John. ((sings))
L2: we are supposed to work not (.) not sing.
L1: e:rm (1.0) >morning bells are ringing morning bells are ringing< ding dang dong ding dang dong.
L2: we are supposed to work not [(1.0) not sing]
L1:   [yes. I just got] to show how good I am to sing
L3: °you are not good at singing.°
L1: I know,=
L3: =you are *elendig* ((tr.: awful))

(Seedhouse, 1996, p. 454)

At this point we need to clarify the relationship between the task-oriented interaction we have been examining and the conception of task in the TBL/SLA literature. We have characterized the typical features of task-oriented interaction as a subvariety based on empirical evidence in the task-in-process of an emic focus on the accomplishment of a task. By contrast, the TBL/SLA literature involves (almost exclusively) an etic specification and conceptualization of task in terms of task-as-workplan prior to classroom implementation. According to Ellis (2003, p. 9) the first criterial feature of a task is that it is a workplan. There are well-known conceptual problems involved in the numerous different definitions of what is (and is not) a task, summarized in Ellis (2003, pp. 2–9). From the perspective of this monograph, however, the problems with the TBL/SLA approach stem from the decision to base the approach on an etic focus on task-as-workplan rather than on task-in-process in the classroom. The vital point to make here is that the empirical characterization of task-oriented interaction employed in this section is not necessarily the same thing as the theoretical/pedagogical specification of task in the TBL/SLA literature. How such specifications in terms of task-as-workplan are operationalized in terms of task-in-process must be determined on a turn-by-turn basis using an emic, holistic analysis. In this monograph we see numerous examples of tasks-as-workplan being reinterpreted by learners or transformed by the interactional organization of the L2 classroom (e.g., Extract 5.8).

When researchers do examine what actually happens in the classroom, they often discover mismatches between TBL/SLA theory and practice. Foster (1998), for example, found that "contrary to much SLA theorizing, . . . 'negotiation for meaning' is not a strategy that language learners are predisposed to employ when they encounter gaps in their understanding" (p. 1). She concludes that

> some current claims in SLA research are of academic rather than practical interest because researchers have lost sight of the world inhabited by language teachers and learners. If language acquisition research wants to feed into teaching methodology, the research environment has to be willing to move out of the laboratory and into the classroom. (p. 21)

Coughlan and Duff (1994) demonstrate that the same task-as-workplan does not yield comparable results in terms of task-in-process when performed by several individuals, or even when performed by the same individual on two different occasions. This also means that there is a crucial conceptual and methodological problem at the heart of TBL/SLA: Almost all conceptualization and discussion is based on the task-as-workplan, and yet all of the data are gathered from the task-in-process, and the two are not necessarily the same thing at all. We will examine the impact of the problem on TBL/SLA research practice in Section 6.3.

A further conceptual problem in the TBL/SLA literature is the question of what learners focus on during tasks. In the literature there is a general assumption that task-based inter-action is meaning focused (Ellis, 2003, p. 3). However, as we have seen in the analysis of previous extracts in this chapter, it may be that the participants' focus in task-oriented interaction is neither on form nor meaning, but rather narrowly on getting the task finished. This is in accordance with the definition of task cited previously (D. Willis, 1990, p. 127). Duff (1986) distinguishes between convergent tasks, such as those illustrated here, and divergent tasks, such as discussion and debate. The evidence from the database used in this study is that discussion and debate can and do occur in the L2 classroom; Warren (1985) provides some excellent examples. The organization of the inter-action is fundamentally different from task-oriented interaction, and so it is characterized as a separate L2 classroom context in Seedhouse (1996).

Since I may appear to have been very critical of TBL/SLA approaches here, I should clarify that, in my opinion, virtually all of the problems identified stem from TBL/SLA's current etic focus on the task-as-workplan. If the focus shifts to the task-in-process in the classroom (as some studies, such as Ellis [2001], have started to do), then not only should these problems disappear, but TBL/SLA should also be able to make itself much more relevant to classroom practice. See Section 6.4 for proposals on how this shift can be accomplished. The aim of this section has been to sketch the characteristics of task-oriented interaction as a variety of interaction and to balance the rosy TBL/SLA theoretical claims with empirical evidence of some less-than-rosy practical drawbacks. Task-oriented interaction is a particularly narrow and restricted variety of communication in which the whole organization of the interaction is geared to establishing a tight and exclusive focus on the accomplishment of the task. There are a multitude of different varieties of interaction in the world outside the L2 classroom, where there is certainly a lot more to communication than "performing tasks." We can also see in this monograph that there are various different subvarieties of communication which can occur in the L2 classroom.

One aim of this monograph is to provide technical characterizations of these L2 classroom contexts and also to show that each subvariety has its own peculiar advantages and disadvantages and limitations from a pedagogical and interactional point of view. CA methodology is particularly well suited to the task, as its origins have nothing to do with language teaching, and so it is pedagogically neutral. Despite the seemingly impressive theoretical arguments put forward to promote TBL, it remains to be proven that task-oriented interaction is more effective than other subvarieties of classroom interaction. This section concludes that it would at present be unsound to pursue a strong TBL approach which promoted task-oriented interaction at the expense of the other subvarieties and took task as the basis for an entire pedagogical methodology and for course and materials design. This monograph suggests that it is time to take a more *holistic* approach and to examine dispassionately the pros and cons of each and every subvariety of L2 classroom interaction on the basis of the empirical interactional evidence and its relationship to learning processes. We could then consider, for any particular group of learners, what balance and mixture of subvarieties of L2 classroom interaction might be most suitable within their curriculum, and we could promote task-oriented interaction as one element in the mixture.

To summarize, in this task-oriented context the pedagogical focus is appropriate to the speech exchange system in that both are oriented to the completion of the task. The pedagogical focus is on the outcome of the activity, and the turn-taking system is reflexively related to the task-in-process and oriented to the successful completion of the task. It is generally not relevant to talk of topic or meaning in this context; the learners' focus is on the task.

3.4 Turn Taking and Sequence in Procedural Contexts

The three L2 classroom contexts discussed in the previous three sections are optional—they do not occur in every lesson. However, the procedural context is obligatory; it occurs in every lesson as a precursor to another L2 classroom context. The teacher's aim in this L2 classroom context is to transmit procedural information to the students concerning the classroom activities which are to be accomplished in the lesson. In the database, this information is overwhelmingly delivered in a monologue, as in Extract 3.12:

(3.12)

T: I'd like you to discuss the following statements. and then you read them, >I don't read them< those for you. if there are words you're not sure of (1.0) in these statements you can ask me. but the ((coughs)) statement and you can pick out the statements you want to to erm start with. you don't have to do it in in the (.) way in the (.) way ((coughs)) I have written them. so if you find out that one of them erm you'd like to discuss more thoroughly you just pick out the the statement that you think is most (.) or is easier to discuss. (1.0) maybe there will be so much (.) disagreement that you will only be able to discuss two or three of them, that's what I hope. (.) so if you just start now forming the groups, (1.0) should I help you to do that? ((T divides learners into groups.))

(Seedhouse, 1996, p. 373)

The turn-taking system in the procedural context is therefore probably the most simple and straightforward and by far the most homogenous of all the L2 classroom contexts. In the majority of transcripts there is no turn taking at all. The teacher has the floor and is in little danger of being interrupted, so we can often find pauses during the teacher's monologue. In Extract 3.12 there are three pauses lasting 1 s each. It is not necessary for the teacher to indicate at the TRPs that her turn is continuing by means, for example, of fillers or rising intonation. As McHoul (1978, p. 192) says (with reference to L1 classrooms), teachers need not be concerned with having their turns cut off at any possible completion point by any other parties. Nonetheless, teacher monologues must be viewed as jointly constructed, with the learners actively cooperating by withholding their talk.

This does not mean that the procedural context invariably consists of an unbroken monologue from start to finish, however. Three possible variations are evident in the data. First, a student may wish to take a turn during the procedural monologue, often in order to ask a question concerning the procedure, as in Extract 3.13:

(3.13)

T: you were supposed to prepare for today (.) e:r by answering (.) the last of
     the questions in your (.) e:rm this volume, (.) the the company volume.(.)
L1: *men eg har'kkje faatt gjort leksa eg?* ((tr.: but I haven't done my
     homework?))
T: um well, (.) that's your problem not mine?

(Seedhouse, 1996, p. 372)

Typically, the student will indicate his or her wish to take a turn by raising a hand. Secondly, the teacher may elect to make the procedural context more interactive by altering the turn-taking system so that the students are able to take turns, as in Extract 3.14:

(3.14)

T: today, er, we're going to um, we're going to do something where, we, er, listen
     to a conversation and we also talk about the subject of the conversation er, in
     fact, we're not going to listen to one conversation, how many conversations are
     we going to listen to?
L: three
T: how do you know?
L: because, er, you will need, er, three tapes and three points
T: three?
L: points
T: what?
L: power points

(Nunan, 1988, p. 139)

In Extract 3.14 the teacher is asking display questions instead of transmitting procedural information in a monologue in order to involve and interest the learners in the activity and maximize motivation and the potential for interaction in that particular stage of the lesson. Thirdly, the teacher may, having explained the procedure, ask a learner to verify the procedure, as in Extract 3.15:

(3.15)

T: what do we have to do? Karine, can you explain?
L: we have, er (.) to describe what it's wrong, er (.) in the object.

(Lubelska & Matthews, 1997, p. 118)

When a researcher records a well-established class, the procedural context may be of minimal length, in that the teacher has, over the previous class sessions, established procedural routines with which the students are, by the moment of recording, well familiar. Abdesselem (1993) characterizes procedural context interaction (which he calls classroom management) in the following way: "Most moves are similar in all lessons and tend to be produced and reacted to automatically. Thus, students and teacher operate within a narrow range of language, much of which is formulaic" (p. 229). In Extract 3.16 we can see formulaic language of minimal length used to outline procedures in a well-established class:

(3.16)

T: now you're going to do the pair work, (1.5) *foerst saa spoer dokker saa svar dokker saa skifter dokker ut* (0.8)*, dokker trenger ikke aa ta New York for eksempel dokker kan bytte ut tidene og navnan, skjoenner dokker?* (0.8) *noen som ikke forstaar?* ((tr.: first you ask then you answer then change, . . . you don't have to say New York for instance and you can change the times and the names, . . . do you understand? . . . anyone who doesn't understand?)) (1.5) ok.

(Seedhouse, 1996, p. 498)

This extract also introduces an interesting phenomenon, namely, whether procedural information is transmitted in the L1, the L2, or a mixture of both, as in the extract. The evidence from my Norwegian database is as follows. In Lessons 1, 2, 3, and 4 (i.e., secondary and tertiary schools), procedural context interaction was conducted solely in English. In Lessons 5, 6, and 7 (primary schools) there are a variety of strategies. In Lesson 6 the teacher uses Norwegian almost exclusively to transmit procedural information. In Lessons 5 and 7 teachers sometimes use exclusively English, and sometimes exclusively Norwegian, to transmit procedural information. However, there is a frequent *double-checking* strategy which involves giving the procedural information first in English and then in Norwegian, as in Extract 3.17:

(3.17)

T: and <u>here</u>, (.) here are (1.5) the (0.5) eleven words. (.) now you are going to write down four of these words >*no skal de skriva ned fire av de orda som staar nede paa arket*< ((tr.: now you write down four of those words on your paper))

(Seedhouse, 1996, p. 477)

The evidence from the Norwegian schools' database is therefore that procedural information is more likely to be transmitted exclusively in the L2 the greater the age and the greater the level of linguistic proficiency of the learners. The basic focus in this procedural context, then, is on the transmission of procedural information, and the basic system of teacher monologue is appropriate to this focus. There is generally little or no turn taking involved in this context, and there is very little variation in the database in terms of the manifestations of this context.

3.5 Methodological Issues

In this chapter we have seen examples of L2 classroom contexts which are fairly clearly delimited. However, since teachers' and learners' motivations and orientations do not always coincide, struggles for control of the pedagogical focus and hence the L2 classroom context sometimes occur. The most common tension between contexts in the data occurs between form-and-accuracy and meaning-and-fluency contexts. One could also express this in pedagogical terms as tension between a pedagogical focus on form and a focus on meaning. A common scenario in the data is for learners to protest (generally in an indirect or oblique way) that the form-and-accuracy context interaction which they are involved in bears little resemblance to real-world meaning and that they have little interactional space to express personal meanings. In other words, learners often seem to hint that they would like to move more toward a meaning-and-fluency context. Sometimes there is also evidence in the data of a simultaneous dual focus on both form and meaning, an issue which is currently of great interest to researchers and practitioners. These issues are discussed in detail in Seedhouse (1996) and Seedhouse (1997b) but cannot be included here for reasons of space.

Chapter 5 provides a full discussion on methodological issues, but it is worth drawing attention at this point to some of the differences between the CA approach to ordinary conversation outlined in Chapter 1 and the approach to L2 classroom interaction taken in this chapter. The dimensions and nature of "applied CA" in relation to institutional interaction are controversial issues, and space does not permit a full discussion here; see, however, Drew (in press), ten Have (1999, 2001), and Richards (in press). CA methodology is always concerned with making explicit the interactional orientations and concerns of participants. Clearly participants' concerns will inevitably vary in each institutional setting, and so CA methodology will evolve in a slightly different way in each such setting in order to portray the participants' different concerns and orientations. For example, Drew (1992, p. 472) explicates a device for producing inconsistency in, and damaging implications for, a witness's evidence during cross-examination in a courtroom trial. Clearly these participants' interactional concerns are unique to this institutional setting. Although Drew is using a CA methodology, he is in effect simultaneously developing a subvariety of CA methodology appropriate to the analysis of cross-examination in courtroom settings; he is selecting for analysis a device which is unique to that institutional setting and explicating the interactional work unique to that setting which the device accomplishes. In exactly the same way, this study uses an over-all CA methodology while in effect simultaneously developing a subvariety of CA methodology appropriate to the analysis of interaction in L2 classrooms. This study will select for analysis those concerns and competences which are unique to the L2 classroom and attempt to explicate how the interaction is accomplished in the institutional setting and to uncover the machinery which produces the interaction.

When studying institutional varieties, CA practitioners have inevitably adopted some technical terms used by professionals in the particular institution they are studying to describe aspects of the interaction. For example, Drew's (1992) study of cross-examination in rape trials starts with an explanation of legal practices and employs many legal (i.e., non-CA) terms. From the ethnomethodological standpoint, analysts are supposed to be representing the participants' perspective, which may include the terms they use to describe their practices. Also, if we invented new "CA" terms to replace professionals' technical terms, we would create a new set of problems, including the problem of the professionals themselves not understanding them. For these reasons I am employing in this monograph a number of terms such as *meaning and fluency* and *form and accuracy* which originate in the applied linguistics (AL) literature and are not CA terms.

3.6 Chapter Summary

In this chapter I have sketched the basic overall speech exchange system of four different L2 classroom contexts and attempted to portray the reflexive relationship between the pedagogical focus of the interaction and the organization of turn taking and sequence. As the pedagogical focus varies, so the organization of turn and sequence varies. The chapter has attempted to show that a dynamic and variable approach to context is necessary to portray the multiplicity of speech exchange systems which we find in the data. It is clear from the data presented here that it would be totally untenable to talk about "the speech exchange system of the L2 classroom." We have seen that in some L2 classroom contexts, the learners manage turn taking locally and creatively to a great extent,[8] and it would be quite inaccurate to state that only teachers can direct speakership in any creative way (McHoul, 1978, p. 188) in the L2 classroom. We have seen great variety in relation to the speech exchange systems of the L2 classroom contexts examined here. At one end of the spectrum, in procedural contexts there is a very high degree of homogeneity; we generally find a teacher monologue with no turn taking at all. At the other end of the spectrum, in meaning-and-fluency contexts, there is enormous heterogeneity in terms of systems of turn taking and sequencing. Again this is rationally linked to pedagogical focus; conveying instructions favors a monologue, whereas expressing meanings, feelings, and opinions favors a diversity of organizations.

In this chapter we have also seen that the architecture of L2 classroom interaction is so flexible that it is able to adopt virtually any speech exchange system (to suit a particular pedagogical focus) and still remain identifiably L2 classroom interaction. We will see in Section 5.1 that this is because certain properties are manifest in the interaction whatever the L2 classroom context and whatever particular speech exchange system is in operation. For reasons of space I have discussed only four L2 classroom contexts; further characterizations are available in Seedhouse (1996).

Notes

[1]See the final section of this chapter for notes on the use of terminology.

[2]The notion of "meaning" is inherently problematic. For discussion, see Seedhouse (1996, 1997b).

[3]The analysis of Extract 3.7 presented here was cowritten with Rana Yazigi.

[4]This is not to suggest that learning takes place only when it is "visible" in transcripts. However, teachers in practice constantly evaluate spoken learner interaction and treat it as evidence of progress or lack of it.

[5]Bygate (1988), however, suggests that such talk may "enable learners to produce dependent units appropriately in the context of discourse, without

imposing the additional processing load implied by the requirements of having to produce complete sentences" (p. 74).

[6]In this section I am moving away from a CA of interactional data to discuss issues of a pedagogical and theoretical nature, since they are complex and require some elaboration.

[7]The following definitions are based on Ellis (1994). Problems often arise in communication involving L2 learners. *Negotiation of meaning* is work undertaken to secure understanding. This often involves *modified interaction*, including comprehension checks and clarification requests. *Input* is the language learners are exposed to. This can be made *comprehensible* by various means, including simplification and using context.

[8]See Seedhouse (1996) for further examples of such contexts.

CHAPTER FOUR

The Organization of Repair in Language Classrooms

In this chapter, I consider the role of repair in language teaching. It is a central issue in that it tends to bear a greater load in the L2 classroom than in other institutional settings and also because of its importance in the concept of negotiation of meaning in work on the interaction hypothesis.[1] As Markee (2000) observes, "Conversational repair is viewed by SLA researchers as the sociopsychological engine that enables learners to get comprehended input" (p. 31). It therefore follows that a clear understanding of how repair is organized in the L2 classroom is vital to this strand of SLA research. Van Lier (1988a) points out that repair is a generic term, with correction or error replacement being one kind of repair, and identifies three different goal orientations for repair in L2 classrooms and four basic kinds of repair. Van Lier concludes his chapter on repair by suggesting that "we must bear in mind that certain types of activity naturally lead to certain types of repair, and that therefore the issue of how to repair is closely related to the context of what is being done" (p. 211). Kasper (1986) contrasts the organization of repair in language-centered and content-centered phases of L2 lessons and concludes that

> talking about repair in FL teaching as such is inconclusive: rather, preferences and dispreferences for specific repair patterns depend on the configuration of relevant factors in the classroom context.... The teaching goal of the two

141

phases turned out to be the decisive factor for the selection of repair patterns. (p. 39)

A "variable" approach to repair in the L2 classroom, in which the organization of repair varies with the pedagogical focus, has been suggested by van Lier (1988a), Kasper (1986), and Jung (1999). The present chapter can be seen as an attempt to extend van Lier's and Kasper's variable approach by describing how repair is organized within different L2 classroom contexts (Seedhouse, 1999a). As with turn taking and sequence, it is argued that there is no single, monolithic organization of repair in the L2 classroom. There is a reflexive relationship between the pedagogical focus and the organization of repair; as the pedagogical focus varies, so does the organization of repair. Furthermore, what constitutes trouble varies with the pedagogical focus, which means that what is repairable is different in each context.

In this chapter, I sketch several L2 classroom contexts and show that each has its own particular organization of repair which is appropriate to the pedagogical focus (Seedhouse, 1999a). The analyses suggest that it is possible to outline the organization of repair within a particular L2 classroom context in terms of (a) typical participants in the repair, (b) typical repair trajectories, (c) typical types of repair, and (d) typical focus of repair, that is, what is repairable. This is not a comprehensive investigation of all the L2 classroom contexts which can occur, nor is it a comprehensive examination of repair organization; it is an illustrative sketch of the organization of repair within some L2 classroom contexts intended as evidence to support the main argument of this chapter: that each L2 classroom context has its own peculiar organization of repair and this is reflexively related to the pedagogical focus of the context. The L2 classroom contexts which I discuss are form-and-accuracy contexts, meaning-and-fluency contexts, and task-oriented contexts. In Section 4.11 I also show how interactional organization can transform pedagogical focus by examining a case of preference organization in relation to repair in form-and-accuracy contexts.

It is worth considering at the start of the chapter what is meant by the terms *repair, trouble,* and *repairable item.* In Chapter 1, I defined *repair* as the treatment of trouble occurring in interactive language use. *Trouble* is anything which participants judge to be impeding their communication, and a *repairable item* is one which causes trouble for participants. Any element of talk may in principle be the focus of repair, even an element which is well-formed, propositionally correct, and appropriate. Schegloff et al. (1977) point out that "nothing is, in principle, excludable from the class 'repairable'" (p. 363). Repair, trouble, and repairable items are participants' constructs, for use in interaction how and when participants find appropriate. Their use may be related to institutional constraints, however. In courtroom cross-examination of a witness by an opposing lawyer, for example, a failure by the witness to answer questions with "yes" or "no" may constitute trouble within that institutional setting (Drew, 1992). Such a failure is therefore repairable (for example, by the lawyer and/or judge insisting on a "yes/no" answer) and even sanctionable. So within a particular institutional subvariety, the constitution of trouble and what is repairable may be related to the particular institutional focus.

The same perspective applies to L2 classrooms. Within each L2 classroom context, the definition of what is trouble and what is repairable is related to the particular pedagogical focus. Because error analysis is a matter of interest to applied linguists and language teachers, one might assume that the organization of repair in L2 classrooms would be based primarily on the occurrence of and correction of linguistic errors. However, as we will see in the analysis of extracts in this chapter, the organization of repair is primarily related to pedagogical focus.

4.1 Repair in Form-and-Accuracy Contexts

In L2 classroom contexts which focus on linguistic form and accuracy, personal or real-world meanings do not enter into the picture to any great extent. Typically, the teacher's pedagogical focus will aim at the production of a specific string of linguistic forms by the learners, and the learners produce utterances so that the teacher can assess whether they have absorbed that information. We noted in Section 3.1 that turn taking and sequence are tightly controlled in form-and-accuracy contexts, and the same applies to the organization of repair. The major feature of the organization of repair in such contexts is the very tight connection between the linguistic forms and patterns of interaction which the learners produce in the L2 and the pedagogical focus which the teacher introduces. In other words, repair may be initiated by the teacher if the linguistic forms and patterns of interaction produced are not exactly identical to those intended by the teacher's pedagogical focus. In Extract 4.1 the teacher's pedagogical focus is to get the learner (via L2 prompts) to produce a specific string of linguistic forms:

(4.1)

1 T: right, the cup is on top of the box. ((T moves cup))
2   now, where is the cup?
3 L: in the box.
4 T: the cup is (.)?
5 L: in the box.
6 T: the cup is in (.)?
7 L: the cup is in the box.
8 T: right, very good, the cup is in the box.

(Johnson, 1995, p. 10)

Even though the answers which L produces in Lines 3 and 5 are linguistically correct and sequentially appropriate, T initiates repair in Lines 4 and 6 until L produces exactly the targeted string of linguistic forms in Line 7.

Since the focus in form-and-accuracy contexts is on the learners' production of specific strings of linguistic forms, it follows that when the learners produce utterances which are linguistically correct and appropriate, those utterances may still be subject to repair by the teacher, as in Extract 4.2. From the evidence of the database, repair of linguistically correct and appropriate utterances seems to be peculiar to form-and-accuracy contexts within the L2 classroom.

(4.2)

T: *Wohin ist Susan gefahren?* ((tr.: where has Susan gone to?)) Michelle.
L: *Sie ist mit dem Zug nach Edinburg gefahren.* ((tr.: she's gone to Edinburgh by train))
T: *Ja. Gut. Können wir genauer sein? Ich habe nur gefragt: Wohin? Nicht womit? Nur wohin?* ((tr: yes. good. only can we be more precise? I only asked where? not: how? only where?))
L: *Sie ist nach Edinburg gefahren.* ((tr: she's gone to Edinburgh))
T: *Gut.* ((tr: good))

(Westgate, Batey, Brownlee, & Butler, 1985, p. 278)

In Extract 4.2 we see the teacher conducting repair in a form-and-accuracy context even when the learner utterance not only is correct and appropriate but also contains precisely the targeted string of linguistic forms: The only problem is that the learner has added information ("by train") which is extraneous to the target string and therefore deemed superfluous by the teacher. Although we might view this as unnecessarily pedantic teacher behavior, the point to be emphasized is that such repair is perfectly "rational" within a form-and-accuracy context, in which repair may be initiated by the teacher if the linguistic forms and patterns of interaction produced are not exactly identical to those targeted by the teacher's pedagogical focus, even if they are linguistically correct and appropriate. This is by no means an isolated instance in the data; see also Extracts 5.2 and 5.10.

We noted in Chapter 1 the four trajectories or routes by which repair is accomplished: self-initiated self-repair, self-initiated other-repair, other-initiated self-repair, and other-initiated other-repair. In conversation, according to Schegloff et al. (1977), there is an order of preference with respect to repair trajectories, with self-initiated self-repair being most preferred and most common and other-initiated other-repair being most dispreferred and least common. Repair in form-and-accuracy contexts is overwhelmingly initiated by the teacher (other-initiation). In the data, there are more instances of other-initiated self-repair than of other-initiated other-repair; this corresponds with McHoul's (1990, p. 353) find-ings for L1 classrooms. Often the teacher initiates repair several times before the target string of linguistic forms is attained, as in Extract 4.3:

(4.3)

```
1 L1: they are watch televi—television
2 T:   okay now. yesterday at eight o'clock (.) they (.)
3 L1: they ar[e   they watche[ s   watched[   they were=
4 T:          [ they—          [ they:::    [they ( )
5 L1: =(.) watching
```

(van Lier, 1988a, p. 197)

The teacher is targeting a particular string of linguistic forms involving the continuous past tense: for example, "they were watching television." In Lines 1 and 3 the learner starts to pro-duce a string involving a tense which is not the targeted one; the teacher therefore initiates repair in Lines 2 and 4. The repair initiation technique used involves repeating the word which the learner used immediately prior to the error, which has the effect of locating the error (see also Section 4.5). Other-initiated other-repair trajectories are also common, as in Extract 4.4:

(4.4)

```
1 L: it bug me to have=
2 T: =it bugs me. it (bugzz) me
3 L: it bugs me when my brother takes my bicycle.
```

(Lightbown & Spada, 1993, p. 76)

In Extract 4.4, the other-initiated other-repair is performed by the teacher producing the correct linguistic form in Line 2. In effect, Line 2 is a double repair. The first utterance in Line 2 ("It bugs me") offers the correct linguistic form, whereas the second utterance ("It bugzz me") highlights the error (the missing −s ending) by stressing and lengthening the final sound. In both other-initiated self-repair and other-initiated other-repair trajec-tories in a form-and-accuracy context, the teacher is initiating repair in order to obtain the learner production of a precise string of linguistic forms. As Kasper (1986, p. 27) points out, self-initiated self-repair is relatively rare in this context, because it is the teacher who evaluates the accuracy of the learner's forms and who therefore predominantly initiates the repair.

Self-initiated other-repair is also fairly common in the data, and in fact van Lier (1988a) notes, "It may be a special feature of L2 classrooms that this trajectory occurs there quite regularly" (p. 201). Van Lier provides three extracts to illustrate this trajectory, and there is an interesting phenomenon in each case: The learner starts off in the L2 and then initiates other-repair by using the L1.

(4.5)

L1: (where is the way) *is dat goed?* ((tr.: is that correct?))
L2: *ja*: where is the way to the cinema

(van Lier, 1988a, p. 201)

We can try to provide a functional explanation as to why this repair trajectory should occur in form-and-accuracy contexts. The learner has to produce a precise string of forms which will correspond to those targeted by the teacher. The learner will initiate other-repair if he or she reaches a point at which he or she is no longer able to proceed or alternatively to verify that the forms produced are in fact those targeted.

There is another very interesting and unusual repair trajectory. When one learner has failed to produce the string of linguistic forms which the teacher is targeting, the teacher invites the other learners to repair the learner's error; this is other-initiated other-repair, the other-repair being conducted by a third party. It could also be termed teacher-initiated peer-repair:

(4.6)

L1: *Erm, sie sind im Schirmgeschäft, weil, erm (.) sie (.) möchten eine [sic] Schirm kaufen.* ((tr.: er, they're in the umbrella shop because, er, they want an umbrella to buy))
T: *Was meinen die anderen? Ist das richtig, was Mary sagt?(.). Roger, Sie Schütteln den Kopf. Verstehen Sie? Sie schütteln den Kopf.* ((tr.: what do the others think? is what Mary says correct? Roger, you're shaking your head. do you understand? you're shaking your head shaking your head.))

Wie sagen Sie es? Warum sind sie im Schirmgeschäft? ((tr.: how do you
say it? why are they in the umbrella shop?))
L2: *Erm, weil sie einen Schirm kaufen möchten.* ((tr: er, because they want to
buy an umbrella))

(Ellis, 1992, p. 115)

This repair trajectory is interesting for two reasons. First, there
is no evidence that this trajectory ever occurs in ordinary conversation; it is not reported in any of the CA works on repair in
conversation. Secondly, this trajectory appears to occur in the
database only in form-and-accuracy contexts, which means that
it may be a context-specific repair trajectory.[2] This peculiar
organization of the interaction can be explained in terms of
rational design in relation to the pedagogical focus to which it
is appropriate. The pedagogical focus in this context is on the
production of a string of precise linguistic forms by learners. If
one learner fails to produce that string, then the teacher may
require another learner to produce it. The advantage of this
technique from an interactional viewpoint is that it appears to
allow the learners some measure of interactional space (which is
normally very restricted in a form-and-accuracy context) in that
it allows learners to perform interactional actions (evaluation
and repair/correction) which are normally reserved for the
teacher in this context. The advantages of this technique from
a pedagogical point of view are summarized by Edge (1989):

> Firstly, when a learner makes a mistake and another
> learner corrects it, both learners are involved in listening
> to and thinking about the language. Secondly, when
> a teacher encourages learners to correct each other's
> mistakes, the teacher gets a lot of important information
> about the students' ability. Thirdly, the students become
> used to the idea that they can learn from each other.
> Fourthly, if students get used to the idea of peer correc-
> tion without hurting each other's feelings, they will be
> able to help each other learn when they work in pairs and
> groups, when the teacher can't hear what is said. (Edge,
> 1989, p. 26)

It is only in the form-and-accuracy context that the teacher requires the production of a precise string of linguistic forms. This is a functional explanation, then, as to why this trajectory appears to be peculiar to this context, and the point reinforces the argument of this chapter that each L2 classroom context has its own peculiar organization of repair which is reflexively related to the pedagogical focus of the context. In form-and-accuracy contexts, any learner contribution which does not correspond exactly to the precise string of linguistic forms required by the teacher may be treated as trouble by the teacher and may be treated as repairable. So, according to the emic logic of this context, even learner utterances which are entirely correct in linguistic terms may still be subject to repair by the teacher, as in Extract 4.2.

4.2 Repair in Meaning-and-Fluency Contexts

The pedagogical aim of the meaning-and-fluency context is to maximize the opportunities for interaction presented by the classroom environment and the classroom speech community itself. The focus is on the expression of personal meaning rather than on linguistic forms, on fluency rather than on accuracy. The focus of repair in this context is on establishing mutual understanding and negotiating meaning; in contrast to form-and-accuracy contexts, repair of correct and appropriate linguistic forms never occurs in meaning-and-fluency contexts in the data. Moreover, it appears that incorrect linguistic forms and interlanguage forms are frequently ignored, unless they lead to a breakdown in communication. Sometimes the type of repair used is embedded correction,[3] as we saw in Extract 2.2. Exposed and overt correction of incorrect or inappropriate linguistic forms does occur, but it appears to be used only when there is trouble which prevents the interaction from continuing. In other words, repair is being conducted in a way which is more similar to ordinary conversation, and in a completely different way from the form-and-accuracy context. In van Lier's (1988a) terms, we see conversational repair in this context, whereas we saw didactic repair in the form-and-accuracy context. In Extract 4.7, the focus is clearly not on linguistic form and accuracy; although linguistic errors occur, the teacher does not attempt to repair them at all:

(4.7)

```
 1 T:    could you tell me something about marriage in Algeria?
 2       who is married here?
 3 L1:   Azo, only Azo.
 4 T:    alright, your opinion about that.
 5 L2:   he will marry.
 6 T:    oh, he is engaged, engaged. tell me something about the
 7       institution of marriage in Algeria. tell me something
 8       about it.
 9 L3:   there are several institutions.
10 T:    you don't have marriage in Algeria. what do you have
11       then?
12 L4:   only women and men.
13 T:    yes, that's what marriage is.
14 L1:   the marriage in Algeria isn't like the marriage in
15       England.
16 T:→   what do you mean?
17 L2:   for get marriage you must pay two thousand.
18 L5:   yes more expensive than here.
19 T:→   why do you have to pay money?
20 L6:   no. it's our religion.
21 L7:   not religion but our tradition.
22 L8:   no, religion, religion. in religion we must pay women,
23       but not high price, but tradition.
24 L5:   between women, women does not like to married to a low
25       money because it is not, it is (.)
26 T:    oh, dowry, oh dear.
```

(Hasan, 1988, pp. 258–259)

The learners in this extract are able to express information which is new to the teacher, as evidenced by the two "oh"s which the teacher utters. So when the teacher initiates repair in this context in Lines 16 and 19, it is a clarification of the message or meaning which the teacher is aiming at.[4] The teacher is not repairing in order to obtain a linguistically correct string of linguistic forms from the learner. The form of repair initiation is identical to clarification requests found in ordinary conversation. That is, they are *wh*-questions which initiate repair without implying that an error has occurred. It is not only the teacher who is conducting repair; we can also see the learners repairing each other's statements (other-initiated other-repair) in Lines 21 and 22 using overt correction techniques. However, the repair is focused on establishing the factual accuracy of statements rather than on linguistic form. In Extract 4.8 we see one possible outcome in this context when the teacher adopts an "extreme" meaning-and-fluency focus:

(4.8)

```
 1 T:   what about in China? well, Hong Kong. China. do you have a milk van?
 2 LL:  er, China (.) no, no milk.
 3 T:   no milk?
 4 LL:  yeah, shop, er, city, city.
 5 T:   ah, at the shop, the shop.
 6 LL:  er, yes, yes.
 7 L:   Hong Kong. Hong Kong.
 8 T:   yeah, in Hong Kong, yes.
 9 LL:  in China, yes er ( ) city.
10 T:   in the big cities.
11 LL:  big city (.) city, yeah.
12 T:   ah huh!
13 LL:  Guangdong. Peking. Shanghai, Shanghai.
14 L:   yes, er city, very big, big milk car.
15 T:→  big milk van. ah! and city, country. in the country, no?
16 LL:  no.
17 T:   no. shh, shh, shh ((gestures))
18 L:   that's right.
19 T:   yes (laughs)
20 L:   I'm, er, I'm (.) no, is China, er city.
21 T:   uh huh!
22 L:   er, I'm house, near, near city er, I'm go to city shopping, er, how many?
23 T:   buy milk.
24 L:   buy milk, yeah. buy milk.
25 T:   buy milk.
26 L:   buy milk, go to home, yes.
```

(Nunan, 1989, p. 142)

In the extracts involving form-and-accuracy contexts earlier in the chapter, sometimes we saw examples of linguistically correct and appropriate learner utterances being subject to repair because they were not the forms which the teacher was targeting. In form-and-accuracy contexts, then, the teacher is typically attempting to upgrade the learners' interlanguage until it corresponds perfectly with the L2. What we sometimes find in meaning-and-fluency contexts, by contrast, is the teacher downgrading expectations of the linguistic forms which the learner produces, making concessions to accept, understand, and praise the learners' interlanguage. In Extract 4.8 we can see the teacher accepting minimal, pidginized interlanguage forms as valid contributions. Sometimes the teacher performs embedded correction (correction done in the context of a conversational action) on errors, as in Line 15. Here, the teacher substitutes "milk van" for "milk car" in the context of an action of acknowledging new information with "ah." Mostly, however, the teacher accepts minimalized, reduced contributions reminiscent of a pidgin without comment or any attempt at repair. What happens in Lines 3, 5, 8, 10, 15, 23, and 25 is interesting: The (NS) teacher is actually downgrading his or her own language to a minimalized, reduced interlanguage devoid of verbs in accommodation to the learners' interlanguage. This is by no means an isolated example—see Nunan (1989, pp. 142–149) for around 30 other examples within the same lesson.

Although Nunan suggests that the lesson in which Extract 4.8 occurs is beginning to be "truly communicative," many teachers would have serious reservations about the instructional value of the interaction in the extract. The teacher is producing some minimalized interlanguage himself or herself which is functioning as both input and model and is accepting any interlanguage forms which the learner produces, which could of course result in fossilized errors.[5] It is probably most satisfactory to see Extracts 4.8 and 4.2 as being at the two opposite extremes of the continuum from exclusive focus on form to exclusive focus on meaning, moving from upgrading to downgrading of expectations concerning the production of linguistic forms by the learners. Most extracts in the database, whether in form-and-accuracy or meaning-and-fluency contexts, are located somewhere between the two extremes.

So we have seen that the focus of repair in meaning-and-fluency contexts is on establishing mutual understanding and negotiating meaning. In general, overt correction is undertaken only when there is an error which impedes communication. The teacher may adopt a policy of not repairing learner utterances even when they are of a minimalized, reduced nature and full of linguistic errors. According to the emic logic of this L2 classroom context, trouble is anything which impedes communication of meaning or content, and any such trouble is repairable. Errors of linguistic form do not necessarily constitute trouble and are not necessarily repairable.

4.3 Repair in Task-Oriented Contexts

In task-oriented contexts, the teacher introduces a pedagogical focus by allocating tasks to the learners and then generally withdraws, allowing the learners to manage the interaction themselves. It appears to be typical in such contexts, therefore, that the teacher does not play any part in the interaction, although learners do sometimes ask the teacher for help when having difficulty with the task. By contrast with the two previous contexts, there is no focus on personal meanings[6] or on linguistic forms. The learners must communicate with each other in order to accomplish a task, and the focus is on the accomplishment of the task rather than on the language used. Therefore, trouble is defined in this context as anything which hinders the learners' completion of the task, and repair is focused on removing any such hindrances.

In Extract 4.9, the task is for the learners to sort 20 vocabulary items (written on cards) into groups in any way which makes sense to them. In Lines 8–12, the learners are trying to decide whether the "Darwin" card fits into the "Science" semantic field:

(4.9)

```
 1 L1: statistic and diagram (.) they go together. you know diagram?
 2 L2: yeah.
 3 L1: diagram and statistic are family (.) but maybe, I think, statistic and
 4     diagram (.) you think we can put in science? or maybe (.)
 5 L2: science, astronomy, (yeah) and er can be agriculture.
 6 L1: agriculture's not a science.
 7 L2: yes, it's similar (.)
 8 L1: no (.) er may be Darwin and science (.)
 9 L2: what's the Darwin?
10 L1: Darwin is a man.
11 L2: no, it's one of place in Australia.
12 L1: yes, but it's a man who discover something, yes, I'm sure.
13 L2: OK.
```

(Nunan, 1993, p. 60)

The repair in Extract 4.9 is directed toward the accomplishment of the task. The learners needed to understand the semantic connection between the words and to reach agreement on the connections. The repair therefore aims to establish understanding (as in the case of the question in Line 9) and to reach consensus on how to group the words through bald expressions of agreement and disagreement; other-initiated other-repair is used by both students, in Lines 6, 7, 8, and 11. In Line 8, L1 suggests grouping "Darwin" and "science." L2 identifies this as possible trouble in relation to the accomplishment of the task (they may not be groupable words) and uses an open type of repair initiator in Line 9 in order to elicit L1's understanding of the meaning of "Darwin." In Line 10, L1 displays an understanding of "Darwin" as being a man. In Line 11, L2 conducts other-initiated other-repair and displays an alternative understanding of "Darwin" as being a place. In Line 12, L1 insists on "Darwin" being a man and this time adds a membership categorization device (a discoverer). In Line 13, L2 confirms that agreement has been achieved on grouping the words.

In the details of the talk, then, we can see how the inter-actants start out with different understandings of the same term. Through mutual displays of understanding and through use of the mechanism of repair, they manage to negotiate intersubjectivity and reach a shared understanding of the term. The mechanism of repair, then, has been employed to further the accomplishment of the task. Although there are errors of linguistic form, the learners do not attempt to repair them. In task-oriented contexts in the data, there is never any attempt by a learner in learner-learner interaction to correct another learner's linguistic forms; this occurs in the data only in form-and-accuracy contexts.[7]

Throughout the data in task-oriented contexts, repair is primarily conducted by the learners. Occasionally the learners call on the teacher as a resource to assist in repairing trouble, in which case a self-initiated other-repair trajectory is common, using the teacher as the "other." In Extract 4.10, the learners are engaged in a computer simulation in which they have to make sense of screen data and reach decisions about what to do next. The task is to enable a village to survive by deploying villagers to the dyke to prevent floods and to the fields to grow rice:

(4.10)

```
 1 LL:  Paul what's this?
 2 T:   it's a flood you had a flood
 3 L1:  what's a flood?
 4 T:   inundación ((tr.: flood))
 5 L1:  uh uh
 6 T:   OK?
 7 L2:  and why?
 8 T:   ah well (.) how many people did you have?
 9 L1:  in the field?
10 L2:  in the dyke?
11 T:   in the dyke
12 LL:  100
13 T:   100 not enough
14 LL:  ah ha
```

(Seedhouse, 1994, p. 309)

Here we can see self-initiated other-repair in Lines 1, 3, and 7, using the teacher to repair trouble which is hindering the accomplishment of the task. In Line 3, L1 initiates repair since the meaning of the English word "flood" is not clear to him. At this point, then, the trouble for the learners is a linguistic item. In Line 4, T repairs the trouble by means of a translation of the word into Spanish, and the teacher's contribution enables the learners to progress with the task. However, we can see in Line 7 that not only linguistic problems impede the learners' accomplishment of the task. L2 asks why they had a flood, and at this point the learners constitute trouble differently. In order to complete the task successfully next time, they need to know which of their decisions caused the flood so that they can use a different strategy.[8] After T has provided the necessary repair in Lines 8–13 (that is, that too few villagers were on the dyke) the learners demonstrate with a marker of change of information state in Line 14 that the trouble has been resolved for them. So clearly repair in a task may be focused on a variety of linguistic, procedural, or cognitive issues; whatever the learners find to be hindering their accomplishment of the task is defined as trouble and is repairable.

In Extract 4.10, the teacher's repair was initiated by the learners, whereas in the following extract, the teacher initiates the repair. The learners are listening to a cassette and trying to identify a location on their map which might correspond to the silk mill mentioned on the tape. There are three possibilities on their map: one item marked "tower'" and two marked "factory":

(4.11)

Cassette:	the last stop on the tour is the silk mill.
LL:	silk mill?
L1:	it is the tower or . . . ?
L2:	it's better to—uh—we need more information.
L1:	the silk mill in the tower or not?
T:	do you know the meaning of mill?
L3:	milk?
L4:	mill.

L5:   mill? it's the postman.
L2:   mail.
T: yes, that's one kind.
L4:   air or wind mill.
T: but this mill is for making silk—do you know silk?—cloth.
L2:   it's cloth.
T: a kind of cloth.
L5:   yeah—elegant.
L3:   can you write?
T: silk mill ((writes on board)).
L5:   ah, I think he go to the factory.
L2:   to factory, but which factory?
L1:   you have two factory.
L6:   yes, near factory is there.
L2:   if we go on maybe we will know.

(T. Lynch, 1989, p. 123)

Lynch, in his analysis accompanying this extract, points out that the learners are focused on completing the task and regard it as a listening (and logical) problem; they can solve the problem by listening to the cassette. The teacher, however, regards it as a language problem. Lynch points out that the teacher's intervention is a digression from the task and is inappropriate. From the perspective of this monograph we could say that her repair strategy would have been more appropriate to interaction in a form-and-accuracy context than to interaction in a task-oriented context. The learners appear to feel that they are able to solve the task on their own (as evidenced by the final line) and are not interested at this point in using the teacher as a resource. It appears that self-initiation of teacher repair is more common and often more appropriate to the pedagogical focus than is teacher initiation of repair in this context. We noted in Section 3.3 that the organization of turn taking and sequence in this context is related neither to form nor to meaning but to the accomplishment of the task, and the same can be said of the organization of repair. We saw in Section 3.3 that SLA research on modified interaction has suggested that task-oriented interaction may feature numerous clarification requests, confirmation checks, and comprehension checks. Extracts 4.9–4.11 also feature these social actions. However, they are merely the social actions or functions performed by the repair and constitute only one small part of the overall organization of repair in task-oriented contexts as described in this section. From the perspective of this monograph, then, SLA research on modified interaction has deprived itself of the analytical power of the CA approach to repair by using only one small and isolated component of this complex organization. This subvariety of interaction needs to be evaluated as a whole, and from a holistic perspective, rather than through selecting superficially isolable features of the interaction for quantification.

4.4 Discussion

We have seen that it is possible to outline the organization of repair within an L2 classroom context in terms of (a) typical participants in the repair, (b) typical repair trajectories, (c) typical types of repair, and (d) typical focus of repair. In form-and-accuracy contexts, repair appears from the data to be overwhelmingly of the exposed or overt type, whereas a variety of repair trajectories can be observed. A trajectory which appears to be peculiar to this context is teacher-initiated peer-repair. Repair is generally initiated by the teacher, and the focus of the repair is on the production of specific sequences of linguistic forms. In meaning-and-fluency contexts we can observe a mixture of repair types and a mixture of repair trajectories. The focus of the repair, however, is on enabling learners to communicate personal meanings and to repair breakdowns in communication. The repair in task-oriented contexts is focused on the accomplishment of the task. Since learners generally work on the tasks in pairs or groups, it is generally the learners who conduct repair. However, self-initiated other-repair involving the teacher seems to be more common in the data in this context than in others.

The analyses of extracts presented thus far in this chapter suggest, then, that repair is organized differently within the different contexts which occur in L2 classrooms. Each context has its own particular pedagogical focus and its own typical organization of repair which is reflexively related to that pedagogical focus. Each context has its own emic logic and hence its own definition of what constitutes trouble and hence of what is repairable. The organization of repair in the L2 classroom can best be understood in relation to the evolving and reflexive relationship between pedagogy and interaction. An error analysis or contrastive analysis approach, by contrast, cannot explicate why it is that L2 teachers sometimes correct learner utterances which are linguistically correct and at other times praise learner utterances which are riddled with linguistic errors.

4.5 Practical Applications of a Contextual Approach to Repair

Ellis (1994) points out that "probably the main finding of studies of error treatment is that it is an enormously complex process" (p. 585). Chaudron (1988, pp. 146–148) lists 31 different types of corrective reaction which a teacher can make. Allwright (1988) writes of the "fundamental and surprisingly complex problem of defining what is meant by an error in the language classroom context" (p. 202). The whole area of error analysis and treatment can seem dauntingly difficult, vast, and unapproachable if L2 classroom interaction is viewed as a monolithic, undifferentiated whole. I would now like to suggest that a context-based approach to repair might be able to provide an appropriate means of simplifying and focusing issues and creating points of reference for further research. There is now a considerable literature on error analysis in L2 classrooms. However, if we treat the L2 classroom as a single, monolithic "context," it may indeed prove impossible to define what is meant by an error or create a coherent perspective on error treatment. For example, we saw that in form-and-accuracy contexts, we find teachers repairing linguistically correct and appropriate learner utterances.

In this monograph I argue that the only way to create a coherent perspective on errors and their treatment is to abandon the idea of error as something etically specifiable by an outside analyst and develop an emic perspective by focusing on what constitutes trouble and hence what is repairable in each L2 classroom context. For example, in form-and-accuracy contexts, the focus of the repair is on the production of specific sequences of linguistic forms. Anything which the learners produce which does not conform exactly to the target string of forms which the teacher requires is repairable, even if it is linguistically correct. By contrast, in meaning-and-fluency contexts, major linguistic errors may be ignored unless they impede communication. From an emic perspective, both of these policies make sense in terms of the rational design of each L2 classroom context. An approach based on such a perspective would also have the advantage of integrating the study of error analysis and treatment into the organization of L2 classroom interaction, instead of in isolation from the interactional environments in which they occur, which is how they have often been analyzed.

A context-based approach to repair may have some practical applications. For example, it would be useful to know which specific repair techniques are helpful and unhelpful in different contexts in the L2 classroom. One way of initiating repair is for the teacher to use an open kind of next-turn repair initiator (Drew, 1997) such as "pardon?" "eh?" or "what?" Discussing the merits of using such a repair initiation technique in the L2 classroom without reference to contexts would be fraught with problems, as it is unclear what basis one could have for evaluation. A context-based approach, however, can provide such a basis. In Extracts 4.12 and 4.13 we can see examples of this technique being used in two different contexts.

(4.12)

18 L: and if er the rules e:r were e:r easier
19   in the sense you can (0.2) hire or .hhh suck off people
20   (1.0) e:rm=
21 T: =what did you say?
22 L: if the rules for hiring people (.) or .hhh e:r lay off or sack
((6 lines omitted))

29 T: no I heard (.) suck *que es chupar*= ((tr.: which is suck))
30 L: no=
31 T: =ha ha and suck off eh suck off is a bit like Monica Lewinsky.

(Woolley, 2002)

In the discussion in Extract 4.12 on employment policy in a meaning-and-fluency context, L is trying to communicate an opinion. T does not understand the propositional content of L's statement in Line 19 and is initiating repair in Line 21 on L's statement using an open kind of next-turn repair initiator to elicit clarification of the meaning.

(4.13)

1 T: er, Mr. P, er what's the man doing (.) he's sitting, but what's he doing with
2   his hand?
3 L1:   she's pointing their hand.
4 T:→ pardon?
5 L1:   he is pointing his hand.
6 T: OK, he's pointing his hand and what
7 L1:   and he is showing the seat in front of him.
8 T: OK, he's pointing his hand and what
9 L2:   the menu (.) the menu (.)
10 T: the menu or ((gestures)) look at the picture, look at the picture (.) he's
        pointing at this watch. why is he pointing at his watch?

(Riley, 1985, p. 54)

By contrast, in Extract 4.13 we are in a form-and-accuracy context. Throughout the lengthy extract (only a short section is reproduced) T expects the learners to produce a specific string of linguistic forms and initiates repair until the required string has been produced. In Line 4 T uses an open repair initiator. Having briefly examined how this particular repair initiation technique functions in context, we are now in a position to consider its appropriateness in the different contexts.

In meaning-and-fluency contexts an open kind of next-turn repair initiator may be very appropriate when it functions as a clarification or repetition request in the case of communication breakdown, if the exact nature of the trouble is unclear, as in Extract 4.12. This is because open repair initiators have just this function in conversation: "A speaker indicates that he/she has some difficulty with the other's prior turn, but without locating specifically where or what that difficulty is" (Drew, 1997, p. 71). In form-and-accuracy contexts, the use of nonspecific or open repair initiators when the specific trouble has been located (as in Line 3 of Extract 4.13) might be less appropriate. As Tsui (1995) points out, "If the teacher decides to get the student to self-correct, then the teacher can point out to the students the presence of an error, the location of an error or the identity of an error" (p. 52).

There are two reasons why an open repair initiator might be less appropriate in a form-and-accuracy context. First, there are several repair initiation techniques which locate or identify the error and are therefore far more useful to the learner than open repair initiation in the process of self-repair when a specific string of linguistic forms is being targeted; see, for example, Extracts 4.16 and 4.18, as well as Chaudron (1988), Edge (1989), and Tsui (1995). Secondly, open repair initiators do not even indicate the presence of a linguistic error: They are frequently used by listeners to initiate repair when the speaker has clearly not made a linguistic error. In situations in which the hearer realizes that the speaker has made a linguistic error, the hearer generally uses a different type of repair initiator (Drew, 1997). The use of open repair initiators by the listener may therefore actually imply to the speaker that some form of trouble other than a linguistic error has occurred.

A contextual analysis of a specific type of repair initiation enables us to conclude, then, that that type of repair initiation would be appropriate in certain circumstances in one L2 classroom context but unhelpful and potentially confusing in certain circumstances in another L2 classroom context. With a contextual analysis there is a basis for evaluation, namely, whether there is a match between the pedagogical focus of the context and the repair technique.

4.6 The Preference Organization of Repair: The Case of the Missing "No"

My main thesis in this monograph is that there is a reflexive relationship between pedagogy and interaction. Generally I have expressed this in terms of the organization of the interaction varying as the pedagogical focus varies. In this section, however, we see the pedagogical focus being transmuted by the organization of the interaction as we explore the concept of preference organization in relation to repair in form-and-accuracy contexts (Seedhouse, 1997a). This section focuses on the structure of repair in form-and-accuracy contexts in the L2 classroom and on the preference organization associated with the structure of repair in such contexts; see Section 4.1 for the organization of repair in this context. When the context in operation is form and accuracy and a learner makes an error of oral production which is an error of linguistic form, regardless of whether it is an error on the level of syntax, lexis, phonology, or discourse, then a lay observer might expect the teacher to frequently employ the words "no" or "wrong" as a negative evaluation (or at least some form of direct and overt negative evaluation) prior to an attempt to repair the error, in order to mark the presence of an error. It has frequently been suggested (Johnson, 1995) that much L2 classroom interaction follows an IRF/IRE pattern. The data show, however, that this in general only applies (in a form-and-accuracy context) when learners supply a linguistically correct reply, as in Extract 4.14:

(4.14)

```
L1:  excuse em (.) which way is the bus station?
T:   good okay (.) theatre (.) just use one of these. yes?
L2:  er excuse me er where is the theatre?
T:   good cinema.
```

(van Lier, 1988a, p. 151)

When a learner produces a linguistically correct response to a teacher initiation, the teacher sometimes[9] produces an overt and direct positive evaluation. Most frequent terms used are "good," "yes," "OK," "that's right," and "fine." However, when learners supply a linguistically incorrect reply in response to a teacher initiation, the data show that direct, explicit, overt negative evaluation tends to be avoided, and "IRF/IRE" is in no way an accurate description of the interactional sequence in these cases. Although teacher repair of learners' linguistic errors is a prevalent feature of L2 classroom interaction in the database, I can find only one case of the use of bald, unmitigated, direct, overt negative evaluation involving the words "no" or "wrong" by teachers. In all other cases there is some form of mitigation involved, and the data show teachers using a wide variety of strategies to avoid bald, unmitigated, direct, overt negative evaluation. In other words, teachers appear to be doing interactional work specifically in order to avoid using unmitigated negative evaluation. This is a case of relevant absence which requires explication in terms of rational design. As Schegloff et al. (1977) put it, "what speakers avoid doing is as important as what they do" (p. 361). In order to investigate this phenomenon I detail the strategies which teachers use to repair errors while avoiding direct negative evaluation. I exemplify the use of mitigated negative evaluation, explain why there is a dispreference for direct negative evaluation, demonstrate a different preference structure in relation to procedural problems, and then place the discussion in a pedagogical perspective.

4.7 Strategies for Conducting Repair Without Using Direct Negative Evaluation

First of all, I will detail the great variety of strategies which teachers employ to conduct repair (when a learner makes a spoken error of linguistic form in a form-and-accuracy context) without performing an explicitly expressed unmitigated negative evaluation. I will provide a single example of each strategy together with references to other examples of the strategy.

1. *Use a next-turn repair initiator to indicate (indirectly) that there is an error which the learner should repair.* This is a method of nonevaluatory repair initiation:[10] other-initiated self-repair.

(4.15)

```
L:    they runs they runs quickly.
T:→   once more.
L:    they run quickly.
T:    yes, that's better.
```

(Tsui, 1995, p. 42; see also Johnson, 1995, p. 19; Riley, 1985, p. 54)

This is an "open" kind of next-turn repair initiator (Drew, 1997), and "pardon?" "sorry?" and "what?" are also members of this class. One problem with this type of repair initiator in this context is that it does not locate precisely the item to be repaired.

2. *Repeat the word or phrase or part of a word which the learner used immediately prior to the error.* This is another method of nonevaluatory repair initiation: other-initiated self-repair.

(4.16)

```
L:    Er (.) Qu'est-ce que (.) qu'est-ce que vous dési(.) ((tr.: er, what do you,
      what do you desi... ))
T:→   Qu'est-ce que vous (.)? ((tr.: what do you... ?))
L:    Avez comme fruit? ((tr.: have in the way of fruit?))
T:    Comme fruit. ((tr.: in the way of fruit))
```

(Westgate et al., 1985, p. 276; see also British Council, 1985, vol. 2, p. 67; Wright, 1987, p. 55)

In Extract 4.16, T repeats "what do you ... ?" which then targets the following word(s) as the trouble source. By contrast with the previous technique, this repair technique has the advantage of locating the repairable item fairly precisely.

3. *Repeat the original question or initiation.* This is another method of nonevaluatory repair initiation: other-initiated self-repair.

(4.17)

```
1 T:    what is a suffix?
2 L:    beautiful?
3 T:→   this is something we forget all the time. what is a suffix?
```

(Wong-Fillmore, 1985, p. 47; see also Prabhu, 1987, p. 123)

In Line 3, T repeats the original question. The problem with this technique is that it does not locate or treat the error in any way. It could be that L's utterance in Line 2 is in fact providing an example of a suffix and is in fact a reasonable response. T's repetition of the question in Line 3 does not provide the learners with any feedback as to the problem with L's response, however.

4. *Repeat the learner's erroneous utterance with a rising intonation.* This is another method of nonevaluatory repair initiation: other-initiated self-repair.

(4.18)

```
L1:  er and I: I am very good person, and [((laughs)) ] and give she another one.
LL:                                        [((laugh))  ]
T:→  give she?
L1:  (.) give her another one.
```

(British Council, 1985, vol. 2, p. 68)

T repeats the erroneous utterance but changes to a rising intonation. This technique locates the error but has sometimes been criticized for providing the learners with erroneous input. However, as we can see, in Extract 4.18, the learner is able to self-repair correctly.

5. *Supply a correct version of the linguistic forms.* This is another method of nonevaluatory repair initiation: other-initiated other-repair.

(4.19)

```
L:   because she can't
T:→  because she counted (.)
L:   because she counted the wrong number of tourists.
```

(Tsui, 1995, p. 48; see also Lightbown & Spada, 1993, p. 76)

In this extract, the teacher substitutes the correct form for the erroneous form. This is possibly the simplest and fastest repair technique, but of course it does not allow the learner the opportunity to self-repair.

6. *Provide an explanation of why the answer is incorrect without explicitly stating that it is incorrect.* This is another method of nonevaluatory repair initiation: other-initiated other-repair.

(4.20)

```
1 T:    fine, right. the doctor's office. what do we call a doctor's office in
2       English? go on, go on, Louisa fine, say it.
3 L:    consult—consultation.
4 T:→  it's a consultation that they are going to give, it's a very good try,
5   →  a good try. we call it a surgery, a surgery.
```

(Malamah-Thomas, 1987, p. 64; See also Lightbown & Spada, 1993, p. 98)

In Line 4, T gives an explanation as to why consultation is not the correct word, and in Line 5, T provides the correct word. However, T never explicitly states that L's answer is incorrect.

7. *Accept the incorrect forms and then supply the correct forms.* This is, in effect, acceptance of the incorrect forms followed by repair: other-initiated other-repair.

(4.21)

```
1 L:    is your mother play piano?
2 T:→  'is your mother play piano?' OK. well you can say 'is your mother
3   →  play piano?' or 'is your mother a piano player?'
4 L:    'is your mother a piano player?'
```

(Lightbown & Spada, 1993, p. 93; see also Long, 1983, p. 12; J. Willis, 1987, p. 154)

T says that L's erroneous forms are possible and then supplies a version that corrects the erroneous forms. Strange cases like this one are in fact more common in my database than examples of unmitigated overt negative evaluation, which indicates how strong the dispreference is against direct negative evaluation.

8. *Invite other learners to repair.* This may or may not include direct negative evaluation. This is other-initiated other-repair,

the other-repair being by a third party. It could also be termed teacher-initiated peer-repair.

(4.22)

L: don't losing weight.
T: OK. ((to the others)) can you help him? (.) not don't. don't say don't. use the gerund. OK. so.

(Banbrook & Skehan, 1989, p. 142; see also Ellis, 1992, p. 115)

Sometimes teachers appear to be going to great lengths to avoid uttering the words no and wrong. In Line 5 of Extract 4.23, the teacher has to stop himself or herself from uttering the word "no":

(4.23)

```
1 T:    when Emma was making the suggestions about peut-être qu'il est dans sa
2       chambre ((tr.: perhaps he is in his bedroom)), what could you nicely have
3       said? (.) well, whoever said it. what could they have said?
4 L:    d'accord ((tr.: OK))
5 T:→   nn, nn ... something that I mentioned to you earlier on. well, there was
6       d'accord, yeah, but there was something else.
```

(Westgate et al., 1985, p. 274)

So we can see that teachers have developed a wide variety of techniques, in a form-and-accuracy context, to initiate repair of learner utterances while simultaneously avoiding direct and overt negative evaluation.

4.8 Examples of the Use of Mitigated Negative Evaluation

There are examples in the data of teachers using the words "no" and "wrong" as negative evaluations, but in every case but one the negative evaluation is not bald, overt, or direct in that it is mitigated in some way. In the following case "wrong" is prefaced by a positive mitigating comment:

(4.24)

L: I was born in January sixth
T: ok look. wrong preposition

(Dinsmore, 1985, p. 229)

Occasionally in the data we find examples of the use of direct and overt negative evaluation by the teacher in the evaluation slot after the teacher has, immediately previously, initiated self-repair:

(4.25)

```
1 T:    ok, where is John Martin's? Phung? John Martin's?
2 L:    oh, Gawler Place
3 LL:   Gawler Place
4 T:→   John Martin's? ((other-initiation of self-repair))
5 L:    Gawler Place
6 T:→   Gawler Place? no! ((direct negative evaluation))
```

(Nunan, 1988, p. 140; see also Guthrie, 1984, p. 192; Tsui, 1995, p. 47)

In cases such as this one, the force of "no" as negative evaluation is mitigated by virtue of its sequential location.[11] Since T has already made an attempt in Line 4 to prompt self-repair (without negative evaluation), the direct and overt negative evaluation in the second repair slot (Line 6) is mitigated and less face-threatening than if it had occurred in the first repair-relevant slot. The teacher is in effect working his or her way down the preference ranking. We saw similar sequences in relation to interactants working their way down the preference organization of repair in ordinary conversation in Extract 1.21.

In Extracts 4.26 and 4.27, we can see the teacher saying "no" baldly in reply to a learner initiation or question:

(4.26)

L: so can say John's hou—John's house (.) er (.) which which its door is broken.
T: no you can't.

(Hasan, 1988, p. 271)

(4.27)

L: er do you think, 'does she mind', is that er
T: no, you can say to about anyone.

(J. Willis, 1987, p. 181)

In these two extracts, the interactional sequence is different from that in previous extracts, and the "no" does not function as a direct negative evaluation of a learner response. The teacher is simply providing an answer to a learner's question or initiation—we have a question-and-answer adjacency pair rather than an IRF/IRE cycle. With the IRF/IRE cycle the teacher initiates or asks a display question in order to test and evaluate the formal accuracy of the learner's response. The power is in the teacher's hands, and direct negative evaluation of the learner's response is thought by many teachers and methodologists to involve loss of face and demoralization for the learner; the accuracy of this belief is questioned later in this chapter, however. In previous extracts, by contrast, the interactional dynamics are different; the teacher is simply providing an answer to a referential question. Here, a direct negative answer does not function as a negative evaluation and involves no loss of face for the learner, so the teacher can use a bald "no."[12] The learner's unsolicited question in fact can create a potentially face-threatening situation for the teacher; if the teacher does not produce a convincing answer, the teacher may lose face, as in Extract 4.28:

(4.28)

L: three bedroom house.
T: all right.
L: why three bed, er, three bedroom? why we don't say three bedrooms?
T: ahh, oh (.) I don't know, um.
L: is not right.
T: we don't say it. we don't say it. there's no explanation. but we often do that in English. three bedroom house.
L: don't ask for it.
L: yes.
T: well, do ask why. ask why, and 99 per cent of the time I know the answer. one per cent of the time, nobody knows the answer. if I don't know, nobody knows.
LL: ((laugh))
T: ah, no, I don't know the answer, sorry.

(Nunan, 1989, p. 137)

There are also examples in the data in which the learner response is negatively evaluated in what appears to be the evaluation slot of an IRF/IRE cycle, as in Extract 4.29:

(4.29)

T: there was also eh some years ago ah a Greek American who tried to become
   president do you remember his name?
L: Theodorakis?
T: Theodorakis, no, it wasn't him

(Seedhouse, 1996, p. 402; see also Chaudron, 1988, p. 130)

In such cases the learners are intoning their contributions as a question, which in effect enables the teacher to make a direct negative evaluation "camouflaged" as an answer to a question—mitigation is thereby involved. It appears that both teacher and learner are treating the exchange as a question-and-answer adjacency pair rather than as an IRF/IRE cycle. The format being used by the learner is what Schegloff et al. (1977, p. 379) call a guess, a candidate, a try, or a correction-invitation format; the format supplies the most accommodating environment for other-correction. In the entire database I can find only one occasion (Extract 4.30) in which a teacher uses a completely bald, unmitigated, overt negative evaluation, that is, "no" in the evaluation slot of an IRF/IRE sequence. (Even here, I cannot be certain that the "no" is completely unmitigated, since the published extract does not include the interaction prior to this sequence.)

(4.30)

T: after they have put up their tent, what did the boys do?
L: they cooking food.
T: no, not they cooking food, pay attention.
L: they cook their meal.
T: right, they cook their meal over an open fire.

(Tsui, 1995, p. 52)

So the evidence from the database is that teachers perform a great deal of interactional work to avoid performing direct and overt negative evaluation of learner linguistic errors. When negative evaluation does occur, it is predominantly mitigated in some way.

4.9 Why Is There a Dispreference for Direct and Unmitigated Negative Evaluation?

Having established the interactional evidence for a strong dispreference for direct and overt negative evaluation of learner errors in form-and-accuracy contexts, we need to consider why such a dispreference should exist. The preference structure appears to be motivated by and derived from pedagogical recommendations, in that explicit negative evaluation of learner responses in a form-and-accuracy context is strongly disfavored in current L2 pedagogy:

> If the teacher decides to correct the error, he or she can repeat the student's response with correction. This kind of modeling can be very effective because it avoids providing explicit negative evaluation and exposes students to the correct form. (Tsui, 1995, p. 51; see also Edge, 1989, p. 17; Harmer, 1983, p. 63)

In general, then, there is a close correspondence between pedagogical recommendations and the interactional evidence from the transcripts concerning what teachers actually do. The pedagogical recommendations spring from a humanistic, communicative paradigm in which learners' feelings and emotions are taken into account. Negative evaluation, then, is thought to offend and demotivate learners. So at this stage it appears that pedagogy and interaction are working together in harmony, although I will later argue that this is an illusion.

4.10 A Different Preference Structure in Relation to Procedural Trouble

It sometimes happens that trouble occurs in form-and-accuracy contexts which has nothing to do with linguistic form—the trouble relates to misunderstanding or misinterpretation by learners of the lesson procedure which the teacher wishes to follow. In these cases the preference organization in relation to repair in form-and-accuracy contexts which has been described does not apply at all. When repairing procedural problems, teachers very commonly use bald "no"s in conjunction with other-initiated other-repair, as we can see in Extracts 4.31–4.33:

(4.31)

```
1 T:     what are you?
2 L:     I am a student.
3 T:→    no, not you, what is she? ((pointing to the textbook))
4 L:     student.
5 T:     well, it looks like a school but if she's not a teacher she's not going to work
6        in a school (.) she's a lawyer (.)
```

(Johnson, 1995, p. 44)

L believes that T is asking a genuine or referential question in Line 1 and responds in Line 2 with a genuine answer. However, L has got the procedure wrong; T wanted L to reply as if she were a character in the textbook. In Line 3, T uses unmitigated negative evaluation.

(4.32)

```
LL:     she asks when he came (.)
T:→     no, no, look at the text, not not the question, look at the question.
L:      have you been waiting long?
T:      yeah have you been waiting long?
```

(Riley, 1985, p. 57; see also J. Willis, 1987, p. 169)

In Extracts 4.31 and 4.32, "no" does not function as a direct negative evaluation of learner linguistic performance. It indicates that there is trouble which needs repairing in connection with nonlinguistic procedures and hence does not seem to involve loss of face for the student.

In all of the previous cases, the repair is teacher-initiated teacher-repair: Nowhere in the data does a teacher initiate self-repair in the case of procedural problems. There is a very revealing section in J. Willis's (1987) transcript of one entire lesson. Throughout the 55 pages of transcript, the teacher meticulously avoids direct and overt negative evaluation of learner utterances when operating in form-and-accuracy contexts. There are several instances of the teacher stating that erroneous forms are acceptable and then supplying the correct forms (as in Extract 4.21). In one case, however, the teacher does say "no" in an evaluation slot. The learners here are constructing questions and answers based on prompts from a textbook:

(4.33)

L1:   erm. does Fred ((a book character)) like being a soldier?
T: yes. that's right. and what do you think's the answer to that one? Constantine?
L2:   uh! he doesn't like being a soldier.
T: no. ((in agreement)) I don't think he does.
L2:   he hates being soldier.
T: well done! he hates being a soldier. Mohavi, ask Virginia er if she likes being a student.
L3:   er does
T: do
L3:   ah! sorry. do you, do you like er a sol—being a soldier?
T: no, she's not a soldier
LL: ((laughter))

(J. Willis, 1987, p. 155)

What happened in Extract 4.33 is that there has been a change in procedure—from making questions based on textbook prompts to making questions based on the classroom situation. L3 failed to notice this procedural shift. The teacher's "no" is therefore not a negative evaluation of the linguistic forms produced by the learner; the utterance is in fact linguistically correct. It is merely a repair of a procedural problem and is therefore thought not to demotivate the student. Trouble with linguistic form is regarded as problematic and face-threatening, whereas trouble with procedure is not. Both of these tendencies are evident in the preference organization of repair in classroom interaction.[13] We can conclude here that the preference structure relating to the repair of trouble with linguistic form marks this trouble as problematic and face-threatening. The preference structure relating to the repair of procedural trouble marks this trouble as nonproblematic and non-face-threatening.

4.11 The Paradox: Pedagogy and Interaction in Opposition

As a result of the above analysis we can see that there appears to be a paradox at the heart of recent, broadly "communicative" approaches to repair. On the one hand, teachers tell learners not to worry about making linguistic errors and even encourage them to try out hypotheses and make plenty of linguistic errors (Edge, 1989, p. 17). On the other hand, by avoiding direct and overt negative evaluation of linguistic errors, teachers are marking repair of linguistic errors as a heavily dispreferred sequence; the interactional message is being transmitted that making errors is an embarrassing, face-threatening matter.[14] As Levinson (1983) points out, the implied underlying rule for speech production is "Try to avoid the dispreferred action—the action that generally occurs in dispreferred or marked format" (p. 333). In other words, the pedagogical message (it's OK to make linguistic errors) is being directly contradicted by the interactional message (linguistic errors are terrible faux pas). The words "no," "wrong," "mistake," and "error" in relation to linguistic form seem to be marked as verging on the unmentionable by their relevant absence or extreme mitigation in form-and-accuracy contexts. If one wanted to indicate on an interactional level to learners that linguistic errors were of no importance, one would have to use the same preference organization of repair as is used to treat procedural problems, that is, immediate, unmitigated other-initiated other-repair with use of "no." Teachers are avoiding direct and overt negative evaluation of learners' linguistic errors with the best intentions in the world, namely, to avoid embarrassing and demotivating them. However, in doing so, they are interactionally marking linguistic errors as embarrassing and problematic.

Sections 4.6–4.10 have focused rather narrowly on a single perspective and a single interpretation of the data in order to develop an argument, and it may well have occurred to readers that there are alternative explanations for the phenomena observed in the data. For example, it could be argued that the teachers in Section 4.7 are merely allowing the learners the opportunity to self-repair as part of the language learning process and that the repair of linguistic errors is worth devoting interactional time and effort to. My reply would be that this is certainly what teachers are intending to do from a pedagogical point of view. But the point is that the task-as-workplan rarely translates directly into the task-in-process, because there is a reflexive relationship between pedagogy and interaction and because there is an intervening level of organization: the interactional organization of the L2 classroom. So from an interactional point of view, what teachers are actually doing in practice is operating a preference organization which marks linguistic errors as embarrassing and face-threatening. We have seen in Section 4.10 in the case of procedural errors that it is perfectly possible to operate a preference organization which marks errors (of a different kind) as nonembarrassing and non-face-threatening.

4.12 Conclusions

Pedagogical recommendations for the L2 classroom do not take its interactional architecture into account explicitly or methodically. They are normally made on the assumption that they can translate directly into classroom interaction as if no level of interactional structure existed and as if the task-as-workplan can translate directly into a task-in-process. This was referred to in Section 2.8 as the pedagogical landing-ground perspective. In this chapter, I have argued that, in this particular case, pedagogy and interaction work in direct opposition to one another. The pedagogical recommendation that teachers should avoid direct and unmitigated negative evaluation of learners' linguistic errors, so that those errors will be treated as unimportant and unembarrassing, directly produces the consequence that errors are treated as important, problematic, and embarrassing because of the preference structure of the interaction. In this case, then, pedagogy ignores the interactional organization of the L2 classroom to its detriment. By contrast, direct and unmitigated other-repair by the teacher would mark linguistic errors as unimportant and unembarrassing on an interactional level; pedagogy and interaction would then be working in tandem. It is not the aim of this section to make the somewhat simplistic pedagogical recommendation that teachers ought to change their habits and always conduct direct, unmitigated other-repair of learners' linguistic errors in order to mark them as unimportant and unembarrassing. Rather, the discussion should be understood to illustrate the following important points.

First, it is possible, using a CA methodology and a large and varied database of L2 lessons, to trace the interactional consequences of particular pedagogical recommendations. For example, this chapter provides many examples of different repair techniques employed by teachers, and it will be evident to the reader that the different techniques have different effects on the flow of the interaction. Pedagogical recommendations which are accompanied by transcript evidence of what actually happens in the classroom (i.e., evidence concerning the task-in-process) may well appear more convincing than recommendations presented on a conceptual level and without any recognition of their interactional consequences (i.e., in terms of a task-as-workplan).

Secondly, some pedagogical recommendations appear to be made on the basis of the implicit assumption that L2 classroom interaction has the same interactional structure as conversation. For example, Edge (1989) justifies self-correction by stating that "people usually prefer to put their own mistakes right rather than be corrected by someone else" (p. 24). Now in conversation, unmitigated other-initiated other-repair is indeed heavily dispreferred and face-threatening and occurs relatively rarely. When it does occur, it often leads to arguments, as in Extract 1.23. However, the point is that repair in the L2 classroom is organized in a different fashion than in conversation. If pedagogical recommendations concerning repair are motivated by the assumption that L2 learners will be offended by direct, unmitigated other-initiated other-repair, then the evidence presented in this section suggests that the assumption may be mistaken.

Thirdly, there has been strong recent interest in why learners don't learn what teachers teach (Nunan, 1994) or why it is that the task-in-process (what actually happens) is sometimes different from the task-as-workplan (what is supposed to happen). From the perspective of this monograph, one answer is that pedagogy can never be translated directly into classroom interaction, because there is an intervening level of organization: the interactional organization of the L2 classroom. The pedagogical focus inherent in the task-as-workplan becomes transformed by the interactional organization of the L2 classroom to become the task-in-process. Sections 4.6–4.11 have illustrated the point by showing how the pedagogical intention to persuade learners that it is all right to make linguistic errors becomes transformed by the interactional organization of the L2 classroom into the message that errors are embarrassing.

The general implicit assumption in much current pedagogical literature appears to be that the relationship between pedagogy and interaction is a simple, unproblematic, and unidirectional one in which pedagogy is translated directly into interaction. In Section 2.7 we called this the pedagogical landing-ground perspective on the L2 classroom. Sections 4.6–4.11 have attempted to show that the relationship between pedagogy and interaction is a complex and reflexive one and that pedagogical recommendations may have quite unforeseen interactional consequences which may work in opposition to the pedagogical effort. It is essential to understand the interactional organization of the L2 classroom not only to understand instructed language learning processes, but also so that any resultant pedagogical recommendations may be effectively implemented.

4.13 Chapter Summary

This chapter described how repair is organized within the different L2 classroom context. As with turn taking and sequence, it was argued that there is no single, monolithic organization of repair in the L2 classroom. There is a reflexive relationship between the pedagogical focus and the organization of repair; as the pedagogical focus varies, so does the organization of repair. Furthermore, what constitutes trouble varies with the pedagogical focus, which means that what is repairable is different in each context. The organization of repair within particular L2 classroom contexts was specified in terms of (a) typical participants in the repair, (b) typical repair trajectories, (c) typical types of repair, and (d) typical focus of repair, that is, what is repairable. In Sections 4.6–4.11, I showed how the interactional organization can transform the pedagogical focus by examining a case of preference organization in relation to repair in form-and-accuracy contexts.

Notes

[1] A discussion of the interaction hypothesis is available in Ellis (2003, pp. 79–83). Briefly, it states that negotiation of meaning and comprehensible input assist acquisition.

[2] However, Markee (2000) contains data in a different context in which a teacher asks one learner to help other learners repair trouble.

[3] In Chapter 6 we explore the similarities between embedded correction and the SLA notion of "recast."

[4] I am grateful to an anonymous reviewer for pointing out that Line 19 might be analyzed as not involving repair, but rather a request for further information. I analyze it as repair initiation since it is not evident to T in Line 17 what the "two thousand" is payment for: marriage tax, wedding expenses, or what? T initiates repair as this lack of understanding constitutes trouble for him. The evidence for this analysis is that in Line 26 T finally understands that the money is for a dowry and displays the resolution of this trouble by using a change of information state marker: "oh, dowry, oh dear."

[5] It should be noted that the construct of fossilized errors is a problematic one.

[6] The notion of "meaning" is problematic; see Seedhouse (1997b) for further discussion.

[7]An anonymous reviewer has pointed out that, in his or her data, learners sometimes correct each other's pronunciation.

[8]I am grateful to an anonymous reviewer for pointing out that Line 7 could be analyzed as not repair initiation at all. I agree that this instance is on what Schegloff (2000b) calls the "fuzzy boundary" of repair (p. 207). My point is that, in a task-oriented context, learners can treat as trouble anything which they identify as hindering the accomplishment of their task.

[9]However, positive evaluation is often not overtly supplied; see Section 3.1.

[10]By this I mean that there is no explicit, verbalized use of evaluation in the surface forms of the repair initiation by the teacher. However, it may be that some evaluation is nonetheless implicit in the teacher's turn, since the institutional role of teachers makes it hard for teachers to avoid being seen as evaluators.

[11]See Extract 1.21 for an example of "sequential mitigation" in ordinary conversation. Once repair initiation has been attempted, subsequent repair strategies can be more direct and "bald" without risking disaffiliation, as the person repairing is "moving down" the preference structure of repair.

[12]I am grateful to Richard Young for pointing out that politeness theory provides a very good explanation of the phenomena in these extracts.

[13]I am grateful to an anonymous reviewer for pointing out that it would be interesting to consider whether "content" activities and procedural activities constitute learner-teacher power and distance relations differently. I feel that the question is beyond the scope of the present study.

[14]Heritage (1984b), in a discussion of preference, observes that "plainly issues of 'face' [Brown and Levinson, 1987] are closely associated with our maintenance of the relevant forms and observances" (p. 268). Brown and Levinson (1987, pp. 38–42) suggest that face issues motivate the organization of preference and presequences. So ethnomethodological conceptions of affiliation and disaffiliation are broadly compatible with Brown and Levinson's conceptions of face and politeness. Since the explanatory system of ethnomethodology underpins CA, analyses do not tend to make massive use of face and politeness, but neither is it necessary to shy away from mention of these concepts.

CHAPTER FIVE

The Organization of Language Classroom Interaction

In Chapters 3 and 4, I portrayed the organization of turn, sequence, and repair in different L2 classroom contexts. In this chapter the perspective broadens as I describe the overall organization of L2 classroom interaction. I introduce the concept of the rational design of institutional interaction and identify the institutional goal as well as three interactional properties which derive directly from the goal. I then identify the basic sequence organization of L2 classroom interaction as well as an emic methodology for its analysis. Next I exemplify how the institution of the L2 classroom is talked in and out of being by participants. The concept of the L2 classroom context, which was introduced in Chapters 3 and 4, is then problematized and located in a broader, three-way perspective on context. Finally I show how teachers create L2 classroom contexts and how they shift from one context to another.

In this chapter, the interactional architecture of the L2 classroom is portrayed as an example of the rational design of institutional interaction, balancing invariant underlying institutional characteristics with extreme flexibility and variability. CA attempts to understand the organization of the interaction as being *rationally* derived from the core institutional goal. Levinson (1992) sees the structural elements of institutional discourse as

> rationally and functionally adapted to the point or goal of the
> activity in question. ... In most cases apparently ad hoc and
> elaborate arrangements and constraints of very various sorts
> can be seen to follow from a few basic principles, in particular
> rational organization around a dominant goal. (p. 71)

In this monograph, I attempt to portray the interactional architecture of the L2 classroom as rational, in Levinson's terms, in
that it is functionally oriented to and derived from the core goal.
There is an overall attempt in this monograph not only to
describe interactional devices, but also to explain why those
elements are as they are and why indeed they must be that
way as part of a rational overall design. It is not sufficient,
then, in CA methodology to merely describe or model interactional devices. One should also try to "provide functional
explanations, or expositions of rational design, for the existence
of the device in question" (Levinson, 1983, p. 319). A related
methodological precept is that one should "search for the raison
d'être of a particular conversational organization, and the implications that the existence of one device has for the necessity for
others" (Levinson, 1983, p. 322). This acts as an antidote to
the tendencies of language teachers and theorists to consider
particular interactional devices in isolation and label them
desirable or undesirable for pedagogical reasons and without
considering the *interactional* consequences of such devices or
how a particular device relates to the interactional organization
of the L2 classroom as a whole. For example, we saw in Section
4.9 that current pedagogy considers the direct and overt
negative evaluation of learner errors to be highly undesirable.
However, it is argued that this choice creates serious new
problems on the interactional level and may be counterproductive. It should also be understood that the description of
the organization of L2 classroom interaction in this chapter has
a status similar to that of the interactional organizations
described in Section 1.6. Although the organization is described
in context-free terms, it is employed by interactants as a
normative resource to display the meaning of their social actions.

5.1 A Sketch of the Interactional Architecture of the Second Language Classroom

The first step toward describing the interactional architecture of L2 classroom interaction[1] is to identify the core institutional goal, which is that *the teacher will teach the learners the L2*. This core institutional goal remains the same wherever the L2 lesson takes place and whatever pedagogical framework the teacher is working in. This is a most important point. In many kinds of institutions, for example, businesses, the institutional goal may vary considerably even among businesses in the same town. However, in L2 teaching the institutional goal of the teacher's teaching the L2 to the learners remains constant whatever the teaching methods, whatever the L1 and L2, and wherever in the world the L2 is taught. It remains the same if the teacher delegates some responsibility to learners in a learner-centered or learner autonomy approach. From this core goal a number of consequences issue which affect the way in which L2 classroom interaction is accomplished. Drew and Heritage (1992b) suggest that each institutional form of interaction may have its own unique *fingerprint* "comprised of a set of interactional practices differentiating [it] both from other institutional forms and from the baseline of mundane conversational interaction itself" (p. 26). There are three interactional properties which derive directly from the core goal, and these properties in turn necessarily shape the interaction. The three properties follow in rational sequence from each other and constitute part of the unique fingerprint of L2 classroom interaction and part of its context-free machinery:

1. Language is both the vehicle and object of instruction.

2. There is a reflexive relationship between pedagogy and interaction, and interactants constantly display their analyses of the evolving relationship between pedagogy and interaction.

3. The linguistic forms and patterns of interaction which the learners produce in the L2 are potentially subject to evaluation by the teacher in some way.

5.1.1 Property 1

Language is "both the vehicle and object of instruction" (Long, 1983, p. 9) in the L2 classroom. This property springs rationally and inevitably from the core goal of the L2 classroom, which dictates that the L2 is the object, goal, and focus of instruction. It must be taught, and it can be taught only through the medium or vehicle of language. Therefore language has a unique dual role in the L2 classroom in that it is both the vehicle and object, both the process and product, of the instruction (see Section 5.6.3 for exemplification of this point). In other forms of classroom education (such as in history or engineering), language is only the vehicle of the teaching. This is not to suggest that all of the teaching in L2 classrooms is conducted in the L2; the data clearly show this not to be the case. However, this monograph is concerned with explicating *only* those periods of an L2 lesson in which the L2 is spoken by both teacher and learners.

5.1.2 Property 2

There is therefore a reflexive relationship between pedagogy and interaction in the L2 classroom. This relationship is explicated throughout the monograph as its principal theme. This means that as the pedagogical focus varies, so the organization of the interaction varies. This point is illustrated through the analyses in Chapters 3 and 4. However, this relationship also means that the L2 classroom has its own interactional organization which transforms the pedagogical focus (task-as-workplan) into interaction (task-in-process)—see Extract 2.7 for an example of this. The omnipresent and unique feature of the

L2 classroom is this reflexive relationship between pedagogy and interaction. So whoever is taking part in L2 classroom interaction and whatever the particular activity during which the interactants are speaking the L2, they are always displaying to one another their analyses of the current state of the evolving relationship between pedagogy and interaction and acting on the basis of these analyses. Although this may sound complicated, we can see how this works even in the first exchange a Chinese L1 beginner makes in his first English class in Extract 5.1:

(5.1)

```
1 T:   OK my name's,
2 LL:  my name's,
3 T:   OK, (.) er, hello, ((addresses L1)) my name's John Fry.
4 L1:  (.) my name's John Fry,
5 T:   oh!
6 LL:  ((laugh))
7 L1:  my name's Ping. Ping.
8 T:   Ping? yes hello, °you say° ((whispers)) hello.
9 L1:  hello my name is my name's Ping.
```

(British Council, 1985, vol. 1, p. 15)

We can see in Line 4 of Extract 5.1 4 that L1 displays an analysis of the current relationship between pedagogy and interaction as being that he must repeat whatever the teacher says. It is easy to see how this occurs, since in Lines 1 and 2 the required relationship between pedagogy and interaction was just that. T, however, displays in Lines 5 and 8 that his analysis is that this is not the required relationship and that L1 should instead produce a specific string of forms including L1's own name. L1 then changes his analysis of the relationship between pedagogy and interaction so that in Line 9, it finally conforms to that required by T. In this extract we see that the linguistic forms and patterns of interaction which the learners produce in the L2 are normatively linked to the pedagogical focus which the teacher introduces. In Section 5.2, I go into more detail about the implications of this property in relation to sequence organization.

5.1.3 Property 3

The linguistic forms and patterns of interaction which the learners in an L2 classroom produce in the L2 are potentially subject to evaluation by the teacher in some way. As van Lier (1988a) puts it, "everyone involved in language teaching and learning will readily agree that evaluation and feedback are central to the process and progress of language learning" (p. 32). This property does *not* imply that all learner utterances in the L2 are followed by a direct and overt verbalized evaluation by the teacher, as the data show this clearly not to be the case. It means that all learner utterances are *potentially* subject to evaluation by the teacher. This third property derives rationally from the second property; since the linguistic forms and patterns of interaction which the learners produce in the L2 are normatively linked in some way to the pedagogical focus which is introduced, it follows that the teacher will need to be able to evaluate the learners' utterances in the L2 in order to match the reality to the expectation. In classrooms in which history or geography, for example, is being taught, learners' work is subject to evaluation in the same way, but in those classrooms the linguistic forms and patterns of interaction which the learners produce are only a vehicle for, not the aim or the focus of, the lesson; it is the propositional content which they carry that is evaluated.

Sometimes a teacher in an L2 classroom does not express any observable evaluation of learner utterances during a lesson. This does not mean, however, that learner utterances were not subject to evaluation by the teacher. For example, I recorded a lesson (Seedhouse, 1996) in which a particular group was not taking its task too seriously. The teacher did not express any evaluation of the learners' discourse whatsoever during the lesson. However, the teacher informed me (6 months later) that she had reprimanded that group of learners during a subsequent lesson for their poor performance. She further informed me that some groups which I had not recorded had very interesting discussions. So learner utterances are potentially subject to teacher evaluation, although the evaluation is not always directly or overtly expressed. An L2 teacher may even avoid any explicit evaluation during lessons altogether, and then give learners an end-of-year grade or report for oral performance.

This study proposes that these three properties are universal in L2 classrooms; that is, they apply to all L2 classroom interaction, and they are inescapable in that they are a rational consequence of the core institutional goal and the nature of the activities in L2 classrooms. Furthermore, the data from many different countries, types of institutions, and types of lesson which are analyzed in the course of the monograph demonstrate the universality of these properties. These properties, then, form the foundation of the rational architecture and of the unique institutional fingerprint of the L2 classroom.

5.2 The Basic Sequence Organization of Second Language Classroom Interaction

We saw in the previous section that the omnipresent unique feature of the L2 classroom is that there is a reflexive relationship between pedagogy and interaction. So whoever is taking part in L2 classroom interaction and whatever the particular activity during which the interactants are speaking the L2, they are always displaying to one another their analyses of the current state of the evolving relationship between pedagogy and interaction and acting on the basis of these analyses. In this section we look at what this means in practice in terms of manifestations of sequence organization. Although we have seen that L2 classroom interaction is extremely diverse and fluid, it is nonetheless possible to state a basic sequence organization which applies to all L2 classroom interaction:

1. A pedagogical focus is introduced. Overwhelmingly in the data this focus is introduced by the teacher, but it may be nominated by learners.

2. At least two persons speak in the L2 in normative orientation to the pedagogical focus.

3. In all instances, the interaction involves participants' analyzing this pedagogical focus and performing turns in the L2 which display their analysis of and normative orientation to this focus in relation to the interaction. Other participants analyze these turns in relation to the pedagogical focus and produce further turns in the L2 which display this analysis. Therefore, participants constantly display to each other their analyses of the evolving relationship between pedagogy and interaction.

Through this sequence the institution of the L2 classroom is talked into being, because introducing the pedagogical focus is directly implicative of the institutional goal: to teach the learners the L2. There are three specific actualizations of this sequence in the data, depending on social dynamics. Although they are different from one another in a number of respects, they all conform to the basic sequence organization just detailed.

The *first actualization* is as follows. If the teacher has introduced the pedagogical focus to the learners, then they analyze what the target production is (i.e., the required relationship between pedagogy and interaction) and then attempt to produce it. The teacher matches the linguistic forms and patterns of interaction which the learners produce to the pedagogical focus and analyzes and evaluates them on the basis of the match or mismatch. The teacher may conduct repair until the targeted patterns of interaction are produced. Then the teacher may introduce a further pedagogical focus on the basis of his or her analysis and evaluation, which the learners analyze again, and so on. In Extract 5.2, for example, the teacher's pedagogical focus is to get the learners (via L2 prompts) to produce a specific sequence of linguistic forms:

(5.2)

```
 1  T:   Gerda. can you tell me the way to the bank please?
 2  L1:  yes straight (.) along the street
 3  T:   straight along this road
 4  L1:  this road
 5  T:   uhuh
 6  L1:  e:n:: den to: the: traffic lights
 7  T:   okay
 8  L1:  and then (1.0) (str—)=
 9  T:   =straight along this road—till the traffic lights
10  L1:  till?
11  T:   yes
12  L1:  till the traffic light—and then
```

(van Lier, 1988a, p. 210)

In Lines 2 and 6, L1 produces answers which would be perfectly acceptable in conversation; the meaning is clear and the linguistic forms are correct: "straight along the street ... to the traffic lights." However, these are not the target forms which the teacher's pedagogical focus is aiming to produce, and the teacher repairs the answer in Lines 3 and 9. The teacher uses other-initiated other-repair techniques and exposed correction (Jefferson, 1987), in which correction becomes the interactional business; the flow of the interaction is put on hold while the trouble is corrected. Sequences of this type account for the vast majority of the data in the database. This does not mean, however, that such sequences always involve a focus on form and accuracy.

The *second actualization* is as follows. If learners are interacting with each other in pair work or group work, then the learners analyze the pedagogical focus and produce turns in the L2 in normative orientation to it. They listen to each other's turns, link the pedagogical focus to the linguistic forms and patterns which their partners produce, analyze them, and respond normatively on the basis of their analyses. We can see how this works by examining Extract 5.3 from a communicative lesson, in which the teacher is physically absent from the interaction. Young Malaysian learners were given an unfinished story and asked to speculate as to how the story would continue:

(5.3)

L1: he saw what happened (1.0) he saw what happened (.) in the house
L2: he tell the villagers that he a saw a: old man=
L3: =maybe he didn't because er he he can't find the: (.) door handle isn't it?
L4: [why, why he ran]
L3: [maybe maybe ma] ybe maybe the thief don't know he's in there, because it's very dark is it [and] maybe maybe only lightning lightning only can
L1:   [but]
L3: maybe every time the lightning came, (.) maybe the: (.) thief didn't notice anything or not. maybe only
L2: [maybe Nazri Nazri kicked the]
L3: [only Nazri maybe only Nazri]maybe or maybe a [scrap] or something like that.
L2: I think maybe Nazri kicked the table. (1.0)
L4: [Nazri ran (.) cannot open the door,]
L3: [I don't think so because he just bec] ause the little you know
L4: (1.0) ( ) because he didn't find the door handle. (.) why is it he can (.) go out from the house, and ( ) the villagers.
L5: (1.0) the robbers must have stolen Nazri then.

(Warren, 1985, p. 234)

The interaction in Extract 5.3 seems highly "communicative"; in fact the interaction corresponds neatly (on the surface) to Nunan's characterization of "genuine communication" (see Section 2.2). The learners are clearly managing the speech exchange system themselves and expressing themselves freely. The point is, however, that the basic sequence organization remains constant. The linguistic forms and patterns the learners produce are still normatively related to the pedagogical focus which the teacher introduced, even though the teacher does not participate in the interaction. Warren states clearly what his pedagogical focus was with these learners: They were given an unfinished story and asked to speculate as to how the story would continue. The students were left alone with a tape recorder. The writer devised the activity "to activate natural discourse in the classroom" (Warren, 1985, p. 45), and "the only condition imposed on the students was that the medium for all that might be said had to be English" (p. 46). He hoped that the exercise "would encourage the students to speculate" (p. 45). We can clearly see the link between the teacher's pedagogical focus and the linguistic forms and patterns of interaction produced by the learners: The learners speak only in English and speculate about the end of the story. The discourse is natural when compared with that in Extract 5.2, for example.

My point is, then, that whatever methods the teacher is using—and even if the teacher claims to be relinquishing control of the classroom interaction—the linguistic forms and patterns of interaction which the learners produce are normatively linked in some way to the pedagogical focus which is introduced. I do not wish to suggest that it is the sole prerogative of the teacher to introduce a pedagogical focus. Current process-syllabus, learner-centered, and learner autonomy approaches stress the importance of allowing learners to be involved in organizing their learning and in selecting materials, methodology, and other components of the curriculum. Also we see in many extracts in the database (e.g., Extract 5.4) that learners can and do introduce their own pedagogical focus, which may be adopted by the teacher or other learners. Whoever introduces the pedagogical focus and however it is introduced, the point is always the same at this level of analysis: A pedagogical focus is introduced, and the learners produce linguistic forms and patterns of interaction in the L2 which relate normatively to that pedagogical focus. We should be clear that the claim is not that learners' production always relates directly and perfectly to the pedagogical focus introduced. Rather, this is a *normative point of reference* in the CA sense. Sometimes learners misunderstand or reinterpret or reject the teacher's pedagogical focus. Sometimes inexperienced teachers are unable to establish a pedagogical focus. These all then become interesting deviant cases, and I investigated a number of these in detail in Seedhouse (1996).

The *third actualization* is as follows. Learners may nominate their own pedagogical focus at any time, which may or may not be validated by the teacher. If validated, the teacher must analyze what the learner's pedagogical focus is and hence what kind of turn he or she should produce in response to realize the pedagogical focus. This sequence is in effect the reverse of the first two sequences. In those sequences the teacher knows what the pedagogical focus is, and the learners have to conduct an analysis to determine what kind of turn they should produce in orientation to this. However, in the third actualization, *the learner* knows what the pedagogical focus is, and *the teacher* has to conduct an analysis to determine what kind of turn he or she should produce in normative orientation to this. Nonetheless, the basic sequence organization remains the same. The common feature is that a pedagogical focus is introduced, in orientation to which other participants produce turns in the L2. In Extract 5.4 the teacher has already introduced a pedagogical focus, but we find that a learner[2] has a different agenda, and he wants to present new information about his country to the class:

(5.4)

```
174  T:   yeah. OK. what does this mean? 'get to'? uh.
175  LL:  ( )
176  T:   OK. it says the group has been trying to get the government,
177       the city government, to help uhm draw special lanes,
178       lanes like this ((draws on board)) on the street. OK these
179       are for cars. these are for bikes ((points to blackboard)).
180  L:   you know, in Moscow they reproduce all all cab.
181  T:   uhm?
182  L:   they reproduced all cabs
183  T:   they produce?
184  L:   reproduce
185  T:   d'you mean uh they they use old cabs, old taxis?
186  L:   no, no, no. they reproduced all all! cabs.
187  T:   all the cabs?
188  L:   yeah, all the cabs for electric (electric you know)
189       electric points.
190  T:   cab. oh you mean they made the cabs in down in
191       downtown areas uh uh use electric uh motors?
192  L:   yeah, no downtown, all cabs in Moscow.
193  T:   where?
```

194 L: in Moscow.
195 T: oh. and it's successful?
196 L: yeah.
197 T: OK. uhm. just a second, Igor. let's what does this
198   mean? if you get someone to do something. uhm.

(Allwright, 1980, p. 180)

The teacher's pedagogical focus in Lines 174–179 of Extract 5.4 is to convey the meaning of "get to," and he or she tries first to elicit the meaning in Line 174. As Allwright (1980, p. 182) says, it appears in Line 175 that the students are not able to cope with the task, and the teacher starts a contextualization of the item in Lines 176–179. Rather than concentrating the mind on the item and giving clues as to its meaning, the explanation appears to lead away from the linguistic item to the carrier topic (traffic). This then provides a favorable environment for L to self-select and nominate an alternative pedagogical focus in Line 180.

T has various choices at this point. T can simply regain control of the pedagogical focus and of the speech exchange system by telling L, for example, that he is out of line, or T can validate L's attempt to introduce real-world information by showing interest in the utterance and by engaging with the topic. However, there is an initial problem in that the meaning of L's utterance is unclear. The problem in communication is that L has made an error in lexis ("reproduce" instead of "convert") which obscures the intended meaning. T in effect validates L's taking the floor and shifting the pedagogical focus by helping to repair L's statement in order to clarify the meaning. The repair process is complex and is certainly a cooperative effort: L repairs T's candidate rephrasings in lines 184, 186, 188, and 192 in an attempt to convey his meaning, and T initiates repair in Lines 181, 183, 185, 187, 190, and 193 in order to clarify L's meaning. The repair is successfully managed on a cooperative basis in that L finally manages to make his meaning clear with the help of T: that all cabs in Moscow have been converted to electricity. In Line 195, T displays a change of information state, shows interest by engaging very briefly with the topic, and then shifts back to a focus on the lexical item in Line 197.

What the extract illustrates is the fluidity and mutability of L2 classroom interaction and the tension, interplay, and dialectic between a focus on form and a focus on meaning; we should note that the meaning of L's utterance in Line 180 was obscured by a problem with linguistic form. The extract also demonstrates the complexity of the interactional work undertaken by language teachers (Seedhouse, 1998b), particularly when learners unexpectedly nominate their own pedagogical focus and topic.

Although Extracts 5.2, 5.3, and 5.4 seem very heterogeneous at first, they all conform to the basic sequence organization previously identified, which is universal because it derives directly from the three properties of L2 classroom interaction as outlined in Section 5.1.

5.3 A Methodology for the Analysis of Second Language Classroom Interaction

The idea that an analytical procedure or methodology can emerge from the structure of interaction is a familiar one in CA, as we saw in Chapter 1. When Sacks et al. (1974) examined the organization of ordinary conversation, they discovered that subsequent turns after the first emerged from the structure of conversation as an analytical tool and proof procedure. The same procedure and methodology is used in institutional settings, in which we find additionally that professionals and clients or laypersons perform analyses which are related to the institutional business and focus. For example, Drew (1992) shows how witness and opposing counsel in courtroom cross-examination use the next-turn proof procedure in relation to the legal focus (testing the validity of testimony) to analyze each other's turns and make responsive moves in orientation to that focus. In institutional interaction, then, interactants display analyses not only of their partners' turns, as in ordinary conversation, but also of the evolving relationship between the institutional focus and the interaction; in our case this is the pedagogical focus.

Our analytical task, then, is to explicate how L2 classroom interactants analyze each other's turns and make responsive moves in relation to the pedagogical focus. The description of the interactional architecture of the L2 classroom in Sections 5.1–5.2, specifically, the properties and basic sequence organization, provides the analyst with a ready-made emic analytical procedure. The participants display in their turns their analyses of the evolving relationship between pedagogy and interaction, that is, how the pedagogical focus relates to the turns produced in L2. Therefore, the methodology can be stated in this way: *The analyst follows exactly the same procedure as the participants and traces the evolving relationship between pedagogy and interaction, using as evidence the analyses of this relationship which the participants display to each other in their own turns.*

So the methodology which is used for the analysis of L2 classroom interaction is the next-turn proof procedure in relation to the pedagogical focus. This methodology is exemplified in all of the analyses in Chapters 3–5. In regard to the vast majority of cases in the database, we can state the procedure more specifically as follows. The classroom teacher compares the linguistic forms and patterns of interaction which the learner produces with the pedagogical focus which he or she originally introduced and performs an analysis and evaluation on that basis. The analyst can do exactly the same thing, comparing the teacher's intended pedagogical focus with the linguistic forms and patterns of interaction which the learner produces, and then analyzing the interaction on the basis of the match or mismatch. As it is a normative methodology, it is able to explicate the interaction in examples in which inexperienced teachers fail to establish a pedagogical focus, in cases in which learners reject or reinterpret the teacher's focus, and in cases in which experienced teachers flout the norms (Seedhouse, 1996).

Clearly, in order for this kind of analysis to be achieved, it is necessary to be able to specify what the pedagogical focus is. In practice, this can be achieved using three types of evidence, some of which appear preferable to CA practitioners and others to applied linguists.

Type 1. In many lessons there is a text-internal statement by the teacher of the *intended* pedagogical focus. In many cases this focus is stated explicitly by the teacher, for example, "Today's class is going to be about describing objects and we're going to look at 3 different types of description" (Seedhouse, 1996, p. 272). This type of text-internal evidence is often (but certainly not always) available in the data in that it is generally accepted to be good pedagogical practice for teachers to state the intended aims of the classroom activity both at the outset of the lesson and before each activity.

Type 2. There are now increasing amounts of classroom data available (e.g., Lubelska & Matthews, 1997) which provide, in addition to video and transcript lesson data, a detailed description of lesson aims and other text-external or ethnographic evidence of intended pedagogical focus. So, for example, in Section 5.7 I analyze an extract and use as evidence of intended pedagogical focus a statement made by the teacher in a video interview after the lesson depicted in the extract. This evidence of pedagogical focus does provide text-external, independent evidence which would tend to be convincing to applied linguists. By contrast, it is likely that CA practitioners would have reservations about this kind of background or ethnographic evidence, as it does not orig- inate in an emic perspective. However, as we saw in Section 2.6, analysts such as Silverman (1999) and Arminen (2000) have tried to create a rapprochement between CA and ethnography and argue that CA practitioners do inevitably make use of some ethnographic knowledge in their analyses of institutional inter- action. For this reason, this monograph does make some use of ethnographic evidence where appropriate.

Type 3. The most acceptable type of evidence to CA practi- tioners is that which is evident in the details of an interaction. In their turns, participants display their analyses of the evolving

relationship between the pedagogical focus and the organization of
the interaction. So, for example, in Extract 5.5 the process of analysis
of and orientation to pedagogical focus by the participants is manifest and available to us in the details of the interaction:

(5.5)

```
 1 T:   now again (1.0) listen to me (1.0) <I've got a lamp>
 2 LL:  [I've got] a lamp
 3 T:   [wha— ]
 4 T:   don't repeat now, don't say after me now. alright I say it and you and you
 5      just listen. I've got a lamp. what have you got? (1.0) raise your hands.
 6      what have you got Eirik?
 7 L1:  e:r I've=
 8 T:   =can you say=
 9 L1:  =I've got a book.=
10 T:   =alright, fine. I've got a telephone. what have you got? (2.5) Trygve.
11 L2:  I've got a hammer.
```

(Seedhouse, 1996, p. 472)

In Line 1, T introduces a new pedagogical focus, which is for T to
say what he has got and then to nominate one learner to say what
he or she has got. However, we see in Line 2 that the learners
display their analyses of the pedagogical focus as being to repeat
whatever T says. In Lines 4–6, T displays his analysis of LL's turn
in relation to the pedagogical focus as being a mismatch and
restates the pedagogical focus. In Line 9, we see that L1 reana-
lyzes the pedagogical focus as being for him to say what he has
got, and we see in Line 10 that T analyzes L1's turn as matching
the pedagogical focus, and so T is able to continue with the same
pedagogical focus. We should note that all of the evidence for the
evolving pedagogical focus is endogenous to the details of the talk;
the participants are displaying their analyses of and orientations
to the pedagogical focus in their turns at talk.

This text-internal form of evidence of pedagogical focus may
be subject to a criticism of circularity by applied linguists, as the
evidence for the pedagogical focus comes from the interaction
itself. However, this type of evidence is most convincing to CA
practitioners precisely because it is endogenous to the talk and

derives from an emic perspective—the evidence relating to the participants' concerns inhabits the details of the talk. Moreover, the CA objection to evidence of Types 1 and 2 would be that they are merely statements of *intended* pedagogical focus or task-as-workplan. As we saw in Extract 5.4 and have seen in a number of other cases in this monograph, the *actual* pedagogical focus or task-in-process can turn out rather differently from the way anticipated; indeed, this happens as well in Line 2 of Extract 5.5. Furthermore, the pedagogical focus can be switched from one turn to another by learners as well as by teachers, and the reflexive relationship between pedagogy and interaction means that the evolving patterns of interactions affect the pedagogical focus. So we should be aware that explicit statements of intended pedagogical focus (evidence of Types 1 and 2) do not necessarily reflect the reality of how participants actually analyze and orient to the pedagogical focus.

Our task as analysts is to match the evolving pedagogical focus with the evolving patterns of interaction in the same way as the participants do and using the same evidence that they do: each other's turns at talk. Therefore, in this monograph, every analysis is undertaken primarily using Type 3 evidence; Type 1 and 2 evidence are also cited where available and appropriate, particularly as the monograph is aimed partly at an AL readership.

To further illustrate the nature of the reflexive relationship between pedagogy and interaction, we will consider Extract 5.6. The pedagogical focus at this point is for L4 to ask L11 questions using the present perfect (third-person form of the verb), to which L11 should respond with a lie, in this case by answering "yes." L4 should then follow up with questions in the simple past (second-person form of the verb) to try to expose the lie:

(5.6)

```
1 T:     lie okay who is coming? .hh now you ask the questions not me. (2.0)
2        °Özgür gel hadi° ((tr.: come here come on)) please (3.0) okay, (.)
3        ↑ let's ask:: the third question. third one. okay ask him.
4 L21:   (.) him?
5 T:     yes ask Özgür have you ever::?
```

```
 6 L4:    (.) go to Trabzon
 7 T:     okay ask yes ask him.
 8 L4:    (.) have you ever: err went to—
 9 T:     third form third ↑form!
10 L4:    uh sorry have you ever gone to Trabzon?=
11 T:     =°yes yes [yes°] (whispers)
12 L11:→          [no ] I haven't=
13 T:     =↑ah:::: ((strangulated voice quality)) you must say ↑YES
14 LL:    ((laughter))
15 T:     you must say yes yes [yes]
16 L11:                        [yes]
17 T:     you ↑lie you say yes yes okay? (0.5) ask another question
18        (0.5) ask another question have you ever dut-dut-dut ((using fillers))
```

(Üstünel, 2003, pp. 73–75)

Extract 5.6 illustrates two points. First, the overriding consideration for everyone involved in L2 classroom interaction is to follow the evolving relationship between pedagogy and interaction and to match the pedagogical focus to the patterns of interaction. In Line 12, L11 gives an answer which is not only correct in terms of truth or meaning and sequentially appropriate, but also correct in terms of linguistic form. However, the teacher analyzes it as wrong and corrects it in an exaggerated fashion because it does not correspond to the pedagogical focus. Moreover, his fellow students laugh at L11's "mistake." Secondly, we cannot take the intended pedagogical focus as stated by the teacher (task-as-workplan) for granted, as learners may interpret it in different ways in the task-in-process.

In this section I have stated the methodology used for the analysis of L2 classroom interaction. During the course of the monograph, its use is illustrated through the analysis of numerous extracts.

5.4 Talking the Institution of the Second Language Classroom in and out of Being

At this point it may be objected that Sections 5.1–5.3 contain an a priori, static, and acontextual description of the organization of interaction, whereas according to CA methodology, it cannot be assumed that a particular interaction which occurs is institutional or that the identities *teacher* and *learner* are relevant. However, the description which I have given previously is of the context-free structure to which interactants may or may not orient and which they may use normatively in context-sensitive ways to perform their social actions. So the above organization of language classroom interaction applies as and when the institutional context and identities are talked into being by the participants. It can be determined only by turn-by-turn emic analysis whether the institution is being talked in or out of being. Not all talk in an institutional setting evokes an institutional context (see Sections 1.8 and 2.6). Social, interpersonal, noninstitutional chat may take place in hospitals between doctors, in which case it is not medical discourse (Schegloff, 1987, 1992). It can also take place in the L2 classroom and have nothing to do with any pedagogical focus, in which case it is not L2 classroom interaction and does not fall within the scope of this study.

The institutional context is talked into being by introducing an institutional focus; in a hospital this would be a medical focus, and in the L2 classroom this is a pedagogical focus which requires the production of the L2. *By introducing a pedagogical focus in orientation to which turns in the L2 are produced, the institutional context of the L2 classroom is talked into being, and the interaction produced is L2 classroom interaction.* So a CA does not make any a priori assumptions that talk which occurs in L2 classrooms is institutional talk or that the identities of teacher and learner are omni-relevant. Through a turn-by-turn emic analysis we uncover whether the participants in a particular extract orient to their institutional identities and produce L2 in relation to a pedagogical focus and hence in relation to the institutional goal. On that basis we consider whether the extract can be considered L2 classroom interaction or not:

(5.7)

T: ok ok I think we stop there. unless you have something else you want
to say >and you're not leaving yet < because I have a message for you
(22.0)

T: *eh Oivind ta og ti still naa for det en viktig beskjed som eg er noedt til aa
gi* ((tr.: Oivind keep quiet now because there is an important message I
have to give))
((12 lines omitted))

T: *eg har diskutert med* (name) (1.0) *kor mye er klokka og tida? Men eg faar
ta det muntlig allikevel—odet er vanskeligt for oss aa sei at pga at der er
tri I klassen som- eller fire som er saa opptatt av ( ) eh kanskje
kan vi ikkje legge turen der, heller ta den seinere* ((tr.: I have discussed
with (name) (1.0) what time is it time? But I will do it verbally anyway—
and it is hard for us to say that because there are three in the class that—or
maybe four that are so concerned about ( ) eh can't we make the trip
then, make it later instead))

(Norwegian data)

Looking at Extract 5.7, T has been speaking L2 English for the whole lesson, but then switches back to L1 Norwegian in order to give an administrative message. So the background context remains identical, with the same participants in the same room. But in a CA we take a major part of context to be created by participants in the details of their talk. By switching from L2 to L1 and by moving from a pedagogical focus to an administrative focus, T talks out of being the identity *L2 teacher* and the institutional business *L2 classroom interaction* and talks into being the identity *teacher as administrator* and the institutional business *local administration*. By disengaging from the pedagogical focus, the institutional context of the L2 classroom is talked out of being, and so the interaction is no longer L2 classroom interaction. In this monograph I am explicating *only* L2 classroom interaction, that is, talk produced by teachers and learners in L2 in orientation to a pedagogical focus. We can also see that in terms of the ontology of the construct *L2 classroom*, an etic specification is not possible. We have to consider the emic perspective and uncover whether participants are talking the institution in or out of being at any moment by making it procedurally relevant or not in the details of their interaction.

Learners as well as teachers can also talk the institution in or out of being from one turn to the next.[3] In Extract 5.8, Markee demonstrates how learners recorded while working on a pair work task can switch instantly from on-task institutional talk to off-task social talk:

(5.8)

```
 1 L9:   this writer has a ra[ther— com— pli—] this is [co— ] writer has a
 2 L11:                      [I slept five ho—  ]      [huh ]
 3 L9:   complicated uh,
 4 L11:  yea:h  [(h) ] ((L11 looks left, lifts his left hand to his mouth
 5          and looks down))
 6 L9:          [h   ] heh heh .hhh
 7 L11:  (what'd I say.)
 8          (1.0) ((L9 scratches his forehead with his right hand.
 9          Simultaneously, L11 drops his hand back to his lap.
10          As L11's hand reaches his lap, he begins his turn at Line 11))
11 L11:  I'm so tired I slept five hours ((L11 looks at his watch))
12 L11:  that night ((L11 drops his hand back to his lap))
13          (0.6 )
14 L9:   a:::h. ((L9 uses a tone of mock sympathy))
```

(Markee, in press)

In Lines 1 and 3, L9 tries to continue the official on-task topic of discussion (the writer Günter Grass's position in the debate on German reunification). But as L9 harks back to this previous topic, L11 overlaps L9 at Line 2 with the announcement that he only slept five hours and introduces off-task social talk. L11 later (in a portion of the extract not reproduced here) invites L9 to a party that night where free beer is available. The social chat is in L2 English, as the two learners have different L1s. This extract illustrates the point made in Section 5.1 that even when the teacher is not participating in the talk, we can see that institutional talk is that which is on-task in that it orients to the pedagogical focus introduced by the teacher. Noninstitutional talk (whether conducted in L1 or L2) can and often does occur in the L2 classroom and is talked into being precisely by abandoning the connection to the teacher's pedagogical focus. So we determine whether or not the talk which occurs in L2 classrooms is institutional by relating it to the pedagogical focus.

How do we know that the learners orient to the distinction between on-task and off-task with regard to the teacher's pedagogical focus? Markee demonstrates how the learners in the Extract 5.8 carefully disguise their social talk from the teacher and are able to instantly switch back on-task when required. This type of switching back and forth surfaces quite often in the data as an issue among learners engaged in tasks in the absence of the teacher, as is illustrated by Extract 5.9:

(5.9)

L1:   teacher said don't use Malay are you? so you don't use Malay.
LL: (1.0) ((laugh))
L2:   very difficult I don't know answer to the question.
      ((scuffles, laughter))
L1:   >OK OK never mind, never mind, don't worry, discuss, discuss, come on
      don't laugh.<
LL: ((laugh))

(Warren, 1985, p. 238)

So the perspective on L2 classroom interaction in this monograph is a dynamic and variable one. The CA methodology is able to portray how the institutional context and institutional identities are talked into being and out of being on a turn-by-turn basis through normative orientation to a pedagogical focus. The description of the interactional organization in this chapter is of a context-free structure. Interactants such as those in Extracts 5.7 and 5.8 use this structure in a normative and context-sensitive way to perform their social actions. In those extracts they talk the institution out of being precisely by moving away from the pedagogical focus in their talk. Similarly, in Extract 5.8, L11 talks the identity *L2 learner* out of being and talks into being the identity *party animal*. So the discussion in this section leads to an operational definition of L2 classroom interaction: *L2 classroom interaction is interaction which is produced in the L2 by teachers and / or learners in normative orientation to a pedagogical focus.* Many other varieties of interaction can occur in the physical setting of an L2 classroom, but the type of interaction described in this definition is the sole focus of this monograph.[4]

5.5 The Concept of Second Language Classroom Contexts

We saw in Chapters 3 and 4 that it was possible to derive characterizations of typical L2 classroom contexts, such as a form-and-accuracy context, inductively from data. In this section we will examine the concept of L2 classroom contexts more closely. In order to explicate this concept, we first need to consider what is meant by an institutional variety and an institutional subvariety of discourse. Institutions conduct their institutional business by means of an overarching variety of discourse which is suited to the overarching institutional aim. Courtroom business, for example, is conducted by means of the variety of courtroom English, which has developed over the centuries to be suited to the overarching institutional aim of administering justice to the cases which come before the court, and this has certain common features. When all of these features are taken into account, they constitute the distinguishing features of the institutional variety. As noted earlier in the chapter, Drew and Heritage (1992b) suggest that each institutional variety may have its own unique fingerprint "comprised of a set of interactional practices differentiating (it) both from other institutional forms and from the baseline of mundane conversational interaction itself" (p. 26).

We have seen in Section 5.1 that L2 classroom interaction has its own unique fingerprint in terms of three properties. However, an institutional variety cannot realistically be treated as an undifferentiated, homogenous entity. A court case, for example, is divided into the swearing-in of jurors, a statement of the case, direct and cross-examinations, the passing of sentence, and so on (Levinson, 1992, p. 71). Each of these subvarieties has a different legal subaim and different organization of the interaction which is appropriate to that aim. So, for example, cross-examination of a witness has the legal subaim of establishing the credibility of a witness's evidence, and the organization of the interaction is essentially that of question by the lawyer and answer by the witness. A subvariety of institutional interaction is understood here as one which combines an institutional subaim with an interactional organization appropriate to that subaim. A subvariety has certain common, distinguishing features (Atkinson & Drew, 1979, p. 195) and may also have its own unique fingerprint.

Let us now revisit the concept of the institutional variety and subvariety. Courtroom talk as an overarching institutional variety has certain common features. So when we focus on an extract as being a product of its *institutional context*, we consider what it has in common with other extracts from the same institutional context. However, each legal subvariety (e.g., cross-examination) has its own particular institutional subaims and an organization of the interaction which is appropriate to those subaims and therefore its own unique fingerprint. When we focus on an extract as being a product of its *subvariety context*, we consider what it has in common with other extracts from the same institutional subvariety.

Similarly, in the L2 classroom there is an overarching variety, L2 classroom interaction, by means of which the core business of teaching the learners an L2 is conducted. Equally, L2 classroom interaction is not an undifferentiated whole but can be divided into a number of subvarieties or L2 classroom contexts, in which a particular pedagogical aim enters into a reflexive relationship with a particular organization of the interaction. The different L2 classroom contexts or subvarieties need to be understood, then, as *different actualizations of the reflexive relationship between pedagogical focus and interactional organization*.

However, we now need to consider the major differences between courtroom discourse and L2 classroom interaction. The courtroom is recognized as a very formal discourse setting (Atkinson & Drew, 1979). In the courtroom, subvarieties such as, for example, cross-examination have technical, formal labels or names, and there are a strictly limited number of subvarieties which may occur. Courtroom professionals are trained in the kinds of interaction which are and are not permissible during each subvariety. In the majority of other institutional settings, however, subvarieties do not have such commonly agreed-upon technical or formal labels or names. In L2 classrooms, there is no agreement in respect to the terminology used to name subvarieties. Furthermore, in many L2 teaching settings, there is no limitation in principle on the kinds of interaction which may occur. Indeed, innovation is highly prized in many (particularly Western) countries, and so invention and variety in terms of interaction may be encouraged. Teachers may try to produce interaction which is as different as possible from traditional lockstep interaction (Warren, 1985). Therefore, there is in principle no limit to the potential number of L2 classroom contexts which could occur around the world. In practice, though, the L2 classroom has an interactional organization which tends to limit what actually happens. I do not suggest that I have characterized all of the L2 classroom contexts which occur; I have merely sketched in Chapters 3 and 4 the organization of several which occur in the database.[5]

It is suggested that L2 classroom contexts should be understood not only as institutional subvarieties, but also as the *interfaces* between pedagogy and interaction, and thus as the environments through which institutional business is accomplished. Although we talk of institutional varieties such as courtroom and classroom talk, whenever we examine an instance of interaction, we see that institutional business is carried out by means of a subvariety. So L2 classroom contexts are modes of interactional organization through which institutional business is accomplished. There is no suggestion that all instances of interaction within a particular L2 classroom context will appear to be almost identical. As we see in Section 5.6, there is a constant tension between homogeneity and heterogeneity in L2 classroom interaction, and an L2 classroom context needs to be understood as *one instance of the reflexive relationship between pedagogy and interaction*. It is the instantiation of a particular pedagogical focus and a particular organization of the interaction. One would not, for example, expect all courtroom cross-examinations or all doctor-patient consultations to evolve in an identical way; one would expect a certain degree of homogeneity and a certain degree of heterogeneity, and this is also the case within an L2 classroom context.

It should also be stressed that the concept of L2 classroom contexts is not a static and invariant one in which a single L2 classroom context covers a whole lesson. Contexts can shift with great rapidity and fluidity from turn to turn during an L2 lesson and can be generated by learners as well as by the teacher—see the analysis of Extract 5.4 for an illustration. The reason that L2 classroom contexts are included in this study is that they are demonstrably elements of the interactional organization of the L2 classroom to which participants orient. In Section 1.9 we saw that it has become quite common for linguists to mistake the interactional organizations uncovered by CA for the methodology of CA and to apply turn taking, adjacency pairs, and so on to interaction as a kind of coding scheme. At this point, therefore, we need to be quite explicit about L2 classroom contexts. They are modes of interactional organization; they are not a methodology for analysis, and they are not intended as a coding scheme.

The methodology for the analysis of language classroom interaction is that described in Section 5.3 and it involves a turn-by-turn, holistic, emic analysis of the sequential environment. Heritage (1997) expresses a similar point in the following way: "Overall structural organization, in short, is not a procrustean bed to fit data into, rather it is something we're looking for and looking at because the parties orient to it in organizing their talk" (p. 168). The argument is not that L2 classroom contexts are discrete entities cast in stone and that as soon as one has identified which context participants are operating in, then one has explained the interaction and finished the analysis. Rather, the L2 classroom context is only one part of the overall interactional architecture of the L2 classroom and one manifestation of the complex, reflexive relationship between pedagogy and interaction which is its cornerstone.

As we saw in Chapter 1, CA does not see findings in terms of interactional organizations such as turn taking and adjacency pair as a fixed set of prescriptive or regulative rules which must be followed. Rather, they are constitutive norms or interpretive resources which interactants make use of in order to orient themselves within and to make sense of an ongoing interaction. In the same way, L2 classroom contexts are findings: interactional organizations which have emerged from the analysis of data and function as constitutive norms. As usual in CA methodology, deviant cases are particularly illuminating, or as Heritage (1995, p. 399) puts it, deviant cases often serve to demonstrate the normativity of practices.

In the data there are four kinds of deviant cases in relation to L2 classroom contexts. In the first, teachers and learners struggle for control of the pedagogical focus and hence the kind of context which is established. In the second, there is confusion as to which context is in operation. In the third, inexperienced trainee teachers fail to establish a pedagogical focus and L2 classroom context. In the fourth, experienced teachers "flout" the normal organization of the L2 classroom in order to create particular effects. A discussion of these deviant cases is presented in Seedhouse (1996) but is not included here for lack of space.

5.6 A Three-Way View of Context

At this point we need to broaden the perspective to be able to portray and explain any instance of L2 classroom interaction as having a *complex personality*, as simultaneously displaying both homogeneity and heterogeneity and as functioning on a number of different levels at the same time: This property is called *complementarity*. Lest I be accused of sounding unscientific or even mystical, I should add that this concept derives from the natural sciences, namely, physics. Descriptions of fundamental entities such as photons and electrons as being particles *and* waves are said to be equally valid, complementary descriptions of the same reality. Neither description is complete in itself: "This idea of wave and particle being two complementary facets of the particle's complex personality is called complementarity" (Gribbin, 1991, p. 118). Although we are of course in a completely different area here, the concept of complementarity is nonetheless a useful one to describe the way in which *institutional discourse simultaneously displays both uniqueness and institutional commonality along with a complex personality*. It is therefore necessary, at this stage of the argument, to present a model which sketches a fuller and more complex picture of *context* in the L2 classroom.

We should be clear that this model is not a method of analysis.[6] Rather, it is a means of explicating and conceptualizing the complementary levels on which an instance of L2 classroom interaction can be viewed, as well as its simultaneous heterogeneity (or unique nature) and homogeneity (or institutional sameness). This fuller picture could best be termed a *three-way view of context*, since it involves three perspectives on context represented in decreasing circles (see Figure 5.1).

Every time a teacher introduces a pedagogical focus in orientation to which learners produce turns in the L2, an L2 classroom context is talked into being. On one level, the particular context produced is quite unique. On another level, the particular context has some features in common with other L2 classroom contexts which have occurred—for example, with other form-and-accuracy contexts. On yet another level, the particular interaction produced has features in common with all other instances of L2 classroom interaction.

We always start at the *micro context* by focusing closely and narrowly on the microinteraction, and at this level the context is unique. We explicate the sequential environment on a turn-by-turn basis and derive a technical characterization of context from the details of the talk: "The CA perspective embodies a

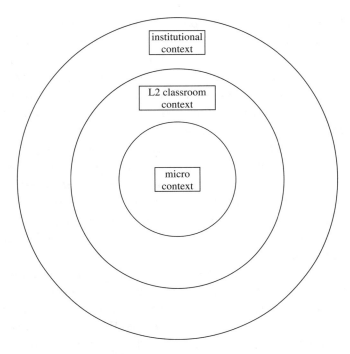

Figure 5.1. A three-way view of context

dynamic approach in which 'context' is treated as both the project and product of the participants' own actions and therefore
as inherently locally produced and transformable at any moment"
(Drew & Heritage, 1992b, p. 19). We determine what the
pedagogical focus is and how the interaction is organized in
relation to it. At this level of context we view the interaction as
a singular occurrence, and the emphasis is on heterogeneity.

When the perspective starts to broaden, we can examine
the particular combination of pedagogical focus and organization
of the interaction (*L2 classroom context*) which is currently in
operation and see whether this instance may have something in
common with other instances which are organized in a similar
way. For example, if the focus is on form and accuracy, in which
ways is this instance similar or dissimilar to other such
instances?

When the perspective broadens further we can see the *institutional context*, in this case that of an L2 classroom. At this level we can see that the instance has properties in common with all other instances of L2 classroom interaction; in any instance the three properties outlined in Section 5.1 are inherent in the interaction, and therefore there is a degree of institutional sameness. At this level of context we view the interaction as an example of L2 classroom discourse, and the emphasis is on homogeneity.

So there is always a tension among (a) a description of an extract of L2 classroom interaction as a unique occurrence, locally produced by the participants, (b) a description of it as an example of interaction within a particular L2 classroom context, and (c) a description of it as an example of institutional L2 classroom discourse. To put it another way, there is always a tension between a description of an extract of L2 classroom interaction as something homogeneous or similar to other instances and as something heterogeneous or different from other instances.

We will now examine a classroom conversation to show how all three levels of context are simultaneously manifested in the conversation:

(5.10)

```
 1 T:  what did I dream? can you remember?
 2 L1: you turned into a toothbrush
 3 T:  can I have a full sentence, Hugo?
 4 L1: that you turned into a toothbrush
 5 T:  OK. you (.)?
 6 L2: you turned into a toothbrush.
 7 T:  you (.)?
 8 L2: you turned into a toothbrush.
 9 L3: you dreamed.
10 T:  you dreamt.
11 L3: you dreamt.
12 T:  everyone
13 LL: dreamt
14 T:  OK. I dreamt that I turned into a toothbrush.
```

(Ellis, 1984, p. 105)

5.6.1 Micro Context

At the micro level of context, we view the interaction as a singular occurrence. Although Extract 5.10 is clearly typical both of an L2 classroom and of a form-and-accuracy context, the extract is nonetheless unique on a micro level; even a teacher giving the same prompts as the teacher in the extract would never receive exactly the same replies from the learners. At this level of context the emphasis is on heterogeneity, uniqueness, and the "instanced" nature of the interaction.

5.6.2 Second Language Classroom Context

At the L2 classroom level of context, we view the interaction as an example of communication within a particular L2 classroom context. The interaction in Extract 5.10 is typical of a form-and-accuracy context, in which the pedagogical focus is on the production of strings of correct linguistic forms by the students and personal meanings tend to be disregarded; Extract 5.10 bears many similarities to other instances in the database. The organization of repair is suited to the pedagogical focus in that the teacher will initiate repair if the linguistic forms produced by the learner are not identical to those targeted by the teacher; we can see evidence of this in Lines 3 and 10. The organization of turn taking and sequence is again appropriate to the pedagogical focus. Since the teacher needs to prompt the learners to produce specific strings of linguistic forms, it follows that the teacher will allocate turns to the learners and constrain the content of those turns, which implies a rigid, lockstep approach. So the pedagogical focus and organization of the interaction is fairly typical of the form-and-accuracy context.

5.6.3 Institutional Context

At the institutional level of context, we view the interaction as an example of L2 classroom discourse, any instance of which manifests the three properties of L2 classroom interaction discussed earlier in the chapter. The first of these properties, as noted previously, is that language is both the vehicle and object of instruction. So in Extract 5.10, we can see T both managing the interaction in the target language (vehicle) and treating learner responses as texts to be corrected (object). The second property is that there is a reflexive relationship between pedagogy and interaction. In particular, the linguistic forms and patterns of interaction which the learners produce in the L2 are normatively linked in some way to the pedagogical focus which the teacher introduces. Extract 5.10 demonstrates the very tight connections which can occur between the teacher's pedagogical focus and the linguistic forms and patterns of interaction which the learners produce. In Line 2, L1 produces an answer which would be perfectly acceptable in conversation. However, this is not the target pattern of interaction which the teacher's pedagogical focus is aiming to produce, and the teacher does not accept the answer. Similarly, in Line 9, L3 produces a perfectly acceptable simple-past form, but this particular linguistic form is not the one targeted by the teacher's pedagogical focus, and the teacher corrects it in Line 10. The third property is that the linguistic forms and patterns of interaction which the learners produce are subject to evaluation by the teacher in some way. In Extract 5.10, the evaluation is implicit as indirect negative evaluation which is understood in the multiple repair initiations by the teacher (see Section 4.1). At this level of context, we view the interaction as an example of L2 classroom discourse, and the emphasis is on homogeneity. So in order to explicate and appreciate fully the complex workings of context in the L2 classroom, one needs to adopt a three-way approach.

Every time participants produce L2 classroom interaction as defined here, they talk these three levels of context into being. All three levels are present and manifest at all times, and when one broadens or narrows one's perspective, one will tend to focus on a different level of context. Context is not seen as something external to the interaction or lurking in the background: "The definition of the situation is not separate and anterior; it inhabits the talk" (Schegloff, 1993, p. 114). We should note, however, that the three levels of context have to be actively talked into being and made relevant through the details of the talk; see Section 5.4. This three-way view of context explicates how it is that instances of institutional interaction display simultaneous homogeneity and heterogeneity; the level of context which one focuses on determines the level of homogeneity or heterogeneity which one discovers.

The model thereby provides the basis for this study's observation that all instances of L2 classroom interaction have the same properties and use the same basic sequence organization, while at the same time portraying the extreme diversity, fluidity, and complexity of the interaction. In addition, the model portrays the relationship between institutional varieties and subvarieties. L2 classroom interaction is an institutional variety of interaction, and L2 classroom contexts are subvarieties.

The three-way model also helps to conceptualize how CA institutional-discourse methodology links the macro and micro levels of social organization. CA is sometimes mistakenly called a "micro" methodology. However, CA works simultaneously on the micro and the macro level, on the general and the particular instance; by emic, turn-by-turn analysis, we uncover the "machinery" which is able to produce the individual instances and hence the organization of the institutional variety of talk. Schegloff (1987, p. 221) suggests that the way in which CA can link the micro and macro levels is by treating modes of interactional organization as contexts themselves, which is what this model attempts to do.

So with the three-way perspective on context proposed here, the micro level, the level of interactional organization, and the macro level can all be analyzed and portrayed simultaneously, with each level feeding the other reflexively. L2 classroom contexts are organizations of the interaction which participants treat as contexts for talk. When we as analysts also treat them as contexts for talk, we are able to provide conceptual links between the micro and macro levels. As we will see in Section 6.3, such a model has practical uses in SLA. Prior to quantifying interactional phenomena (e.g., recasts) in SLA, it is vital to be able to explicate the relative levels of homogeneity and heterogeneity in the naturally occurring instances of the phenomenon. Finally, I should point out that the model is intended merely as an aid to conceptualization; one could add further levels to the model and expand or modify it in a number of ways.

5.7 Creating a Second Language Classroom Context

We will now examine how an L2 classroom context is established or "talked into being" in the CA sense by an experienced teacher in a language school in Mexico. The first main L2 classroom context which the teacher establishes is a meaning-and-fluency context. The teacher has previously asked the learners to bring a personal possession to class which is special to them in some way. The teacher states explicitly her reasons for establishing such an L2 classroom context during an interview prior to the lesson:

> In a lot of classes I like to use ... the so-called humanistic techniques. Students give personal information about themselves or about things that they have, or about their families and so on. These humanistic kinds of activities tend to be good because they break the ice and they make the students find out a bit about each other. For example, in this class the students will be bringing some of their own objects and talking about them. In that kind of activity, the level of the students' English doesn't matter so much because you focus a lot on the content of what they are saying. (British Council, 1985, vol. 4, p. 50)

The teacher's explanation is interesting for a number of reasons. It provides a clear rationale for the use of a meaning-and-fluency context as a contrast to the form-and-accuracy context which was to come after it; in a *proficiency* class[7] in the early 1980s it was inevitable that the bulk of lesson time would be spent on form-and-accuracy work in preparation for the examination. The teacher states that the meaning-and-fluency context is placed deliberately at the start of the lesson as an icebreaker. This does not mean that the meaning-and-fluency context normally occurs at the start of the lesson. The data show that it may occur at any stage of the lesson. In this lesson, the meaning-and-fluency context also functions as an introduction to work in a form-and-accuracy context, to which it is thematically related. Again, this is not always the case, and the reverse order also occurs in the data.

So although we should not generalize from this one lesson as to the sequencing of main contexts, the teacher's comments clearly display an orientation to the sequential organization of contexts within a lesson as serving specific overall pedagogical goals. L2 classroom contexts follow each other for good reason in this teacher's lessons. The teacher also states explicitly that in a meaning-and-fluency context, she focuses on the content of what the learners are saying, and this is implicitly contrasted with the focus on linguistic ability necessary in the rest of the lesson. I will now examine how the teacher establishes the pedagogical focus and context and then manages the context shift.

(5.11)

T: today's class is going to be about describing objects, (.) and we're going to look
   at three different types of description. .hh I'm going to write it here on the board,
   what we'll be doing. ((T writes on board)) (.) the first type will be personal (.)
   OK? objects that have an especial value for you. a personal value. .hh the second
   type will be (.) catalogue (.) type descriptions.

(British Council, 1985, vol. 4, p. 50)

In Extract 5.11, the lesson starts with a procedural context which anticipates that the lesson will involve some kind of change of focus and which provides a link between the two contexts, in that they will both involve description. For the next stage in the establishment of the context, T asks the learners if they have brought personal belongings along as requested and elicits from two or three students the nature of their belongings. Then the teacher produces an enormous embroidery, a personal belonging with personal value for her, and tells the learners about it in Extract 5.12:

(5.12)

T: um, this is a nineteenth-century Japanese embroidery, and it was given to me by my great-aunt. (.) my great-aunt she had a—a funny kind of job really, she was a governess.

(British Council, 1985, vol. 4, p. 51)

This part of the interaction serves multiple functions. It establishes the nature of the context, in that the teacher is demonstrating what the learners are to do during the context: describe their personal possession and its significance to them. It establishes the nature of the speech exchange system: a monologue addressed to the other participants. The teacher has stated that one purpose of this context is for learners to learn a bit about each other, and here the teacher is telling the learners something about herself and thus developing her relationship with the learners.

The teacher then rolls up her embroidery and issues further procedural directions for the establishment of the main context:

(5.13)

T: and what I want you to do is to .hh talk about your things now in the same way as I did about mine. say what it is and give the history of it. how—why have you got it, and maybe also say why is it important (.) to you. for this ... we're going to work in two groups. so, would you be a group of six here you two, and you four. (.) OK, it doesn't matter who begins whoever wants to can can start. I'm going to come and sit with each group some of the time but just listen.

(British Council, 1985, vol. 4, p. 51)

So the spatial configuration of the learners is altered in preparation for the main context.

How does the teacher ensure that it is in fact a meaning-and-fluency focus which is established rather than any other? This appears to be accomplished in the following ways: first, by explicitly modeling the type of talk which is to be produced, which implicitly establishes a focus; secondly, by giving explicit instructions concerning the nature of the speech exchange system and the topic of the talk; and thirdly, by focusing on the content of the talk and by not mentioning linguistic accuracy. The teacher states, "I'm going to come and sit with each group some of the time but just listen." The use of "but just" implies that the teacher will not be conducting repair of linguistic errors and hence that the emphasis should be on the expression of personal meanings.

We can see from Extract 5.14 that the interaction produced by the learners is as expected within a meaning-and-fluency context:

(5.14)

```
1 L1: OK. as you see this is a music box, (.) .hh and my mother made it. it's=
2 L2: =oh, your mother made it?=
3 L1: =yes, my mother made it. .hh the thing is that when: (.) this is the first
4     thing she did (.) like this, with .hh painting and everything, so nobody.
5     nobody thought that it was going to come out like this.[((laughs))] that's
      the point. that's why
6 LL:                                                        [((laugh)) ]
7 L1: this is special because it took her about three weeks to: to make it, .hh and
8     erm she put erm a really special interest in that
```

(British Council, 1985, vol. 4, p. 51)

The learners express personal meanings, and linguistic errors (as in Line 9) are ignored. We noted in Section 3.2 that "oh" often occurs in a meaning-and-fluency context as a marker of change of information state, since new information is being exchanged. We can also see that the learners are managing the speech exchange system themselves. Although the teacher modeled a monologue, L2 feels able to self-select and disrupt the monologue (Line 2). So the teacher has used multiple methods of ensuring that the correct pedagogical focus and context are created, and in this case the intended context has clearly been successfully talked into being.

5.8 Managing Context Shift

We have seen an example of how contexts are created. A lesson may contain multiple contexts, so it is now necessary to explicate how contexts are shifted. I will now show how a context shift is managed by an experienced practitioner. Looking at the same lesson, we will see how the previous meaning-and-fluency context is shifted to a form-and-accuracy context. The teacher brings the previous context to a close in Extract 5.15:

(5.15)

```
 1 T: OK. CAN I stop you now? I know not all of you have finished but—we
 2     haven't got time for any more so let's: get back into two lines again.
       ((LL move chairs))
       ((11 lines omitted))
 3 T: ↑OK well, remember that I said the second thing we're going to look at
 4     is catalogue type descriptions, sometimes when we're describing things
 5     we need .hh to use a lot of different adjectives. .hh and sometimes we're
 6     not very sure which order we should put the adjectives in. for example do
 7     we say (.) erm <a green felt hat> or <a felt green hat>. OK which way
 8     round should we put the adjectives? so we're going to take a look today at
 9     this chart, ((T points to chart on board)) which gives us an idea of how the
10     order of adjectives should go.
       ((10 lines omitted))
11     all right, well what we're going to do is, (.) I am going to give you a
12     handout, (.) and on the top you've got some jumbled sentences. OK, these
13     are just little descriptions, but the adjectives are all in the wrong order. I
14     want you to work in pairs: to put them into the right order.
       ((2 lines omitted))
15     does everyone understand? all right could you give these out ((LL give out
16     sheets)) (4.0) look up at the chart, use the chart as much as you (.) need to,
17     to help you get the sentences right.
```

(British Council, 1985, vol. 4, p. 51)

In Line 1 of the extract, T explicitly marks a transition. "OK. Can I stop you now?" is uttered with high pitch and high volume. T indicates that there is to be a change in spatial configuration back from group to whole class in Line 2. In Line 3, T arranges the context shift. This starts with "OK well" (which functions as a shift marker; see Seedhouse, 1996), uttered with high pitch and volume, and continues (in Lines 3 and 4) with a reference to the procedural context at the start of the lesson, where it was indicated that the second phase of the lesson would be concerned with catalogue-type descriptions.

The teacher develops a form-and-accuracy context in the following way. There is a focus on linguistic correctness in the expressed concern for the proper order of adjectives (Lines 5–7). The change in focus is symbolized by the presentation of a chart of the correct order of adjectives (Line 9). The teacher distributes materials in which the adjectives are in the wrong order, with the instructions that the learners are to put them in the right order (Line 14). A focus on form and accuracy and linguistic correctness without regard to personal meanings is thus established. Whereas in the previous meaning-and-fluency context, the learners supplied the materials (which were personally meaningful and which they had to hold close to themselves), in this L2 classroom context, the teacher presents the materials in a "logical," impersonal chart format which is placed at some distance from the learners. This change might indicate to the learners that they now have less interactional space to express personal meanings. Finally, the teacher introduces a new pedagogical focus (Line 14) which is incompatible with the focus inherent in the previous context. The new pedagogical focus entails a change of L2 classroom context.

Sections 5.1–5.6 have provided a broad overall sketch of the interactional architecture of the L2 classroom. One goal of this monograph is to portray L2 classroom interaction as rationally and coherently organized. Levinson (1992) suggests that "the various levels of organization within an activity cohere, and can be seen to derive as rational means from overall ends and organizational conditions" (p. 93).

One fascinating feature of L2 classroom interaction is the way that it balances invariant underlying institutional characteristics with extreme flexibility and variability. Teachers may aim to produce very unusual and innovative kinds of interaction (for example, Extract 5.6). They may try to replicate varieties of interaction which occur outside the L2 classroom (for example, Packett, in press, and Warren, 1985). Nonetheless, because of the rational organization of the interaction, whatever L2 classroom interaction is produced manifests the three invariant institutional properties and the basic sequence organization.[8]

5.9 Chapter Summary

In this chapter I have described the overall organization of L2 classroom interaction. I introduced the concept of the rational design of institutional interaction and identified the institutional goal as well as three interactional properties which derive directly from the goal. I then identified the basic sequence organization of L2 classroom interaction as well as an emic methodology for its analysis. Next, I exemplified how the institution of the L2 classroom is talked in and out of being by participants. The concept of the L2 classroom context, which was introduced in Chapters 3 and 4, was then problematized and located in a broader, three-way perspective on context. Finally, I exemplified how teachers create L2 classroom contexts and how they shift from one context to another.

Notes

[1]In this section I am uncovering the rational design of the interaction, following Levinson's precepts as cited previously. Here we are at Stage 8 in the list of CA procedures discussed in Section 1.7. A similar discussion of the overall rational organization of an institutional setting can be found in Atkinson and Drew (1979).

[2]It should be noted that Igor is an unusual learner in terms of his success in obtaining a disproportionate share of turns at talk. See Allwright (1980) for a full discussion.

[3]I am grateful to Richard Young for pointing out that Goffman's concepts of "footing" and "participation formats" are highly relevant to this section.

[4]This is not to suggest that code-switching is not an interesting phenomenon, but simply to specify the limited scope of the monograph.

[5]Further examples of L2 classroom contexts are characterized in Seedhouse (1996).

[6]Graphical models of discourse are not typical of CA, and the model is supplementary to the CA perspective developed in this monograph. It is included because the perspective on heterogeneity and homogeneity is useful to the discussions in Chapter 6. However, I recognize that this model moves the discussion well away from the CA perspective on context presented in Section 1.8. I am grateful to an anonymous reviewer for pointing out that a preferable way of explicating the three-way model might be that "one moves from a single case analysis of actual talk (microanalytic context) to collections of single cases, which establish whether we actually have a phenomenon worth talking about as an instance of L2 classroom talk, which can finally be compared to other institutional contexts to establish how, say, classroom talk is similar to, or differs from, courtroom interaction."

[7]This refers to a class which prepares students for the high-level Cambridge Proficiency Examination in English.

[8]Because of space limitations, this account of the organization of L2 classroom interaction has not included discussion of the following areas: (a) the relationship between contexts and the unit of institutional business known as a lesson, (b) organization below the L2 classroom context in terms of consideration of how contexts themselves may be arranged into episodes, (c) how teachers choose which pedagogical focus to establish, and (d) how teachers mark shifts between L2 contexts. Interested readers are referred to a discussion of these issues in Seedhouse (1996).

CHAPTER SIX

Conversation Analysis, Applied Linguistics, and Second Language Acquisition

So far in this monograph I have explicated the organization of L2 classroom interaction using a CA methodology applied to an extensive database. Although I have considered some issues related to the theory and practice of L2 teaching, I have not so far attempted to relate the study to broader research paradigms, which is the focus of this chapter.

The overall aim of this chapter is to consider how CA can be located in and contribute to the research agendas of AL and SLA. Following Larsen-Freeman (2000), SLA is seen as a subfield of AL:

> AL draws on multidisciplinary theoretical and empirical perspectives to address real-world issues and problems in which language is central. SLA draws on multidisciplinary theoretical and empirical perspectives to address the specific issue of how people acquire a second language and the specific problem of why everyone does not do so successfully. (p. 165)

After introducing the relationship between CA and AL, I consider the latest CA research in the following AL areas: language-teaching task design; language-teaching materials design; language proficiency assessment design; disordered talk and speech therapy; professional discourse; CA in languages other than English; NS-NNS talk; bilingual and multilingual interaction; and grammar, pragmatics, and interaction. A common theme in the research is that competence is coconstructed by participants rather than being fixed and static. I then critique the current SLA research on recasts and form-focused instruction (FFI) and suggest that there is a vacant slot in the SLA project which CA is able to fill. I specify the contributions which CA is able to make and demonstrate why it is necessary to subject interactional data to a qualitative, emic analysis prior to quantification. Finally I position CA in relation to social science research methods and concepts such as validity, reliability, generalizability, epistemology, quantification, and triangulation.

6.1 Conversation Analysis and Applied Linguistics[1]

AL, by definition, has always focused on applications. CA, by contrast, has only relatively recently begun to look closely at applications of CA (Drew, in press; Heritage, 1999; Hester & Francis, 2001; Richards & Seedhouse, in press; ten Have, 1999, 2001). In his review of CA at century's end, Heritage (1999) argued that "part of the claim of any framework worth its salt is that it can sustain 'applied' research of various kinds" (p. 73) and indicated that this aspect might feature prominently in developments within the discipline. There has been a rapid growth of CA studies in institutional settings, following Drew and Heritage's (1992a) important collection, embracing not only traditional professions such as medicine or law (e.g., Heritage & Maynard, in press), but also fields such as business (e.g., Boden, 1994), broadcasting (e.g., Clayman & Heritage, 2002), and counseling (Peräkylä, 1995). It was only natural that professional interest should extend beyond description and toward the potential of such research in terms of training and development interventions, encouraging the emergence of *applied* CA almost by default.

However, the concept of application is by no means straightforward (Heritage, 1999). According to Richards (in press), the model of application which is most consistent with the nature of CA is that of description leading to informed action. Such a model would represent the primary research as oriented mainly to description, allowing for the possibility of unexpected insights arising from the sort of unmotivated investigation recommended by Sacks. In emphasizing description, it would reflect CA's methodological orientation, implying no fundamental distinction between primary research and research undertaken with a view to possible applications, allowing that both might generate insights with the potential to transform practice.

In terms of application, the emphasis on informed practice would have two important implications. The first of these would be the establishment of a relationship in which CA would be seen as performing an enabling rather than an enacting role in professional development. Instead of thinking in terms of narrow prescription, professionals would be encouraged to consider more broadly the ways in which CA might affect their practice. For example, Bloch (in press), discussed later in the chapter, uses CA to reveal the ability of interactants with limited resources to coconstruct meaning in dialogue with partners. The second important implication of a focus on informed professional practice is that it would allow for the possibility that CA would become involved in describing not only aspects of professional practice, but also the processes of training or development that might be associated with these. Markee (in press), for example, shows how CA can be used to reveal aspects of classroom behavior that may have implications for an approach to teaching using tasks, and Packett (in press) demonstrates how CA can be used as part of the teaching process in order to sensitize trainees to aspects of their professional practice. It is conceivable that over time this aspect of applied CA, which takes it closest to the concerns of AL, is one that will grow significantly.

The development of an applied dimension in CA and its fundamental concern with language as a form of social action suggest a natural link with AL. There is currently growing interest within the field of AL in CA methodology. This is evidenced by a growing number of publications in AL journals which use a CA methodology (Boyle, 2000b; Carroll, 2000; Hosoda, 2000; Jung, 1999; Markee, 1995; Mori, 2002; Seedhouse, 1994, 1997a, 1999a;

Wong, 2000a, 2002). Equally, there is growing interest in CA circles in AL, as evidenced by recent publications by Schegloff in *Applied Linguistics* (2000b) and by Schegloff, Koshik, Jacoby, and Olsher (2002) in the *Annual Review of Applied Linguistics*. Schegloff et al. (2002) note that "a small but increasing amount of CA and CA-informed research on talk in educational institutions directly addresses issues of interest to applied linguists" (p. 14). AL, which has its roots in language, finds its realization through action, so a method of inquiry that brings together these two aspects as part of a coherent program of investigation and description offers a perspective to which applied linguists should be particularly receptive. In this section we consider the latest research and possible future directions for CA research in AL in areas other than SLA. Each area will be illustrated by reference to research which has an applied dimension and which creates links between the interactional (micro) and institutional (macro) levels in a similar way to this monograph.

6.1.1 Language-Teaching Task Design

The area of languages for specific purposes can be informed by CA research on institutional discourse. Some of the issues and possibilities are discussed in Jacoby (1998a, 1998b) and Koshik (2000). CA methodology can offer a description of the organization of an institutional setting (for example, Atkinson and Drew, 1979, and the present monograph). CA can identify sequence organizations which may be vital to institutional business and which may need to be understood or learned by novices as part of their induction. An example of a concrete and direct application of CA findings to the English for specific purposes classroom is provided by Packett (in press). Packett worked with students in Portugal who opted to study English as part of their journalism degree and who were required to record a face-to-face interview for potential radio broadcast as part of their assessed coursework. A key and problematic demand on these trainee interviewers was that they needed to manage the interaction for the benefit of the overhearing but absent audience. Packett identified a common *insertion action* in which the interviewer departs very briefly from the question-and-answer turn-taking format in order to add a detail to a description given in the prior turn, specifically for the benefit of the absent audience. These insertions, according to Packett, are constitutive of "doing interview" and directly linked to the institutional goal. An insertion action can be seen in Line 8 of Extract 6.1, which is an example of expert data used to teach students (IR = Interviewer, IE = Interviewee):

(6.1)

```
1 IR:    .hh you say if you'd had (.) Jo::hn's some of John's (.)
2        > abilities or talents and he'd had some of yours <
3        which were those. which would he've [ liked to (  ) between
4        you
5 IE:                                        [ .hhh well I think John—
6        John er (0.2) John no::w (0.2) having obviously been married to
7        Chris an—an— an— =
8 IR:→   = >Chris Evert yah.< =
9 IE:    =yeah, and basically living a lot in—in the states … Howe,
```

(————, 2000)

These insertions are organized so as to interrupt only minimally the question-and-answer format of the interview and to redress the indexicality of the prior description. It was noted that in the learners' assessed interviews, this vital insertion sequence was often absent or delayed, which disrupted the flow of the talk. Both the expert data and the learner data were then used by Packett as classroom materials to demonstrate to students the use of the device in interaction. Packett's paper serves as a model not only for CA-informed pedagogy, but also for CA research in language for specific purposes with the aim of linking sequences to the institutional goal.

6.1.2 *Language-Teaching Materials Design*

Language-teaching materials frequently feature dialogues presented in audio or on video together with a transcription. Issues relating to authenticity of dialogues are complex and have been hotly debated. However, in many countries around the world, writers of such materials continue (for a variety of reasons) to invent dialogues. CA is well positioned to portray the similarities and differences between invented dialogue and naturally occurring interaction, both in terms of ordinary conversation and institutional interaction. Wong (2002) provides a very clear example of an application of CA to an area of AL. She identified four sequence types which typically occur in American English telephone conversations, namely, summons-answer, identification-recognition, greeting, and *how are you?* Examining the presentation of 30 inauthentic phone conversations in ESL textbooks, Wong found that the above sequences were "absent, incomplete or problematic" (p. 37). CA research findings, such as Wong's sequence types, can be fed into future language-teaching materials design.

6.1.3 *Language Proficiency Assessment Design*

Previous CA-informed work in the area of language proficiency assessment design by Young and He (1998) and Lazaraton (1997) examined the American Language Proficiency Interview (LPI). Egbert (1998) pointed out that "LPIs are implemented in imitation of natural conversation in order to evaluate a learner's conversational proficiency" (p. 147). Young and He's collection demonstrated, however, a number of clear differences between LPIs and ordinary conversation. First, the systems of turn taking and repair differ from those in ordinary conversation. Secondly, LPIs are examples of goal-oriented institutional discourse, in contrast to ordinary conversation. Thirdly, LPIs constitute cross-cultural communication in which the participants may have very different understandings of the nature and purpose of the interaction. Egbert's study demonstrated that interviewers explain to students not only the organization of repair they should use, but also the forms they should use to do so; the suggested forms are cumbersome and differ from those found in ordinary conversation. He's (1998) microanalysis revealed how a student's failure in an

LPI can be attributed to interactional as well as linguistic problems. Kasper and Ross (2001) pointed out that their CA of LPIs portrays candidates as "eminently skillful interlocutors" (p. 10), which contrasts with the general SLA view that clarification and confirmation checks are indices of NNS incompetence, and Kasper and Ross (2003) analyzed how repetition can be a source of miscommunication in LPIs.

Future CA research in oral assessment could apply the same approach adopted in Young and He's (1998) volume to oral language assessments in other countries around the world. Of particular interest in future research in assessment may be the perspective that communicative competence is not a fixed and static construct but is variable and coconstructed by participants in interaction (see Young, 2002). As far as practical applications are concerned, CA research can clarify the advantages and disadvantages of assessment formats and inform the design of assessment tasks (Schegloff et al., 2002).

6.1.4 *Disordered Talk and Speech Therapy*

It would be fair to say that, within the broad field of AL, speech therapy has been employing CA as a methodology for a longer period and more widely than has the language-teaching sector of the field. Furthermore, speech therapists tend to have seen the practical relevance of CA to their investigations and to have adopted the methodology into their mainstream to a far greater extent than in the language-teaching sector and in SLA in particular. Bloch (in press) exemplifies applications of CA to the field of disordered talk and speech therapy (see also Goodwin, 2003, and Goodwin, Goodwin, & Olsher, 2002). Close analysis of conversation between a man suffering from severe dysarthria[2] and his mother reveals how the participants have developed two resources to facilitate interaction: joint turn adaptation to coconstruct utterances for meaning and completion of utterances by the nondysarthric participant. Bloch explains that the investigation and management of dysarthria have tended to focus solely on the patient's speech, so that "dysarthria has been understood largely in terms of the deviation of speech from culturally accept-able norms." However, broadening the scope of analysis by using CA to investigate the coconstruction of dialogue with a partner offers new possibilities. It provides complementary information for the assessment process and identifies successful interactional strategies which may be used by others in dialogue with dysarthria patients.

6.1.5 Professional Discourse

CA methodology has spawned studies in a wide variety of professional settings, as evidenced in collections such as Drew and Heritage (1992a), Richards and Seedhouse (in press), and Sarangi and Roberts (1999), as well as some papers in McHoul and Rapley (2001). Settings covered by CA studies include legal hearings, news interviews, phone calls to emergency services and help lines, psychiatric interviews, airplane cockpit talk, mediation, and counseling. Gafaranga and Britten's (in press) study exemplifies how CA is able to link interactional sequences on the micro level to the macro level of the institutional goal. Gafaranga and Britten focus on topic-initial elicitors such as *How are you?* or *What can I do for you?* which occur at the start of medical consultations and which may at first be taken to be insignificant social preliminaries. However, their analysis of 62 consultations shows *How are you?* to be used in follow-up consultations and *What can I do for you?* in new consultations. This difference is shown to be institutionally significant in relation to the concepts of continuity of care and the doctor-patient relationship, and the authors conclude that "through orderly openings, doctors and patients talk the institution of General Practice into being." Gafaranga and Britten's study neatly captures the reflexive relationship between talk and its social and institutional context, which is also the central theme of this monograph.

6.1.6 Conversation Analysis in Languages Other Than English

Early criticisms that CA was biased because it was based exclusively on English native-speaker interaction are no longer founded, as CA studies have been published on talk in a range of languages and including NNSs. Examples of CA studies in non-pedagogical settings include those in German (Egbert, 1996, in press; Golato, 2000), Finnish (Kurhila, 2001, in press; Sorjonen, 1996), Swedish (Lindstrom, 1994), Danish (Brouwer, 2004), Dutch (ten Have, 1999), Japanese (Hayashi, 1999; Hayashi, Mori, & Takagi, 2002; Tanaka, 1999), Chinese (Hopper & Chen, 1996), Korean (Kim, 1999; Park, 1999), and Thai (Moerman, 1988).

Such studies reveal similarities and differences in the organization of talk in different languages which may then feed into comparative and contrastive analyses of languages, as well as into language-teaching materials design. To illustrate this point, Hopper and Chen (1996) compared telephone openings in Mandarin Chinese to those in English. We saw previously that there are four sequence types which typically occur in American English telephone conversations: summons-answer, identification-recognition, greeting, and *how are you?* Hopper and Chen found some similarities, in that the first three sequences regularly occur in Taiwanese telephone conversations. However, they also identify practices and linguistic resources which have not been identified in European languages. In particular, telephone callers in Taiwan use a variety of greeting tokens to index the state of their interpersonal relationship, and intimate callers may speak before the answerer. Such findings can potentially feed into design of materials aimed at learners with specific L1s learning specific L2s.

6.1.7 Native Speaker–Nonnative Speaker Talk

Interest in the CA of NS-NNS or cross-cultural talk outside the classroom has developed in recent years, including Egbert (in press), Hosoda (2000), Kurhila (2001, in press), Seedhouse (1998a), Wagner (1996), and Wong (2000a, 2000b, in press). Gardner and Wagner (2004) is a major collection of work in the area of NS-NNS talk, and Seedhouse (1998a) provides an overview of how CA methodology can be applied to the study of NS-NNS interaction. The CA study of NS-NNS interaction in nonpedagogic settings has broadened in recent years to include languages other than English, for example, German (Egbert, in press; Seedhouse, 1998a; Wagner, 1996), Finnish (Kurhila, 2001, in press), Danish (Brouwer, 2004), and Japanese (Hosoda, 2000). The field has also broadened to include the CA study of interaction between NNS and NNS using English as international lingua franca talk (Firth, 1996; Mondada, 2004; Wagner, 1996) and Finnish as international lingua franca talk (Mazeland & Zaman-Zadeh, 2004), as well as studies which compare the identical interactional phenomenon in NNS talk (Wong, 2000a) and in NS talk (Schegloff, 2000b) in English.

Carroll's (in press) study demonstrates that a CA focus on sequence can sometimes reveal hitherto unnoticed aspects of the talk of NNSs. Japanese speakers of EFL (particularly at the novice level) often add vowels to word-final consonants, for example: "Oldest child-u is-u (0.21) um:: twenty." Generally, English teachers have treated this as a pronunciation problem, resulting from negative transfer from the L1. Although not disputing this origin, Carroll's analysis of his data demonstrates that his participants were employing vowel marking as an interactional resource, particularly during forward-oriented repair (Schegloff, 1979) or word search, as in Extract 6.2:

(6.2)

A: what-o what-o interesting-u (0.43) e:to schoo:l-u festival

(Carroll, in press)

According to Carroll (in press), vowel marking, in delaying the production of some *next item due*, serves to buy the speaker initiating the repair a little more time to achieve self-repair. Furthermore, vowel marking alerts coparticipants to the fact that a search is underway and to their possible role in resolving it. In terms of application, Carroll suggests that training students in the use of interactionally equivalent conversational micropractices, such as the use of *uh* and *um*, would be helpful. Furthermore, Carroll's microanalysis reveals a previously unimagined degree of interactional sophistication in the way the novice NNSs in his study employ their limited resources. Such CA research, then, reinforces a shift away from a linguistic-deficit model focused on individual performance toward a model in which communicative competence is seen to be coconstructed. In this model, many of the interactional competencies of L2 students, NNSs, and speech-disordered patients can be revealed only through painstaking CA.

6.1.8 *Bilingual and Multilingual Interaction*

Recent years have seen a growth in the number of studies which have employed a CA approach to bilingual and multilingual interaction and to code-switching in particular (Auer, 1988, 1998; Gafaranga, 2000, 2001; Gafaranga & Torras, 2001, 2002; Mondada, 2004; Sebba & Wootton, 1998; Stroud, 1998; Torras, 2002, in press; Torras & Gafaranga, 2002; Wei, 2002). Wei (2002) provided an overview of the CA approach to bilingual interaction. Torras (in press) demonstrated how CA can be used to portray the reflexive relationship among language preference, social identity, and institutional context in relation to bilingual and multilingual talk. Torras's study was based on recordings of service encounters in Barcelona, in which the use of Castilian, Catalan, and English is possible. Her study demonstrated how language choice was locally negotiated by the participants and found that service providers routinely adopted the linguistic identity enacted by the service seeker. Torras then drew out the implications for training of service personnel in an increasingly globalized world.

6.1.9 Grammar, Pragmatics, and Interaction

Although CA's main interest has been in how social acts are performed through language, it has always been interested in the reflexive relationship between grammar and interaction and the domain of pragmatics. According to Schegloff et al. (2002), "CA treats grammar and lexical choices as sets of resources which participants deploy, monitor, interpret and manipulate as they design turns, sort out turn taking, co-construct utterances and sequences, manage intersubjectivity and (dis)agreement, accomplish actions and negotiate interpersonal trajectories as real-time talk and interaction unfold" (p. 15). A growing number of recent publications have explored the reflexive ways in which grammar organizes interaction and in which interaction organizes grammar, for example, Clift (2001), Ford (1993), Ford, Fox, and Thompson (2002), Goodwin (1996), Hayashi (1999), Heritage and Roth (1995), Ochs, Schegloff, and Thompson (1996), and Schegloff (1996).

Recent research by Vinkhuyzen and Szymanski (in press) uncovers a reflexive relationship between grammatical formatting and social/institutional context. They recorded interactions between employees of a local reprographics business and customers who make a request for a copying service at the business's drop-off counter. In the case of small jobs which it is unprofitable for the counter employees to undertake, they generally redirect the customer to the do-it-yourself area. Vinkhuyzen and Szymanski found that "the grammatical formatting of these customer requests sets certain constraints on just how employees construct a non-granting response, and determines in part whether the non-granting can be done as an affiliative response to the request." Essentially, when customers formatted their requests as self-oriented declaratives that state a customer's desire or need (e.g., "I'd like [I need] to make three copies of this"), it proved simple for staff to redirect them to the do-it-yourself area. However, when customers formatted their requests as other-oriented interrogatives that inquired after the organization's willingness or capability to produce a document followed by a job description (e.g., "Can you make two copies of this document?"), problems often ensued on the interactional and institutional level, since the staff appeared to be rejecting a request. On the institutional level, this analysis exposes the inherently conflicting goals of many service industries, namely, those of making a profit and satisfying diverse customer needs. In terms of applications, in this particular case the authors suggested altering the spatial organization of the store to guide customers to the appropriate location. Moreover, examination of the interaction of employees who successfully manage nongranting of requests has implications for staff training.

A theme which runs through the studies cited in the foregoing is the contribution which CA can make to the study of competence, which has been accepted as fundamental to AL's interests since the 1970s, when communicative language teaching shifted attention to issues of communicative competence and how this might be developed through teaching. The communicative-competence model proved highly successful in broadening the scope of classroom teaching and AL. However, it is, like all methods before or since, based on a deficit model: The purpose of language teaching, it is generally assumed, is to help students develop linguistic knowledge and skills that will enable them to overcome current limitations and develop their communicative competence to the level of the teacher or an NS. CA offers a very different view of the nature of competence. Instead of working from the static assumption that competence is something that one has a fixed degree of at a point in time, CA provides a means of exploring the variable ways in which such competence is coconstructed in particular contexts by the participants involved. So CA studies such as Bloch (in press), Goodwin et al. (2002), and Carroll (in press) portray how interactants with minimal linguistic resources can nonetheless employ these resources skillfully and innovatively in interaction.

AL is inherently multidisciplinary and does not have a single research paradigm to which all AL research should conform. From the AL perspective, then, CA is one methodology in its array of methodologies which may be brought to bear on problems or issues relating to naturally occurring spoken language. CA, for its part, is increasing its interest in applications (Heritage, 1999). The foregoing review of the latest research demonstrates that there are no major, insurmountable incompatibilities between CA and AL and that there are many possibilities for fruitful future collaboration.

6.2 Conversation Analysis and Second Language Acquisition

The late 1990s saw a CA-motivated debate on a proposed "reconceptualization" of SLA (Firth & Wagner, 1997, 1998; Gass, 1998; Kasper, 1997; Long, 1997; Markee, 2000, 2002; Van Lier, 2000). Kasper's (1997) reply to CA practitioners Firth and Wagner (1997) noted that they did not, in their article, provide any specific proposals about how level of discourse may be incorporated into SLA. In this section, therefore, I will be as specific as possible about the contribution which CA can make to SLA.

Since SLA is a broad area, we should first clarify that CA's only possible contribution would be to those areas of SLA which use spoken interaction (both inside and outside the classroom) as data. Some of the criticisms which Firth and Wagner (1997, 1998) have made of SLA are as follows:

- SLA has neglected the social and contextual aspects of language use and their contribution to SLA processes.
- SLA is becoming a "hermetically sealed area of study" (1998, p. 92) which is losing contact with sociology, sociolinguistics, and DA in favor of a psycholinguistic focus on the cognition of the individual.
- There is an etic rather than emic approach to fundamental concepts.
- The traditional SLA database is too narrow.

Essentially the call is for a holistic approach which includes the social dimension and emic perspectives. Since Firth and Wagner's (1997) article, a number of studies have been published which do incorporate social and contextual dimensions (e.g., Hall & Verplaetse, 2000; Lantolf, 2000; Ohta, 2001) and have established a sociocultural school within SLA. So I should note at the start of this section that (in contrast to the situation with AL) there has been controversy concerning whether CA has any role in SLA at all, and if it does, what that role should be. In order to exemplify the contribution which CA might be able to make to the project of SLA, I will focus on two areas of strong recent interest in SLA research involving classroom discourse: recasts and FFI.

6.3 Recasts

In this section we will focus on SLA research on recasts[3] as an example of SLA work on repair, which is of course an area of potentially significant collaboration between CA and SLA (Markee, 2000). First of all, we need to explicate the CA position on cognition and learning by analyzing interaction involving recasts. I argued in Chapter 1 that the linguistic version of CA has become widespread among linguists. This underpowered version is certainly unable to portray the level of socially distributed cognition or learning, by contrast to ethnomethodological CA, as we will see below. It is therefore understandable that SLA has sometimes dismissed the possibility of CA's having anything to contribute to the study of cognition or learning and hence SLA (e.g., Kasper, 1997; Long, 1997). To practitioners of the ethnomethodological version, however, CA involves the explication of the organization of socially distributed cognition (Drew, 1995; Schegloff, 1991). The organizations of sequence, turn taking, preference, and repair are employed by interactants in order to display to one another not only their social actions, but also their understandings of the other's social actions; these organizations constitute part of the architecture of intersubjectivity.

Since this may sound abstract, I will illustrate how this is operationalized in the L2 classroom by examining Extract 6.3:

(6.3)

1 T: Vin, have you ever been to the movies? what's your favorite movie?
2 L: big.
3 T: big, OK, that's a good movie, that was about a little boy inside a big man, wasn't it?
4 L: yeah, boy get surprise all the time.
5 T: yes, he was surprised, wasn't he? usually little boys don't do the things that men do, do they?
6 L: no, little boy no drink.
7 T: that's right, little boys don't drink.

(Johnson, 1995, p. 23)

As there is a full analysis of this extract in Section 2.1, I will focus here on Lines 4 and 5 only. In Line 4, L displays an understanding of T's turn in Line 3. How do we know what the understanding is which L has displayed in Line 4? We know this by normative reference to the interactional organization. There are two pieces of interactional evidence. The first is the kind of action which L's turn performs: L confirms T's summary of the subtopic and contributes new information which develops the subtopic (the film's plot) and exemplifies what happened in the film's plot ("boy get surprise all the time"). The second piece of evidence is that T's turn in Line 5 confirms that L's turn displays a correct understanding of T's turn in Line 3. So we know what understanding L has displayed in Line 4 by reference to the turn-taking system, a turn having been specifically allocated to L by the tag question in Line 3, and by reference to sequence organization, which tells us that Line 4 is an answer to a question about the plot of the film. In interactional sequences, then, evidence in relation to socially distributed cognition is available and piles up, layer upon layer. The utterance in Line 4 is linguistically incorrect, although we can see that the propositional content is clear to T, since T's turn in Line 5 displays understanding of the content of L's turn in Line 4. T displays understanding by positively evaluating the propositional content of the learner utterance followed by an expansion of the learner utterance into a correct sequence of linguistic forms, using embedded correction in the context of an action of agreement and confirmation. We should also note that T's embedded correction in Line 5 also corresponds to Long, Inagaki, and Ortega's (1998) definition of recast as quoted later in this section.

It should be made quite explicit at this point that CA does not claim to be able to establish the cognitive state of individuals in isolation. What it is able to portray and explicate, however, is the progress of intersubjectivity or socially distributed cognition. CA aims to "identify ways in which participants themselves orient to, display, and make sense of one another's cognitive states (among other things)" (Drew, 1995, p. 79). The point is, then, that the interactants in Extract 6.3 are displaying to each other (and to the rest of the class and to the analyst) their understanding of each other's utterances by means of and by reference to the organization of turn taking, sequence, and repair. This demonstrates what Schegloff (1991) means by "the embeddedness, the inextricable intertwinedness, of cognition and interaction" (p. 152). The CA of Extract 6.3 demonstrates not only what understandings the interactants display to each other, but also how they do so by normative reference to inter-actional organizations. In other words, we gain access to their displays of understanding to each other in the same way that they gain this access: by reference to the interactional organizations. This is what is meant by developing an emic perspective. Psychology, SLA, and CA do not have any means of establishing a direct window into an individual's cognitive state while he or she is engaged in L2 classroom interaction.

We do need to try to conceptualize what this might mean in practice, though: What factors are involved in an individual's cognitive state in such a stream of interaction? Looking at Line 4 of Extract 6.3, L is not merely producing an utterance in the L2; any utterance is a document on many levels, and we saw in Section 2.1 that L2 classroom interaction in particular operates on a number of levels simultaneously. An utterance is a display of the learner's analysis of the prior utterance of an interactant, it performs a social action in response, and it positions the learner in a social system. It displays an understanding of the current context (sequential, social, and L2 classroom context) and also renews it. It documents the learner's cognitive, emotional, and attitudinal states: Note that this does not mean it provides a direct window into these states. In the specific case of the L2 classroom, a learner's utterance may in addition be delivered in the L2 and may thereby document his or her actual developmental level as well.

So we can see that a part of what is meant by the cognitive state of a learner involved in L2 classroom interaction is inextricably entwined and engaged with the unique sequential, social, and contextual environment in which he or she is engaged. It is argued that this part of the individual's cognitive state can be portrayed emically in situ, that is, in that unique sequential environment. This is not to suggest that this provides anything like the whole picture, or that the methods employed by SLA and psychology are not useful in portraying other aspects of the full picture in relation to cognition. The point to be made, however, is that CA is able to make a major contribution to the SLA project in terms of the portrayal of socially distributed cognition (Markee, 2000, p. 3).

Ohta (2001) demonstrates how socially distributed cognition can work in the L2 classroom. Recasts are not necessarily just responses by the teacher to one learner. Ohta shows (by recording and transcribing the private talk of individually microphoned students in a classroom) that other students can use recasts in which they are not personally involved as negative evidence and display uptake in their private talk. Moving the focus back to the general relationship between cognition and interaction, Schegloff (1991) suggests that "the structures of interaction penetrate into the very warp" (p. 154) of cognition, so that, for example, an "understanding-display" device (i.e., the next-turn proof procedure) is built into the organization of turn taking and sequence. In the same way, if we wish to fully understand the processes of cognition in relation to instructed SLA, it is vital to understand how L2 classroom interaction is organized.

6.3.1 Learning

We will now attempt a CA of learning in relation to Extract 6.3 in three stages. First, what can we say about the learner's actual developmental level or current ability in L2? We can note in Lines 4 and 6 that his grammatical resources are fairly limited. Nonetheless, the learner is able to make use of these limited resources to nominate a subtopic (Line 2) and develop the subtopic by exemplifying T's comments (Lines 4 and 6). Although it can be challenging for children to interact with the teacher in a classroom setting, even in the L1, we can see that L is able to use the turn-taking and sequence organization of the L2 proficiently, producing a correct response to a negative tag question (Line 4) and a positive tag question (Line 6). As we saw in Section 2.1, T's turn in Line 5 operates on a number of levels. From the learner's perspective, it is not just a matter of understanding the propositional content of what T says in the L2; it is also a matter of analyzing what social and sequential action T is performing and what an appropriate social and sequential action in response would be. So we can see that L skillfully manages to coconstruct meaning with T in the L2 from his limited grammatical resources.

Secondly, what can we say as a result of the interaction about the learning environment in terms of input to the language learning process and facilitation of upgrading? Line 5 reads: "Yes, he was surprised, wasn't he?" We will break its contribution down into four points:

> 1. First, the utterance places the sequence within the teacher's overall pedagogical plan for the lesson, which was "to allow the students to share their ideas and possibly generate some new vocabulary words within the context of the discussion" (Johnson 1995, p. 23).

2. Secondly, it may promote positive affect and motivation in that the teacher engages with the ideas and personal meanings which the learner chooses to share and produces a conversational action of agreement which validates the utterance. It then demonstrates confidence in the learner by returning the floor to him with the tag question.

3. Thirdly, it makes it possible for the other learners in the class to follow the topic of the interaction and to receive correctly formed linguistic input. There is no evidence in the transcripts as to whether the other learners have done so or not. However, Ohta (2001) shows (by recording and transcribing the private talk of individually microphoned students in a classroom) that students are capable of using recasts in which they are not personally involved as negative evidence and of displaying uptake in their private talk.

4. Fourthly, and most importantly, there is positive evaluation of the propositional content of the learner utterance followed by an expansion of the learner utterance into a correct sequence of linguistic forms or embedded correction.

In terms of input, the teacher provides a corrected version of the learner's turns in Lines 4 and 6 while retaining a focus on meaning. This form of correction and expansion is highly reminiscent of adult-child conversation (see, for example, adult-child conversation transcripts in Peccei, 1994, p. 83, and Painter, 1989, p. 38). The technique being used by the teacher here is often termed scaffolding (Johnson, 1995, p. 75). Ohta (2001) defines Vygotsky's zone of proximal development (ZPD) in relation to SLA in the following terms: "For the L2 learner, the ZPD is the distance between the actual developmental level as determined by individual linguistic production, and the level of potential development as determined through language produced collaboratively with a teacher or peer" (p. 9).

What we can see in this extract, then, is how a ZPD is talked into being through the organization of the interaction.

Specifically, we see a neat juxtaposition of the learner's actual developmental level in Lines 4 and 6 with the potential level in Lines 5 and 7, where the learner's erroneous utterances have been upgraded by the teacher. The SLA literature terms this action a recast, and the action conforms to Long et al.'s (1998) definition of recasts quoted later in the section. So from the perspectives of SLA psycholinguistic theory, L1 acquisition studies, and Vygotskyan social constructivist educational theory, there is agreement that such upgrading sequences are beneficial. A CA demonstrates the same point. The distinctive CA contribution is to show how learning is constructed by the use of interactional resources and to explicate the progress of learning and socially distributed cognition or intersubjectivity. From a broader perspective, CA is able to explicate the reflexive relationship between pedagogy and interaction and hence how learning takes place through the interaction; the monograph as a whole demonstrates this point.

Thirdly, how does the process of instructed L2 learning progress? As we saw in Chapter 5, the canonical way in which an L2 lesson progresses is that the L2 teacher introduces a pedagogical focus and the learners produce specific linguistic forms and patterns of interaction in the L2 in normative orientation to the pedagogical focus. The teacher then evaluates the learners' turns and moves the lesson in a particular direction on the basis of that evaluation. So in Extract 6.3, we can see that the teacher analyzes the learner's contribution positively and continues to promote the learner's nominated topic. The point is, then, that we as analysts have access to the same interactional evidence of a learner's learning states as the teacher has[4] as well as access to the steps the teacher takes in reaction to such evidence. In other words, we have access to the same emic perspective of the learning process in interaction to which the teacher has access. This type of evidence of learning may complement the evidence of learning gathered through mainstream SLA studies. Schegloff (1991) demonstrated that CA gives access to socially distributed cognition. In the same way, CA gives access to socially distributed language learning processes. As with cognition, this is only one part of the whole picture, but a useful one nevertheless.

We now move on to consider the SLA treatment of recasts. The quantitative machinery which is often employed in mainstream SLA studies is certainly robust and well-established in terms of validity and reliability in a quantitative paradigm, and Long (1997) is right to emphasize the importance of construct validity for quantitative SLA. However, all quantitative practitioners agree that the quality of quantitative output crucially depends on the quality of the data which are fed in. Serious problems can and do arise when discoursal data are fed into quantitative machinery without prior qualitative analysis. As the foregoing analyses of Extract 6.3 have demonstrated, any turn at talk in the L2 classroom is inextricably entwined in a complex web of sequence, social action, pedagogy, context, socially distributed cognition, and learning. As I demonstrated in Chapter 5, any turn at talk in the L2 classroom has a complex personality and displays simultaneous homogeneity and heterogeneity.

The point to be made here is that it is invalid to homogenize discoursal data by inputting it into quantitative machinery without first having conducted a case-by-case holistic and emic analysis. This is hardly a new observation; as long ago as 1988, van Lier (1988a) wrote that he had "consistently warned against studies which isolate superficially identifiable features for quantitative treatment" (p. 223; see also Schegloff, 1993). Judging by the number of subsequent SLA studies which have done just that, however, his warnings appear not to have been taken seriously at all.

In view of this, and because it is probably impossible to explicate in the abstract the grave threat to the validity of the quantitative process of inputting unanalyzed discoursal data, it will be necessary to demonstrate this point by examining what I take to be a representative example of quantitative mainstream SLA work in the area of recasts, namely Long et al. (1998). This study has been widely cited (e.g., Doughty & Williams, 1998; Ellis, 2001) as evidence of the effectiveness of recasts. I have also selected this study because, unusually for a mainstream SLA study, it contains transcripts of the task-in-process, which can then be compared with the task-as-workplan. In Long et al.'s quantitative laboratory study, learners of Japanese and Spanish were supposed to receive either recasts or modeling in relation to two new structures, with a posttest revealing that recasts produced more short-term improvement than modeling. According to Long et al. (p. 366),

> Extracts 6.4 and 6.5 exemplify use of the target structures in the recast condition:
>
> (6.4)
>
> Prompt: *A veces*
> (Sometimes)
> Participant: *Elena toma a veces cafe*
> (Elena drinks sometimes coffee)
> Researcher: *Elena toma a veces cafe, si? uhuh*
> (Elena drinks sometimes coffee, right? uhuh)
>
> (6.5)
>
> Prompt: *La guitarra*
> (The guitar)
> Participant: *Pedro tiene la guitarra*
> (Pedro has the guitar)
> Researcher: *La guitarra la tiene Pedro, si? uhuh*
> (The guitar it has Pedro, right? uhuh)

If we analyze the data closely, however, we can see that there are four fundamental problems in terms of construct validity in a quantitative paradigm. First, neither extract is a corrective recast. In both extracts the participant produces a sentence which is morphosyntactically correct, therefore the researcher's subsequent turn cannot possibly be a corrective recast,[5] according to the definition provided by Long et al. in the same article:[6]

> Corrective recasts are responses which, although communicatively oriented and focused on meaning rather than form, incidentally reformulate all or part of a learner's utterance, thus providing relevant morphosyntactic information that was obligatory but was either missing or wrongly supplied, in the learner's rendition, while retaining its central meaning. (p. 358)

We must also question in what way the researcher's turns could possibly be construed as "incidental" and "focused on meaning rather than form." (See the fourth point in this discussion.)

Secondly, the researcher's turns in the two extracts are clearly rather different or heterogeneous as actions. In Extract 6.4, the researcher repeats the participant's turn verbatim, whereas in 6.5 she alters the syntactical structure. However, the two different sequences are homogenized as recasts in the quantitative data treatment. Indeed, in order for SLA to quantify interactional phenomena, it must treat them as if they are homogeneous. These two extracts are presented by Long et al. as typical, and no evidence is presented as to the degree of homogeneity or heterogeneity of the discourse produced by the other 28 participants in the Spanish experiment.

The third problem is that discussed by Nicholas, Lightbown, and Spada (2001): whether learners are able to recognize recasts as corrective feedback, since their corrective nature may be "carefully masked by the teacher" (p. 740; see also Ellis, Basturkmen, & Loewen, 2002, p. 423). Although the researcher repeats the participant's turn verbatim in Extract 6.4 and modifies the syntactical structure in 6.5, the ends of both turns are designed in exactly the same way, namely, "si? uhuh." From the participant's perspective, then, the researcher's identical recipient design may make it very difficult to know whether or not a morphosyntactic correction is intended. So there is homogeneity in terms of the recipient design at the same time as there is heterogeneity in terms of the actions.

Fourthly, there is a major mismatch between intended and actual pedagogy, between task-as-workplan and task-in-process. We can see from Long et al's (1998) definition that the researcher's action is supposed to be "communicatively oriented and focused on meaning." Long et al. (1998) describe the intended pedagogical approach as "communication tasks" (p. 365) and "communicative" (p. 368). However, when we examine the extracts, what we actually find is a prerecorded prompt for the participants to produce a precise string of linguistic forms which is then evaluated for syntactic accuracy by the researcher. In the reference system which I have used in this monograph, this is an example of a form-and-accuracy context, and in language-teaching parlance, it is a structural drill. Extract 6.6, by contrast, contains two examples of recasts which do conform to Long et al.'s definition; by comparing these to the two extracts from Long et al., we can see just how dissimilar the sequential environments are:

(6.6)

```
1    T: Vin, have you ever been to the movies? what's your favorite movie?
2    L: big.
3    T: big, OK, that's a good movie, that was about a little boy inside a big man,
        wasn't it?
4    L: yeah, boy get surprise all the time.
5→   T: yes, he was surprised, wasn't he? usually little boys don't do the things
        that men do, do they?
6    L: no, little boy no drink.
7→   T: that's right, little boys don't drink.
```

(Johnson, 1995, p. 23)

My argument is that such mismatches are virtually inevitable if there is an etic, top-down specification of pedagogy (task-as-workplan) with no corresponding emic, case-by-case analysis of the discoursal data (task-in-process) before quantitative treatment. It is normal practice in SLA studies using interactional data to find a concept or construct specified in terms of task-as-workplan but data that are actually gathered from the task-in-process, which may be (as in this case) rather different. Often any possible mismatches between the two are not "visible," as most studies do not actually publish examples of their raw interactional data, Long et al.'s study being an exception.

The purpose of the preceding discussion is not to challenge the overall validity of Long's considerable work or of the use of quantification in SLA in general. CA does not seek to prohibit quantification—it is *premature quantification* of discoursal data without prior analysis which it seeks to discourage, or as Schegloff (1993) puts it, "we need to know what the phenomena are, how they are organized, and how they are related to each

other as a precondition for cogently bringing methods of quantitative analysis to bear on them" (p. 114). The intention of the
preceding discussion is to propose that if SLA wishes to use
naturally occurring discourse as data for quantification and to
ensure the construct validity of the data obtained through the
research process, then it will need to separate that process into
two stages and to change its focus of analysis from the task-as-
workplan to the task-in-process. The first stage in the research
process would involve the following:

1. Conducting an emic, holistic analysis of each extract as an
instance of discourse in its own right.

2. Adopting qualitative, emic concepts of validity, reliability,
epistemology, and so on in relation to the discourse which it
uses for input which are different to and separate from those
which it uses for the quantification stage. These concepts are
outlined in Section 6.5.

3. Generating any definitions used in a study (including that
of the "task") inductively, bottom-up from the data (in other
words, a shift to the task-in-process).

4. Adopting a perspective on the homogeneity and heterogeneity of discourse which at present it lacks, together with a
model and methodology for analyzing these. We saw in the
foregoing discussion of Long et al.'s (1998) data that it is
possible to explicate the degree and type of homogeneity
and heterogeneity in discourse.

5. Adopting a perspective on socially shared cognition and
learning.

In the second stage of the research process, the analyzed
interactional data (e.g., recasts) could be used for quantitative
treatment with their construct validity assured. CA is able to
provide all that is necessary for the first stage of the process, so
there is a clear role or vacant slot which CA can play in that
part of the SLA project which relates to interaction. Such a

preliminary stage is particularly necessary with phenomena like recasts, which according to Long et al.'s (1998) definition occur incidentally as and when errors occur. Recasts which occur incidentally in the classroom are therefore bound to be unique and heterogeneous and would certainly have to be analyzed as individual instances before quantification.

6.4 Focus-on-Form Instruction[7]

Recent work on FFI[8] in SLA (e.g., Doughty & Williams, 1998; Ellis, 2001) provides a good example of a possibility for future collaboration between CA and SLA. The argument which will again be developed is that there is a vacant slot in the FFI project which CA is able to fill.

FFI adheres to the concept of differentiation in classroom activities, as is evident from Doughty and Williams's (1998), Ellis's (2001), and Long and Robinson's (1998) taxonomies or categorizations of different kinds of pedagogical activities. However, there is a major conceptual problem inherent in the literature on focus on form: Whose focus is it? Is it the researcher's etic focus, the etic focus of the teacher's task-as-workplan, or the learner's emic focus? As Ellis points out,

> Conceptualizing FFI in terms of types and options is not unproblematic. The three types of FFI rest on the distinction between focus on form and focus on meaning. The question arises as to how this focus is to be determined. Whose perspective is to be considered? Is the focus to be determined in terms of the researcher's or teacher's intention or in terms of particular learners' response to instruction?...Classroom learners may or may not respond in the way intended. (p. 26)

Looking at the FFI literature, it seems quite clear that the SLA view is that it should be the learner's perspective which is the vital one. Long's (1996) definition of focus on form is that learners "attend to language as object during a generally meaning-oriented activity," and he notes that "learners need to attend to a task if acquisition is to occur, but...their orientation can best be to both form and meaning, not to either form or meaning alone" (p. 429). According to Doughty (2001), "the factor that distinguishes focus on form from other pedagogical approaches is the requirement that focus on form involves learners' briefly and perhaps simultaneously attending to form, meaning and use during one cognitive event" (p. 211).

Nowhere in the FFI literature, however, do we find any description of the methodology which SLA researchers are to use in order to identify what the learners' focus is on during a lesson. In order to identify the learners' focus, researchers would have to analyze the classroom discourse and develop an emic perspective in order to ascertain what the learners are focusing on. However, FFI has derived its typology of pedagogical activities in a top-down, etic way from theory and pedagogy (Ellis, 2001) rather than in a bottom-up, emic way from interactional data. In other words, FFI has been conceptualized in terms of task-as-workplan (before classroom implementation) rather than task-in-process (what actually happens in the classroom). As we saw in the foregoing extracts dealing with recasts (and as all classroom teachers know), there can be quite a gulf between the two.

There is also now ample evidence in the literature (Coughlan & Duff, 1994; Donato, 2000; Foster, 1998; Mori, 2002; Ohta, 2000) of tasks-as-workplan resulting in different and unexpected tasks-in-process. For example, the FFI literature assumes from an etic theoretical perspective (task-as-workplan) that tasks promote a focus on meaning (Ellis, 2003, p. 3). However, when we look at the interactional evidence in the classroom from the learners' emic perspective (task-in-process), the picture may be very different. Tasks may in some cases promote a focus on meaning, but as we saw in Section 3.3, learners may document a focus on the accomplishment of the task itself rather than on form or meaning. Alternatively, learners may go completely off-task (Seedhouse, 1996; Markee, in press).

The only way to establish what learners actually focus on during a task is through a detailed, case-by-case, emic analysis of the entire interactional data for the whole task. Determining the perspectives of others is a fundamentally constructionist or phenomenologist undertaking belonging to the qualitative paradigm (Bryman, p. 2001, p. 20). The point to be made here, then, is that the TBL/SLA project crucially requires an emic methodology to analyze task-in-process and to ascertain the focus of participants but has as yet not adopted such a methodology. It would not be sufficient to "sample" task-based interaction. As we have seen throughout this monograph, the focus of L2 classroom interaction can shift instantaneously (see also Sullivan, 2000). The only way in which mismatches between talk-as-workplan and task-in-progress can be avoided is to work inductively from the data with an emic perspective to describe interactions which are actually produced in the language classroom and the learners' focus during those interactions. From that starting point it is then possible to construct theoretical or pedagogical categories which correspond to the data, and any quantitative treatment will have a firm basis and a correspondence between theory and practice, between task-as-workplan and task-in-process.

Perhaps the major contribution which a CA methodology can make to the SLA project is to demonstrate that it is possible for SLA to shift its focus from the task-as-workplan to the task-in-process. In fact Ellis (2001) and Ellis, Basturkmen, and Loewen (2001) have already made a start on deriving some instructional categories in FFI from studies of classroom processes. Ellis (2001, p. 22), for example, derives the constructs *preemptive* and *reactive focus-on-form* inductively from classroom data. The threat to validity within a quantitative paradigm is too great for SLA to continue to derive constructs etically from the task-as-workplan and then to gather interactional data from a potentially very different task-in-process.

So in this section I have argued that CA is compatible with SLA and can contribute to its project. Following Kasper (1997) I have been very specific about the vacant slots in the area of discourse within the SLA project which CA can fill. CA can provide the first stage in a two-stage, multistrategy research (Bryman, 2001, p. 444) model. CA can contribute to SLA by providing:

1. A methodology for analyzing and ensuring the construct validity (in a quantitative paradigm) of discoursal data prior to quantification.

2. A methodology for deriving definitions and classifications inductively from discoursal data.

3. A methodology for portraying processes of socially shared cognition and learning.

4. A methodology for the analysis of L2 classroom discourse.

5. An emic methodology to determine learners' focus, which is vital for the FFI project.

6. A direct link to the social dimension. SLA has frequently been criticized (Firth & Wagner, 1997; Roberts, 2001, p. 110) for lack of engagement with sociology and sociolinguistics. CA is an interdisciplinary methodology par excellence and as such could ensure that SLA moves out of its allegedly hermetically sealed state and makes connections with other institutional settings.

7. A description of the interactional organization of L2 classroom discourse and a model for relating to one another the findings in regard to different subvarieties of interaction. It is argued that this is of direct relevance, as this level of organization mediates between pedagogy and learning and in effect transforms the task-as-workplan into the task-in-process. This aspect of the *CA-for-SLA* research agenda is proposed by Markee (2002):

> An important strand of future empirical work on the Interaction Hypothesis should specify in qualitative terms how many different classroom talks are attested in second and foreign language classrooms and provide detailed descriptions of how these speech exchange

systems are organized. Complementary experimental research should establish through factor analysis and other powerful inferential statistical techniques what contributions different classroom talks make to acquisition. (p. 11)

This monograph characterizes some L2 classroom contexts or classroom talks, and others are characterized in Seedhouse (1996).

Finally, it is suggested that some work in a future CA-for-SLA paradigm may (following Kasper, 2002) not be restricted to an agenda defined by existing SLA interests, but rather by unmotivated looking at the data as a discovery procedure and examining issues which emerge from the data. Examples of research focus which have emerged from looking at the data underlying this monograph are the identification of a dual focus on form and meaning (Seedhouse, 1997b) and teachers' reluctance to give unmitigated negative evaluation in form-and-accuracy contexts (Section 4.6).

6.5 Conversation Analysis as a Social Science Research Methodology

At this point I will attempt to position CA in relation to social science research methods and concepts such as validity, reliability, generalizability, epistemology, quantification, and triangulation. The aim of this section is to facilitate mutual understanding among the different paradigms in which CA, AL, and SLA operate. A number of points need to be made beforehand. First, qualitative researchers often object that the concepts of validity and reliability derive from quantitative approaches and sometimes propose that alternative criteria be applied to qualitative research; these issues are discussed by Bryman (2001, pp. 31–32). Secondly, as Peräkylä (1997) notes, "the specific techniques of securing reliability and validity in different types of qualitative research are not the same" (p. 216). Thirdly, the goal of developing an emic perspective on naturally occurring interaction means that CA has had to develop procedures which are sometimes rather different in many ways from those of mainstream research methodologies. Fourthly, Peräkylä notes that, until his own publication, there had been "no accessible discussions available on issues of validity and reliability in conversation analytic studies" (p. 202).

This does not mean that CA practitioners have not been interested in these issues. On the contrary, it may be argued that all CA work has been (on one level) an attempt at a process exposition of what exactly is involved in and meant by ensuring validity and reliability in the analysis of talk. This is clear from Sacks's (1992) aim to produce "methods [which] will be reproducible descriptions in the sense that any scientific description might be, such that the natural occurrences that we're describing can yield abstract or general phenomena which need not rely on statistical observability for their abstractness or generality" (vol. 1, p. 11). However, CA practitioners have often phrased the discussion in terms which are accessible only to other practitioners, with the unintended result that the CA perspective has often been misunderstood by social science and linguistics researchers. In any case, the point to be understood at the outset is that CA's aim to develop an emic perspective on talk means that many of its assumptions and practices will necessarily be radically different from research methodologies operating in an etic paradigm.

Peräkylä (1997, p. 206) identifies the key factors in relation to *reliability* in CA as the selection of what is recorded, the technical quality of recordings, and the adequacy of transcripts; ten Have (1999) provides a very detailed account of this area. However, another aspect of reliability is the question of whether the results of a study are repeatable or replicable (Bryman, 2001, p. 29), and the way CA studies present their data is of crucial significance here. Many research methodologies do not require presentation of the primary data on which a study is based in publications about that study, and hence the reliability of major sections of the analyses of that data is not available for scrutiny. By contrast, it is standard practice for CA studies to include transcripts of the data they employ and increasingly to make audio and video files available electronically via the Web. Furthermore, the conversation analyst makes the process of analysis transparent for readers. This enables readers to analyze the data themselves, to test the analytical procedures which the author has followed and the validity of his or her analysis and claims. In this way, conversation analyses are rendered repeatable and replicable to readers. Also, it is standard practice for CA practitioners to take their data and analyses to data workshops and to send their work to a number of other practitioners for comment before sending them for publication.

I will now consider four kinds of validity in relation to qualitative research: internal, external, ecological, and construct validity (Bryman, 2001, p. 30). *Internal validity* is concerned with the soundness, integrity, and credibility of findings. Do the data prove what the researcher says they prove, or are there alternative explanations? Many CA procedures which seem strange to nonpractitioners are based on a concern for ensuring internal validity while developing an emic perspective. In some research methodologies operating in an etic perspective, it is legitimate for the analyst to invoke concepts such as power and gender in relation to a particular extract without needing to demonstrate that the participants themselves are oriented to such concepts. However, the crucial point in developing an emic perspective is that it is the participants' perspective, rather than the analyst's. Conversation analysts know what the participants' perspective is, because the participants document their social actions to each other in the details of the interaction by normative reference to the interactional organization. We as analysts can access the emic perspective in the details of the interaction and by reference to the same organization. Clearly, the details of the interaction themselves provide the only justification for claiming to be able to develop an emic perspective. Therefore, CA practitioners cannot make any claims beyond what is demonstrated by interactional detail without destroying the emic perspective and hence the whole validity of the CA enterprise.

External validity is concerned with generalizability, or the extent to which findings can be generalized beyond a specific research context. A typical criticism of qualitative studies is that they are context-bound and therefore weak in terms of external validity. Peräkylä (1997) points out that generalizability in CA "is closely dependent on the type of conversation analytic research" (p. 214) being conducted. It is often not appreciated that CA studies of institutional discourse—the subject of this monograph—are often analyzing on the micro and macro level simultaneously. So by explicating the organization of the microinteraction in an institutional setting, CA studies may at the same time be providing a generalizable description of the interactional organization of the setting, because institutional interaction is seen as rationally organized in relation to the institutional goal (Levinson, 1992, p. 71).

For example, in the case of this monograph, CA has revealed the reflexive relationship between pedagogy and interaction to be a generalizable, indeed universal, feature of L2 classroom inter-action because it relates directly to the institutional goal, which is always the same wherever L2 classroom interaction is taking place. All CA studies in effect work on the particular and the general simultaneously. By analyzing individual instances of interaction, the machinery which produced these individual instances is revealed: "The point of working with actual occurrences, single instances, single events, is to see them as the products of a 'machinery'... to generate formal descriptions of social actions which preserve and display the features of the machinery which produced them" (Benson & Hughes, 1991, pp. 130–131).

Ecological validity is concerned with whether findings are applicable to people's everyday life; laboratory experiments in the social sciences can often be weak in terms of ecological validity. CA practitioners typically record naturally occurring talk in its authentic social setting. Furthermore, CA attempts to develop an emic, holistic perspective and to portray how interactants perform their social actions through talk by reference to the same interactional organizations which the interactants are using. Therefore CA studies tend to be exceptionally strong in comparison to studies employing other methodologies in terms of ecological validity. The current study, for example, is based on evidence of what teachers actually do in the classroom, rather than on pedagogical recommendations produced by theorists.

Construct validity is a vital concept in a positivistic, quantitative, etic paradigm, as we saw in Section 6.3. However, in an emic paradigm the question is: Whose construct is it? Typically, descriptivist linguists look for etically specifiable methods of description, so that an analyst can match surface linguistic features of an interaction to constructs and categories. In an emic perspective, however, we are looking for organization to which participants orient during interaction, which is not at all the same thing. The best example of this different orientation is the TCU, as we saw in Section 1.6.3. TCUs are only analyzable emically as social actions. They are quite heterogeneous in terms of linguistic form and do not correspond in any way to single linguistic categories. In whatever way they are packaged in terms of linguistic form, the point is that social actors are able to recognize them in interaction as complete social actions and hence are able to project when they are likely to end. The "construct" of the TCU, then, is an interactant's construct rather than an analyst's one, and it is not etically specifiable.

Lepper (2000, pp. 175–176) suggests that CA research should be accountable in two more ways above and beyond those normal in qualitative research. *Sequential accountability* means that a CA should provide a holistic account of the coherence of a particular text, and *distributional accountability* requires functional explanations as to why a particular phenomenon occurs in one discourse environment but not another.

In relation to *epistemology*, CA is based on ethnomethodology, whose fundamental principles are described in Chapter 1. Ethnomethodology can be located (M. Lynch, 2000) in a phenomenological paradigm, which considers it to be "the job of the social scientist to gain access to people's 'common-sense thinking' and hence to interpret their actions and their social world from their point of view" (Bryman, 2001, p. 14). Ethnomethodology's ontological position can be associated with constructionism or the belief that "social phenomena and their meanings are constantly being accomplished by social actors. It implies that social phenomena and categories are not only produced through social interaction but that they are in a constant state of revision" (Bryman, 2001, p. 18).

The short and simple way to present the CA attitude to *quantification* would be to state that CA is a qualitative methodology which tries to develop an emic perspective, so quantification is generally of peripheral interest to CA practitioners. However, given that one aim of this section is to develop mutual understanding between on the one hand linguists and SLA researchers (who often quantify interaction) and CA practitioners on the other, a more detailed explanation is necessary. In order to introduce the CA attitude to quantification we will examine Schegloff's (1968) study of sequencing in conversational openings.

Schegloff (1968) examined 500 instances of openings of telephone calls to a disaster (emergency) center of the American Red Cross. In examining the first instance he established a norm which worked perfectly for 499 of the calls, namely, that the answerer speaks first. The only deviant case was the following:

(6.7)

((Police makes call))
((Receiver is lifted and there is a 1.0 pause.))
Police: hello.
Other: American Red Cross.
Police: hello, this is Police Headquarters (.) er, Officer Stratton

(Schegloff, 1968, p. 1079)

Now in a quantitative paradigm one would simply say that a norm which worked for 99.8% of cases was an extremely good one and leave it at that. However, the CA approach is rather different, as it is trying to uncover the norms to which participants are orienting and the emic logic or rational basis for their actions. Deviant cases are particularly helpful in this regard and should be explored in detail. The deviant case here pushed Schegloff to a deeper analysis resulting in the identification of a summons-answer sequence which works for all 500 cases. The telephone ring functions as the summons, to which the overwhelming next action is a response by the receiver of the call. In the deviant case the response is not immediately provided, and therefore the caller repeats the summons, this time in verbal form. It should also be noted that the deviant-case analysis resulted in the formulation of a more elegant adjacency pair norm rather than a single-speaker norm.

This is also a good example of a CA account which is both particularized and generalized. The specific features of individual cases (particularly deviant cases) are investigated in depth and are used to build a general account of a phenomenon or interactional organization. It has often been mistakenly reported that quantification is prohibited in CA. However, informal or methodological quantification has been widely used from the beginnings of CA. Schegloff et al. (1977), for example, report self-correction as "vastly more common than other-correction" (p. 362). The classic statement of the CA position on quantification is Schegloff (1993), which warns specifically against premature quantification in relation to superficially identifiable interactional phenomena. In Section 6.3, we saw an example of this from the SLA literature. We can understand the organization of an interaction and its emic logic only through detailed analysis of individual instances, and premature quantification of superficially identifiable and decontextualized phenomena will tend to divert our attention from this. As Schegloff (1993) puts it, "quantification is no substitute for analysis" (p. 114). Nevertheless, Heritage (1999, p. 70) considers the likelihood that CA will become more quantitative during the next period of its development and cites three CA studies in which quantification has proved vital to establishing the nature of an interactional practice. There are, according to Heritage (1995, p. 404), a number of possible uses for statistics in CA:

- As a means of isolating interesting phenomena
- As a means of consolidating intuitions which are well defined, but in which the existence of a practice is difficult to establish without a large number of cases
- In cases in which independent findings about a conversational practice can have indirect statistical support
- In almost all cases in which a claim is made that the use or outcome of a particular interactional practice is tied to particular social or psychological categories, such as gender and status

Readers who have followed the argument thus far will have realized that, given the emic goal of CA, there is no substitute for detailed and in-depth analysis of individual sequences; interviews with participants, questionnaires, and so on are not able to provide this, which is why *triangulation* is not normally undertaken. "Experience shows that participants may not afterwards 'know' what they have been doing or why, and furthermore tend to justify their behavior in various ways.... CA CA tries to analyze conduct 'in its own setting'" (ten Have, 1999, p. 33). The aim, then, is to portray the emic orientations of participants in situ at a particular point in an interaction, rather than from outside the interactional sequence. However, as noted in Section 2.6, there is currently a movement to integrate CA and ethnography, the relationship being first CA, then ethnography. So CA and triangulation are generally compatible and may be mutually reinforcing, with the caveats just stated. It is not that any of these practices are off-limits to CA practitioners, but rather that they should be making it their priority to spend time on serious, detailed, and in-depth analysis.

Finally, I should make it quite clear that CA is not being presented as a methodology which could "revolutionize" AL or SLA. CA's scope is limited to the study of naturally occurring spoken interaction. I have been very specific about the areas in which CA can contribute to existing research agendas and processes. I have also been careful to reveal compatibilities with existing research methodologies and to demonstrate how CA can work with them on a multistrategy research agenda.

6.6 Chapter Summary

After discussing the relationship between CA and AL, I reviewed the latest CA research in the following AL areas: language-teaching task design; language-teaching materials design; language proficiency assessment design; disordered talk and speech therapy; professional discourse; CA in languages other than English; NS-NNS talk; bilingual and multilingual interaction; and grammar, pragmatics, and interaction. A common theme in the research is that competence is coconstructed by participants rather than being fixed and static. I then critiqued the current SLA research on recasts and FFI and suggested that there is a vacant slot in the SLA project which CA is able to fill. I specified the contributions which CA is able to make and demonstrated why it is necessary to subject interactional data to a qualitative, emic analysis prior to quantification. Finally I positioned CA in relation to social science research methods and concepts such as validity, reliability, generalizability, epistemology, quantification, and triangulation.

This chapter has tried to demonstrate that CA is not (as often assumed) incompatible with other approaches such as AL, SLA, critical discourse analysis, ethnography, and psychology, as well as with quantification and triangulation. The point (following Silverman, 1999) is that doing CA first provides a warrant for invoking the relevance of contextual factors and constructs, which is helpful to other methodologies. CA necessarily has a number of unusual characteristics precisely because it aims to develop an emic perspective. Nonetheless, we have seen that it has many features in common with mainstream qualitative social science research methodologies.

Notes

[1]Keith Richards contributed to the writing of this section.

[2]Dysarthria is a speech disorder that results from a weakness or lack of coordination of the speech muscles. Speech is slow, weak, imprecise, or uncoordinated. Dysarthria can affect both children and adults. It is often a symptom of a disease, such as cerebral palsy, Duchenne muscular dystrophy, myotonic dystrophy, or Bell palsy. In both adults and children, it can result from head injury.

[3]Ellis et al.'s (2002, p. 423) definition of recast is "a reformulation of either the whole or part of the student's utterance containing an error in such a way as to maintain the student's intended meaning."

[4]We do not have access, however, to all of the cues which the teacher uses, including nonverbal ones.

[5]Moreover, one of the aims of Long et al.'s study (pp. 358–359) is to investigate whether learners can use recasts as negative evidence. Clearly, negative evidence can be used by learners only in relation to grammatically incorrect sentences.

[6]Note also Ellis, Basturkmen, and Loewen's (2002, p. 423) definition of recast: "a reformulation of either the whole or part of the student's utterance containing an error in such a way as to maintain the student's intended meaning."

[7]Ellis, Basturkmen, and Loewen (2001) define focus on form as having the following five "criterial features":

1. It occurs in discourse that is primarily meaning-centered.
2. It is observable (i.e., occurs interactionally).
3. It is incidental (i.e., it is not preplanned).
4. It is transitory.
5. It is broadly focused (i.e., several different forms may be attended to in the context of a single lesson). (pp. 283–284)

[8]Focus-on-form instruction is abbreviated *FonF* in Doughty and Williams (1998).

CHAPTER SEVEN

Epilogue

The main thesis developed in this monograph has been the reflexive relationship between pedagogy and interaction in the L2 classroom. This relationship has been portrayed as the cornerstone of the context-free architecture of the L2 classroom, and we have seen extreme diversity in the context-sensitive way interactants orient to and employ this architecture. We noted in Chapter 1 that in the 1960s the dominant view in linguistics was the Chomskyan one that conversation was too disordered and degenerate to be studied; that viewpoint is no longer expressed nowadays. However, for many years researchers in the area of language learning have shied away from classroom interaction, regarding it as an excessively complex, heterogeneous, and "particularly messy" (van Lier, 1988a, p. 14) source of data. However, this monograph hopes to have demonstrated that, as with conversation, there is also order at all points in L2 classroom interaction. Following the notion of complementarity, the interaction simultaneously displays simplicity and complexity, homogeneity and heterogeneity, "messiness" and rational design.

In an interview directed specifically to applied linguists (Wong & Olsher, 2000), Schegloff very strongly warns readers against "just reading" about CA and suggests that "it's not until our colleagues actually engage with materials, and try to make sense of them, and understand how they're orderly, how they are

organized" (p. 126) that they will actually achieve an understanding of what CA is about. The potential research agenda in
applying CA to AL and SLA is vast; the major areas are outlined
in Chapter 6. Beyond that specific agenda, however, CA methodology provides a basis for shifting the focus of both L2 pedagogy
and research from the task-as-workplan to the task-in-process,
from intended to actual pedagogy. Debates on the merits and
demerits of language-teaching approaches have generally
focused on the task-as-workplan. However, shifting the focus of
debate to the task-in-process in the classroom provides an
empirical basis for evaluating the effectiveness of teaching
approaches. CA is not a methodology which was designed to
analyze language teaching, and it is therefore neutral and dis-
interested with respect to the different approaches. However, it
can provide evidence, for any particular approach, as to how the
relationship between pedagogy and interaction evolves in the
classroom and how learning takes place (see Section 6.3.1) and
is hence able to provide a basis for evaluation.

Furthermore, learners and teachers document, through the
turns they produce in L2 classroom talk, a theory of language
learning. For example, through the interaction in Section 3.1,
the participants are talking into being an understanding that
languages are learned through a focus on form and accuracy.
The point is that classroom interaction gives us access to the emic
theories of language learning which are actually implemented
by participants in the classroom, and if we take these seriously
and compare them with the top-down, etic theories of learning
produced by theorists, we should have a better basis for reconciling
theory and practice.

In Chapter 6 I outlined how CA can contribute to the
research agendas of AL and SLA. I have presented CA research
into language learning and teaching as being complementary to
existing SLA approaches rather than in competition with them
and, in Section 6.4, I presented proposals for complementary or
multistrategy research. This monograph argues that L2 classroom interaction provides us with ready access to massive

amounts of data on the instructed L2 learning process. Learning is mediated through discourse, and the problem previously has been that we have not had available a model and methodology which has been able to portray how the learning process is accomplished through the discourse. It is hoped that CA will enable research to exploit this data source effectively in the future.

A persistent criticism of AL and SLA research by classroom language teachers has been that it has been top-down, driven by theory and concepts which may have little relevance to classroom practice. Furthermore, little attention or interest has been shown in what language teachers actually do, and classroom practice has not generated theory; in other words, there has been one-way traffic between theory and practice. However, as I argued in the previous paragraph, all L2 classroom interaction embodies a theory of language learning and is displayed as a text to be read. I hope that the model and methodology presented in this monograph will enable pedagogical theory to be generated inductively from interactional data and enable two-way traffic between theory and practice.

Throughout my career first as a classroom language teacher and now as an academic, it has been my constant belief that language teachers perform amazingly complex and demanding interactional and pedagogical work in the classroom, and I have attempted to portray this in the monograph. However, pedagogical and research literature has often conceptualized teachers as intermediaries or "transmitters" who should deliver the pedagogy devised by theorists to learners. Although, as we saw in Chapter 2, researchers have sometimes found teachers at fault for not delivering the results anticipated by the theory, the fault sometimes lies in the theory rather than in the teachers' practice. I hope that this situation will change and that the professional work of language teachers will become both an object of academic study and a source of theory generation.

APPENDIX ONE

Transcription Conventions

A full discussion of CA transcription notation is available in Atkinson and Heritage (1984). Punctuation marks are used to capture characteristics of speech delivery, *not* to mark grammatical units.

Those extracts for which the author had access to original audio- and/or videotapes have been transcribed according to this system. Other extracts are reproduced as they originally appeared with occasional modifications to achieve standardization.

[	Point of overlap onset
]	Point of overlap termination
=	(a) Turn continues below, at the next identical symbol
	(b) If inserted at the end of one speaker's turn and at the beginning of the next speaker's adjacent turn, indicates that there is no gap at all between the two turns
	(c) Indicates that there is no interval between adjacent utterances
(3.2)	Interval between utterances (in seconds)
(.)	Very short untimed pause
<u>word</u>	Speaker emphasis
e:r the:::	Lengthening of the preceding sound
—	Abrupt cutoff

267

?	Rising intonation, not necessarily a question
!	Animated or emphatic tone
,	Low-rising intonation, suggesting continuation
.	Falling (final) intonation
CAPITALS	Especially loud sounds relative to surrounding talk
° °	Utterances between degree signs are noticeably quieter than surrounding talk
↑ ↓	Marked shifts into higher or lower pitch in the utterance following the arrow
< >	Talk surrounded by angle brackets is produced slowly and deliberately (typical of teachers modeling forms)
> <	Talk surrounded by reversed angle brackets is produced more quickly than neighboring talk
( )	A stretch of unclear or unintelligible speech.
(guess)	Indicates the transcriber's doubt about a word
.hh	Speaker in-breath
hh	Speaker out-breath
→	Mark features of special interest

Additional Symbols

((T shows picture))	Nonverbal actions or editor's comments
ja ((tr.: yes))	Non-English words are italicized and are followed by an English translation in double parentheses
[gibee]	In the case of inaccurate pronunciation of an English word, an approximation of the sound is given in square brackets
[æ]	Phonetic transcriptions of sounds are given in square brackets
X___	The gaze of the speaker is marked above an utterance and that of the addressee below it. A line indicates that the party

marked is gazing toward the other;
absence indicates lack of gaze. Dots mark
the transition from nongaze to gaze,
and the point where the gaze reaches
the other is marked by X.

T:	Teacher
L:	Unidentified learner
L1:	Identified learner
LL:	Several or all learners simultaneously

APPENDIX TWO

Resources for Conversation Analysis Research in Applied Linguistics and Second Language Acquisition

In the discussion of database issues in chapter 2, I noted that because of the great variety of L2 classrooms, it is important for CA researchers in AL and SLA to have access to a large and varied classroom database. Fortunately, technology can facilitate this in some respects. It is becoming increasingly common for published research studies to include transcript data and for student theses and dissertations to include not only transcripts but also video or audio data. It is also now simple for researchers to pool data by e-mailing transcriptions, audio, and video data as attachments. Playback machines with foot pedals can help with transcription. Software is now becoming available which claims to transcribe speech and/or digitized audio and video files, but its suitability for CA research has not yet been evaluated. Web sites such as Childes (http://childes.psy.cmu.edu) demonstrate how data in transcript, video, and audio formats can be pooled to create a very large database as a resource for future research. Such a website for AL/SLA interactional data would be of great benefit.

Training in CA Methodology

In Chapter 1 we saw that it is quite common for linguists to acquire a "linguistic" version of CA which employs interactional organizations in isolation from the ethnomethodological principles. Chapter 1 concluded that this version is not capable of conducting conversation analyses of data correctly. It follows that, if CA is to be integrated into the projects of AL and SLA, it will be necessary for researchers in these areas to have access to proper training in CA. Markee (2000) suggests that "learning to become a skilled CA researcher minimally entails completing at least one year of course work in CA, ideally followed up by a continuing apprenticeship with an established CA practitioner" (p. 50). Fortunately, the number of universities offering modules and programs in CA is increasing, as is the number of introductory texts on CA (Hutchby & Wooffitt, 1998; Markee, 2000; ten Have, 1999). Ten Have's text includes training exercises.

A number of Web sites now have resources available for training. Ethno/CA News at http://www2.fmg.uva.nl/emca/ has details about courses, conferences, publications, and bibliographies as well as links to four e-mail discussion lists and downloads for characters used in transcripts. It also has links to an online CA tutorial, to software for transcription of video data, and to sample sound and video files and transcripts. Conversation Analysis.Net at http://www.conversation-analysis.net has extensive data corpora. The Childes Web site at http://childes.psy.cmu.edu has extensive procedures and tools for CA analysis along with an enormous database. Schegloff's home page at http://www.sscnet.ucla.edu/soc/faculty/schegloff/ has a transcription module, sound clips, and access to his classic publications.

References

Abdesslem, H. (1987). *An analysis of foreign language lesson discourse.* Unpublished doctoral dissertation, University of Sheffield, Sheffield, England.

Abdesslem, H. (1993). Analyzing foreign language lesson discourse. *International Review of Applied Linguistics, 31*(3), 221–235.

Allwright, R. (1980). Turns, topics and tasks: Patterns of participation in language learning and teaching. In D. Larsen-Freeman (Ed.), *Discourse analysis in second language research* (pp. 165–187). Rowley, MA: Newbury House.

Allwright, R. (1988). *Observation in the language classroom.* Harlow, England: Longman.

Arminen, I. (2000). On the context sensitivity of institutional interaction. *Discourse and Society, 11,* 435–458.

Atkinson, J., & Drew, P. (1979). *Order in court.* London: Macmillan.

Atkinson, J., & Heritage, J. (Eds.). (1984). *Structures of social action.* Cambridge, England: Cambridge University Press.

Auer, P. (1988). A conversational analytic approach to code-switching and transfer. In M. Heller (Ed.), *Codeswitching: Anthropological and sociolinguistic perspectives* (pp. 187–213). Berlin: Mouton de Gruyter.

Auer, P. (1995). Ethnographic methods in the analysis of oral communication. In U. Quasthoff (Ed.), *Aspects of oral communication* (pp. 419–440). Berlin: De Gruyter.

Auer, P. (Ed.). (1998). *Code-switching in conversation.* London: Routledge.

Banbrook, L., & Skehan, P. (1989). Classrooms and display questions. In C. Brumfit & R. Mitchell (Eds.), *Research in the language classroom* (pp. 141–151). London: Modern English Publications and the British Council.

Barnes, D., Britton, J., & Torbe, M. (1990). *Language, the learner and the school.* Portsmouth, NH: Boynton/Cook–Heinemann.

Benson, D., & Hughes, J. (1991). Method: Evidence and inference— Evidence and inference for ethnomethodology. In G. Button (Ed.), *Ethnomethodology and the human sciences* (pp. 109–136). Cambridge, England: Cambridge University Press.

273

Bergmann, J. (1992). Veiled morality: Notes on discretion in psychiatry. In P. Drew & J. Heritage (Eds.), *Talk at work: Interaction in institutional settings* (pp. 137–162). Cambridge, England: Cambridge University Press.

Bloch, S. (in press). Co-constructing meaning in speech-impaired conversation. In K. Richards and P. Seedhouse (Eds.), *Applying conversation analysis*. Basingstoke, England: Palgrave Macmillan.

Boden, D. (1994). *The business of talk: Organizations in action*. Cambridge, England: Polity Press.

Boyle, R. (1997). Getting along with others: An examination of the ethnomethodological roots of preference organisation and its relationship to complimenting. Unpublished doctoral dissertation, University of Aston, Aston, England.

Boyle, R. (2000a). Whatever happened to preference organisation? *Journal of Pragmatics*, *32*, 583–604.

Boyle, R. (2000b). "You've worked with Elizabeth Taylor!": Phatic functions and implicit compliments. *Applied Linguistics*, *21*(1), 26–46.

Breen, M. (1989). The evaluation cycle for language learning tasks. In R. K. Johnson (Ed.), *The second language curriculum* (pp. 187–206). Cambridge, England: Cambridge University Press.

British Council. (1985). *Teaching and learning in focus. Edited lessons* (Vols. 1–4). London: Author.

Brock, C. (1986). The effects of referential questions on ESL classroom discourse. *TESOL Quarterly*, *20*(1), 47–57.

Brown, P., & Levinson, S. (1987). *Politeness*. Cambridge, England: Cambridge University Press.

Brouwer, C. (2004). Doing pronunciation: A specific type of repair sequence. In R. Gardner & J. Wagner (Eds.), *Second language talk* (pp. 148–178). London: Continuum.

Bryman, A. (2001). *Social research methods*. Oxford, England: Oxford University Press.

Burns, A. (2001). Analysing spoken discourse. In A. Burns & C. Coffin (Eds.), *Analysing English in a global context* (pp. 123–148). London: Routledge.

Bygate, M. (1988). Units of oral expression and language learning in small group interaction. *Applied Linguistics*, *9*(1), 59–82.

Byrne, P., & Long, B. (1976). *Doctors talking to patients*. London: Her Majesty's Stationery Office.

Cameron, D. (2001). *Working with spoken discourse*. London: Sage.

Carroll, D. (2000). Precision timing in novice-to-novice L2 conversations. *Issues in Applied Linguistics*, *11*(1), 67–110.

Carroll, D. (2004). Restarts in novice turn-beginnings: Disfluencies or interactional achievements? In R. Gardner & J. Wagner (Eds.), *Second language talk* (pp. 318–345). London: Continuum.

Carroll, D. (in press). Vowel-marking as an interactional resource in Japanese novice ESL conversation. In K. Richards and P. Seedhouse (Eds.), *Applying conversation analysis*. Basingstoke, England: Palgrave Macmillan.

Chaudron, C. (1988). *Second language classrooms: Research on teaching and learning*. Cambridge, England: Cambridge University Press.

Clayman, S., & Heritage, J. 2002. *The news interview: Journalists and public figures on the air*. Cambridge, England: Cambridge University Press.

Clift, R. (2001). Meaning in interaction: The case of "actually." *Language*, 77(2), 245–291.

Conze, E. (Ed.). (1959). *Buddhist scriptures*. Harmondsworth, England: Penguin.

Cook, G. (1989). *Discourse*. Oxford, England: Oxford University Press.

Coughlan, P., & Duff, P. (1994). Same task, different activities: Analysis of a second language acquisition task from an activity theory perspective. In J. P. Lantolf & G. Appel (Eds.), *Vygotskian approaches to second language research* (pp. 173–194). Norwood, NJ: Ablex Press.

Davidson, J. (1984). Subsequent versions of invitations, offers, requests, and proposals dealing with potential and actual rejection. In J. Atkinson & J. Heritage (Eds.), *Structures of social action* (pp. 102–128). Cambridge, England: Cambridge University Press.

Dinsmore, D. (1985). Waiting for Godot in the EFL classroom. *ELT Journal*, *39*, 225–234.

Donato, R. (2000). Sociocultural contributions to understanding the foreign and second language classroom. In J. Lantolf (Ed.), *Sociocultural theory and second language learning* (pp. 27–50). Oxford, England: Oxford University Press.

Doughty, C. (2001). Cognitive underpinnings of focus on form. In P. Robinson (Ed.), *Cognition and second language instruction* (pp. 206–257). Cambridge, England: Cambridge University Press.

Doughty, C., & Williams, J. (1998). Pedagogical choices in focus on form. In C. Doughty & J. Williams (Eds.), *Focus on form in classroom second language acquisition* (pp. 197–261). Cambridge, England: Cambridge University Press.

Drew, P. (1987). Po-faced receipts of teases. *Linguistics*, *25*, 219–253.

Drew, P. (1992). Contested evidence in courtroom cross-examination: The case of a trial for rape. In P. Drew & J. Heritage (Eds.), *Talk at work: Interaction in institutional settings* (pp. 470–520). Cambridge, England: Cambridge University Press.

Drew, P. (1994). Conversation analysis. In R. E. Asher (Ed.), *The encyclopedia of language and linguistics* (pp. 749–754). Oxford: Pergamon.

Drew, P. (1995). Conversation analysis. In J. Smith, R. Harré, L. van Langenhove, & P. Stearns (Eds.), *Rethinking methods in psychology* (pp. 64–79). London: Sage.

Drew, P. (1997). "Open" class repair initiators in response to sequential sources of trouble in conversation. *Journal of Pragmatics*, *28*, 69–101.

Drew, P. (in press). The contribution of conversation analysis to applied linguistics. In K. Richards and P. Seedhouse (Eds.), *Applying conversation analysis*. Basingstoke, England: Palgrave Macmillan.

Drew, P., & Heritage, J. (Eds.). (1992a). *Talk at work: Interaction in institutional settings*. Cambridge, England: Cambridge University Press.

Drew, P., & Heritage, J. (1992b). Analyzing talk at work: An introduction. In P. Drew & J. Heritage (Eds.), *Talk at work: Interaction in institutional settings* (pp. 3–65). Cambridge, England: Cambridge University Press.

Duff, P. (1986). Another look at interlanguage talk: Taking task to task. In R. Day (Ed.), *Talking to learn: Conversation in second language acquisition*. Rowley, MA: Newbury House.

Duranti, A., & Goodwin, C. (1992). *Rethinking context: Language as an interactive phenomenon*. Cambridge, England: Cambridge University Press.

Edge, J. (1989). *Mistakes and correction*. London: Longman.

Edmondson, W. (1985). Discourse worlds in the classroom and in foreign language learning. *Studies in Second Language Acquisition*, *7*, 159–168.

Edwards, A., & Westgate, D. (1994). *Investigating classroom talk*. London: Falmer.

Egbert, M. (1996). Context-sensitivity in conversation: Eye gaze and the German repair initiator *bitte*? *Language in Society*, *25*, 587–612.

Egbert, M. (1998). Miscommunication in language proficiency interviews of first-year German students: A comparison with natural conversation. In R. Young & A. He (Eds.), *Talking and testing: Discourse approaches to the assessment of oral proficiency* (pp. 147–169). Amsterdam: Benjamins.

Egbert, M. (in press). Discrimination due to non-native speech production? In K. Richards and P. Seedhouse (Eds.), *Applying conversation analysis*. Basingstoke, England: Palgrave Macmillan.

Ellis, R. (1984). *Classroom second language development*. Oxford, England: Pergamon Press.

Ellis, R. (1992). *Second language acquisition and language pedagogy*. Clevedon, England: Multilingual Matters.

Ellis, R. (1994). *The study of second language acquisition*. Oxford, England: Oxford University Press.

Ellis, R. (2001). Investigating form-focused instruction. In R. Ellis (Ed.), *Form focused instruction and second language learning* (pp. 1–46). Malden, MA: Blackwell.

Ellis, R. (2003). *Task-based language learning and teaching.* Oxford, England: Oxford University Press.

Ellis, R., Basturkmen, H., & Loewen, S. (2001). Learner uptake in communicative ESL lessons. *Language Learning, 51*(2), 281–318.

Ellis, R., Basturkmen, H., & Loewen, S. (2002). Doing focus-on-form. *System, 30*(4), 419–432.

Firth, A. (1996). The discursive accomplishment of normality: On "lingua franca" English and conversation analysis. *Journal of Pragmatics, 26,* 237–259.

Firth, A., & Wagner, J. (1997). On discourse, communication, and (some) fundamental concepts in SLA research. *Modern Language Journal, 81,* 285–300.

Firth, A., & Wagner, J. (1998). SLA property: No trespassing! *Modern Language Journal, 82,* 91–94.

Ford, C. (1993). *Grammar in interaction.* Cambridge, England: Cambridge University Press.

Ford, C., Fox, B., & Thompson, S. (2002). Constituency and the grammar of turn increments. In C. Ford, B. Fox, & S. Thompson (Eds.), *The language of turn and sequence* (pp. 14–38). Oxford, England: Oxford University Press.

Ford, C., & Thompson, S. (1996). Interactional units in conversation: Syntactic, intonational and pragmatic resources for the management of turns. In A. Ochs, E. A. Schegloff, & S. A. Thompson (Eds.), *Interaction and grammar* (pp. 134–184). Cambridge, England: Cambridge University Press.

Foster, P. (1998). A classroom perspective on the negotiation of meaning. *Applied Linguistics, 19,* 1–23.

Froehlich, M., Spada, N., & Allen, P. (1985). Differences in the communicative orientation of L2 classrooms. *TESOL Quarterly, 19,* 27–57.

Gafaranga, J. (2000). Medium repair vs. other-language repair: Telling the medium of a bilingual conversation. *International Journal of Bilingualism, 4*(3), 327–350.

Gafaranga, J. (2001). Linguistic identities in talk-in-interaction: Order in bilingual conversation. *Journal of Pragmatics, 33,* 1901–1925.

Gafaranga, J., & Britten, N. (in press). Talking a general practice consultation into being. In K. Richards and P. Seedhouse (Eds.), *Applying conversation analysis.* Basingstoke, England: Palgrave Macmillan.

Gafaranga, J., & Torras, M. C. (2001). Language versus medium in the study of bilingual conversation. *International Journal of Bilingualism, 5*(2), 195–219.

Gafaranga, J., & Torras, M. C. (2002). Interactional otherness: Towards a redefinition of code-switching. *International Journal of Bilingualism*, 6(1), 1–22.

Gardner, R., & Wagner, J. (Eds.). (2004). *Second language talk*. London: Continuum.

Garfinkel, H. (1967). *Studies in ethnomethodology*. Englewood Cliffs, NJ: Prentice Hall.

Gass, S. M. (1998). Apples and oranges: Or, why apples are not oranges and don't need to be. A response to Firth and Wagner. *Modern Language Journal*, 82, 83–90.

Golato, A. (2000). *Und ich so / und er so*: An innovative German quotative for reporting on embodied actions. *Journal of Pragmatics*, 32(1), 29–54.

Goodwin, C. (1996). Transparent vision. In A. Ochs, E. A. Schegloff, & S. A. Thompson (Eds.), *Interaction and grammar* (pp. 370–404). Cambridge, England: Cambridge University Press.

Goodwin, C. (Ed.). (2003). *Conversation and brain damage*. New York: Oxford University Press.

Goodwin, C., Goodwin, M. H., & Olsher, D. (2002). Producing sense with nonsense syllables: Turn and sequence in conversations with a man with severe aphasia. In C. Ford, B. Fox, & S. Thompson (Eds.), *The language of turn and sequence* (pp. 56–80). Oxford, England: Oxford University Press.

Graddol, D., Leith, D., & Swann, J. (1996). *English history, diversity and change*. London: Routledge.

Green, J., & Wallat, C. (1981). Mapping instructional conversations—A sociolinguistic ethnography. In J. Green & C. Wallat (Eds.), *Ethnography and language in educational settings* (pp. 161–252). Norwood, NJ: Ablex.

Gribbin, J. (1991). *In search of Schroedinger's cat: Quantum physics and reality*. London: Black Swan.

Grice, H. P. (1975). Logic and conversation. In P. Cole and J. L. Morgan (Eds.), *Syntax and semantics 3: Speech acts* (pp. 41–58). New York: Academic Press.

Gumperz, J., & Hymes, D. (Eds.). (1986). *Directions in sociolinguistics: The ethnography of communication*. Malden, MA: Blackwell.

Guthrie, E. (1984). Six cases in classroom communication: A study of teacher discourse in the foreign language classroom. In J. Lantolf & A. Labarca (Eds.), *Research in second language learning: Focus on the classroom* (pp. 178–194). Norwood: Ablex.

Hall, J. K., & Verplaetse, L. S. (Eds.). (2000). *Second and foreign language learning through classroom interaction*. Mahwah, NJ: Erlbaum.

Halliday, M. A. K. (1985). *An introduction to functional grammar*. London: Arnold.

Harmer, J. (1983). *The practice of English language teaching*. Harlow, England: Longman.

Harris, M., & Coltheart, M. (1986). *Language processing in children and adults*. London: Routledge and Kegan Paul.

Hasan, A. S. (1988). *Variation in spoken discourse in and beyond the English foreign language classroom: A comparative study*. Unpublished doctoral dissertation, University of Aston, Aston, England.

Hayashi, M. (1999). Where grammar and interaction meet: A study of co-participant completion in Japanese conversation. *Human Studies, 22,* 475–499.

Hayashi, M., Mori, J., & Takagi, T. (2002). Contingent achievement of co-tellership in a Japanese conversation: An analysis of talk, gaze and gesture. In C. Ford, B. Fox, & S. Thompson (Eds.), *The language of turn and sequence* (pp. 81–122). Oxford, England: Oxford University Press.

He, A. (1998). Answering questions in language proficiency interviews: A case study. In R. Young & A. He (Eds.), *Talking and testing: Discourse approaches to the assessment of oral proficiency* (pp. 101–115). Amsterdam: Benjamins.

Heritage, J. (1984a). A change-of-state token and aspects of its sequential placement. In J. M. Atkinson & J. Heritage (Eds.), *Structures of social action* (pp. 299–345). Cambridge, England: Cambridge University Press.

Heritage, J. (1984b). *Garfinkel and ethnomethodology*. Cambridge, England: Polity Press.

Heritage, J. (1988). Explanations as accounts: A conversation analytic perspective. In C. Antaki (Ed.), *Analyzing everyday explanation: A casebook of methods* (pp. 127–144). London: Sage.

Heritage, J. (1995). Conversation analysis: Methodological aspects. In U. M. Quasthoff (Ed.), *Aspects of oral communication* (pp. 391–418). Berlin: De Gruyter.

Heritage, J. (1997). Conversation analysis and institutional talk: Analysing data. In D. Silverman (Ed.), *Qualitative research: Theory, method and practice* (pp. 161–182). London: Sage.

Heritage, J. (1999). Conversation analysis at century's end: Practices of talk-in-interaction, their distributions and their outcomes. *Research on Language and Social Interaction, 31,* 69–76.

Heritage, J., & Maynard, D. W. (in press). *Practicing medicine: Talk and action in primary care encounters*. Cambridge, England: Cambridge University Press.

Heritage, J., & Roth, A. L. (1995). Grammar and institution: Questions and questioning in the broadcast news interview. *Research on Language and Social Interaction, 28*(1), 1–60.

Hester, S., & Francis, D. (2001). Is institutional talk a phenomenon? Reflections on ethnomethodology and applied conversation analysis. In A. McHoul & M. Rapley (Eds.), *How to analyse talk in institutional settings: A casebook of methods* (pp. 206–217). London: Continuum.

Hopper, P., & Chen, C.-H. (1996). Languages, cultures, relationships: Telephone openings in Taiwan. *Research on Language and Social Interaction*, *29*(4), 291–313.

Hosoda, Y. (2000). Other-repair in Japanese conversations between non-native and native speakers. *Issues in Applied Linguistics*, *11*(1), 39–65.

Howe, J. (2000, August 15). *On the ropes* [Radio broadcast]. London: British Broadcasting Corporation.

Hutchby, I., & Wooffitt, R. (1998). *Conversation analysis*. Cambridge, England: Polity Press.

Hymes, D. (1972). Introduction. In C. Cazden, V. P. John, & D. Hymes (Eds.), *Functions of language in the classroom* (pp. xi–lvii). New York: Teachers College Press.

Jacoby, S. (1998a). How can ESP practitioners tap into situated discourse research: And why should we? (Part 1). *English for Specific Purposes News*, *7*(1), 1–10.

Jacoby, S. (1998b). How can ESP practitioners tap into situated discourse research: And why should we? (Part 2). *English for Specific Purposes News*, *7*(2), 4–10.

Jefferson, G. (1987). On exposed and embedded correction in conversation. In G. Button and J. Lee (Eds.), *Talk and social organisation* (pp. 86–100). Clevedon, England: Multilingual Matters.

Johnson, K. (1995). *Understanding communication in second language classrooms*. Cambridge, England: Cambridge University Press.

Jung, E. H. (1999). The organisation of second language classroom repair. *Issues in Applied Linguistics*, *10*(2), 153–171.

Kasper, G. (1986). Repair in foreign language teaching. In G. Kasper (Ed.), *Learning, teaching and communication in the language classroom* (pp. 23–42). Aarhus, Denmark: Aarhus University Press.

Kasper, G. (1997). "A" stands for acquisition: A response to Firth and Wagner. *Modern Language Journal*, *81*, 307–312.

Kasper, G. (2002, March). *Conversation analysis as an approach to second language acquisition: Old wine in new bottles?* Paper presented as part of the Second Language Acquisition and Teacher Education (SLATE) speaker series, University of Illinois at Urbana-Champaign.

Kasper, G., & Ross, S. (2001, May). "Is drinking a hobby, I wonder": Other-initiated repair in language proficiency interviews. Paper presented at American Association for Applied Linguistics (AAAL) meeting, St. Louis, MO.

Kasper, G., & Ross, S. (2003). Repetition as a source of miscommunication in oral proficiency interviews. In J. House, G. Kasper, & S. Ross (Eds.), *Misunderstanding in social life* (pp. 82–106). Discourse approaches to problematic talk. Harlow, England: Longman/Pearson Education.

Kim, K. H. (1999). Other-initiated repair sequences in Korean conversation: Types and functions. *Discourse and Cognition*, *6*(2), 141–168.

Koshik, I. (2000). Conversation analytic research on institutional talk: Implications for TESOL teachers and researchers. *TESOL Research Interest Section Newsletter*, *7*(2), 8–11.

Koshik, I. (2002). Designedly incomplete utterances: A pedagogical practice for eliciting knowledge displays in error correction sequences. *Research on Language and Social Interaction*, *35*(3), 277–309.

Kramsch, C. (1981). *Discourse analysis and second language teaching.* Washington, DC: Center for Applied Linguistics.

Kramsch, C. (1985). Classroom interaction and discourse options. *Studies in Second Language Acquisition*, *7*, 169–183.

Kumaravadivelu, B. (1993). Maximizing learning potential in the communicative classroom. *ELT Journal*, *47*(5), 12–21.

Kurhila, S. (2001). Correction in talk between native and non-native speaker. *Journal of Pragmatics*, *33*, 1083–1110.

Kurhila, S. (in press). Different orientations to grammatical correctness. In K. Richards and P. Seedhouse (Eds.), *Applying conversation analysis.* Basingstoke, England: Palgrave Macmillan.

Lantolf, J. P. (Ed.). (2000). *Sociocultural theory and second language learning.* Oxford, England: Oxford University Press.

Larsen-Freeman, D. (2000). Second language acquisition and applied linguistics. *Annual Review of Applied Linguistics*, *20*, 165–181.

Lazaraton, A. (1997). Preference organization in oral proficiency interviews: The case of language ability assessments. *Research on Language and Social Interaction*, *30*(1), 53–72.

Legutke, M., & Thomas, H. (1991). *Process and experience in the language classroom.* Harlow, England: Longman.

Lepper, G. (2000). *Categories in text and talk.* London: Sage.

Lerner, G. H. (2002). Turn-sharing: The choral co-production of talk in interaction. In C. E. Ford, B. A. Fox, & S. A. Thompson (Eds.), *The language of turn and sequence* (pp. 225–256). Oxford, England: Oxford University Press.

Levinson, S. (1983). *Pragmatics.* Cambridge, England: Cambridge University Press.

Levinson, S. (1992). Activity types and language. In P. Drew & J. Heritage (Eds.), *Talk at work: Interaction in institutional settings* (pp. 66–100). Cambridge, England: Cambridge University Press.

Lightbown, P., & Spada, N. (1993). *How languages are learned.* Oxford, England: Oxford University Press.

Lindstrom, A. B. (1994). Identification and recognition in Swedish telephone conversation openings. *Language in Society, 23*(2), 231–52.

Long, M. (1983). Inside the "black box." In H. Seliger & M. Long (Eds.), *Classroom oriented research in second language acquisition* (pp. 3–36). Rowley, MA: Newbury House.

Long, M. H. (1985). Input and second language acquisition theory. In S. Gass & C. Madden (Eds.), *Input in second language acquisition* (pp. 377–393). Rowley, MA: Newbury House.

Long, M. H. (1996). The role of the linguistic environment in second language acquisition. In W. C. Ritchie & T. K. Bhatia (Eds.), *Handbook of second language acquisition* (pp. 414–468). New York: Academic Press.

Long, M. H. (1997). Construct validity in SLA research: A response to Firth and Wagner. *Modern Language Journal, 81,* 318–323.

Long, M. H., Inagaki, S., & Ortega, L. (1998). The role of implicit negative feedback in SLA: Models and recasts in Japanese and Spanish. *Modern Language Journal, 82*(3), 357–371.

Long, M. H., & Robinson, P. (1998). Focus on form: Theory, research and practice. In C. Doughty & J. Williams (Eds.), *Focus on form in classroom second language acquisition* (pp. 114–138). Cambridge, England: Cambridge University Press.

Long, M. H., & Sato, C. (1983). Classroom foreigner talk discourse: Forms and functions of teachers' questions. In H. W. Seliger & M. H. Long (Eds.), *Classroom oriented research in second language acquisition* (pp. 268–285). Rowley, MA: Newbury House.

Lubelska, D., & Matthews, M. (1997). *Looking at language classrooms.* Cambridge, England: Cambridge University Press.

Lynch, M. (2000). The ethnomethodological foundations of conversation analysis. *Text, 20*(4), 517–532.

Lynch, T. (1989). Researching teachers: Behaviour and belief. In C. Brumfit & R. Mitchell (Eds.), *Research in the language classroom* (pp. 117–127). London: Modern English Publications and the British Council.

Maclure, M., & French, P. (1981). A comparison of talk at home and at school. In G. Wells (Ed.), *Learning through interaction* (pp. 205–239). Cambridge, England: Cambridge University Press.

Malamah-Thomas, A. (1987). *Classroom interaction.* Oxford, England: Oxford University Press.

Markee, N. (1995). Teachers' answers to students' questions: Problematizing the issue of making meaning. *Issues in Applied Linguistics, 6,* 63–92.

Markee, N. (2000). *Conversation analysis.* Mahwah, NJ: Erlbaum.

Markee, N. (2002, April). A conversation analytic perspective on quantification and generalizability in applied linguistics and SLA. Paper presented to the plenary panel at the American Association for Applied Linguistics meeting, Salt Lake City, UT.

Markee, N. (in press). The organization of off-task classroom talk in second language classrooms. In K. Richards and P. Seedhouse (Eds.), *Applying conversation analysis*. Basingstoke, England: Palgrave Macmillan.

Mathers, J. (1990). *An investigation into feedback in an L2 classroom*. Unpublished master's thesis, Canterbury Christ Church College, Canterbury, England.

Mazeland, M., & Zaman-Zadeh, M. (2004). The logic of clarification: Some observations about word-clarification repairs in Finnish-as-a-lingua-franca interactions. In R. Gardner & J. Wagner (Eds.), *Second language talk* (pp. 208–246). London: Continuum.

McCarthy, M. (1991). *Discourse analysis for language teachers*. Cambridge, England: Cambridge University Press.

McHoul, A. (1978). The organization of turns at formal talk in the classroom. *Language in Society, 7,* 183–213.

McHoul, A. (1990). The organization of repair in classroom talk. *Language in Society, 19,* 349–377.

McHoul, A., & Rapley, M. (Eds.). (2001). *How to analyse talk in institutional settings: A casebook of methods*. London: Continuum.

Mehan, H. (1979). *Learning lessons: Social organization in the classroom*. Cambridge, MA: Harvard University Press.

Mitchell, R. (1986). *An investigation into the communicative potential of teachers' target language use in the foreign language classroom*. Unpublished doctoral dissertation. University of Stirling, Stirling, England.

Moerman, M. (1988). *Talking culture: Ethnography and conversational analysis*. Philadelphia: University of Pennsylvania Press.

Moerman, M. (1996). The field of analyzing foreign language conversations. *Journal of Pragmatics, 26,* 147–158.

Mondada, L. (2004). Ways of "doing being plurilingual" in international work meetings. In R. Gardner & J. Wagner (Eds.), *Second language talk* (pp. 27–60). London: Continuum.

Mori, J. (2002). Task design, plan and development of talk-in-interaction: An analysis of a small group activity in a Japanese language classroom. *Applied Linguistics, 23*(3), 323–347.

Moskowitz, G. (1976). The classroom interaction of outstanding language teachers. *Foreign Language Annals, 9*(2), 135–157.

Nicholas, H., Lightbown, P. M., & Spada, N. (2001). Recasts as feedback to language learners. *Language Learning, 51,* 719–758.

Nunan, D. (1987). Communicative language teaching: Making it work. *ELT Journal, 41*(2), 136–145.

Nunan, D. (1988). *The learner-centred curriculum*. Cambridge, England: Cambridge University Press.

Nunan, D. (1989). *Understanding language classrooms*. Hemel Hempstead, England: Prentice Hall.

Nunan, D. (1993). Communicative tasks and the language curriculum. In S. Silberstein (Ed.), *State of the art TESOL essays* (pp. 59–68). Alexandria, VA: TESOL.

Nunan, D. (1994). The role of the learner in the learning process. In D. Baker (Ed.), IATEFL Annual Conference Report (pp. 8–11). Whitstable, England: International Association of Teachers of English as a Foreign Language.

Ochs, A., Schegloff, E. A., & Thompson, S. A. (Eds.). (1996). *Interaction and grammar*. Cambridge, England: Cambridge University Press.

Ohta, A. S. (2000). Rethinking interaction in SLA: Developmentally appropriate assistance in the zone of proximal development and the acquisition of grammar. In J. P. Lantolf (Ed.), *Sociocultural theory and second language learning* (pp. 51–78). Oxford, England: Oxford University Press.

Ohta, A. S. (2001). *Second language acquisition processes in the classroom: Learning Japanese*. Mahwah, NJ: Erlbaum.

Olsher, D. (2004). Talk and gesture: The embodied completion of sequential actions in spoken interaction. In R. Gardner & J. Wagner (Eds.), *Second language talk* (pp. 346–380). London: Continuum.

Packett, A. (in press). Teaching patterns of interaction in English for Specific Purposes. In K. Richards and P. Seedhouse (Eds.), *Applying conversation analysis*. Basingstoke, England: Palgrave Macmillan.

Painter, C. (1989). *Learning the mother tongue*. Oxford, England: Oxford University Press.

Park, Y. Y. (1999). The Korean connective *nuntey* in conversational discourse. *Journal of Pragmatics, 31*, 191–218.

Parsons, T. (1937). *The structure of social action*. New York: McGraw-Hill.

Peccei, C. (1994). *Child language*. London: Routledge.

Peräkylä, A. (1995). *AIDS counselling: Institutional interaction and clinical practice*. Cambridge, England: Cambridge University Press.

Peräkylä, A. (1997). Reliability and validity in research based on transcripts. In D. Silverman (Ed.), *Qualitative research: Theory, method and practice* (pp. 201–220). London: Sage.

Pica, T., & Doughty, C. (1988). Variations in classroom interaction as a function of participation pattern and task. In J. Fine (Ed.), *Second language discourse: A textbook of current research* (pp. 41–56). Norwood, NJ: Ablex.

Pica, T., & Long, M. (1986). The linguistic and conversational performance of experienced and inexperienced teachers. In R. Day (Ed.), *Talking to learn: Conversation in second language acquisition* (pp. 85–98). Rowley, MA: Newbury House.

Pike, K. (1967). *Language in relation to a unified theory of the structure of human behaviour*. The Hague, Netherlands: Mouton.

Pomerantz, A. (1984). Pursuing a response. In J. M. Atkinson & J. Heritage (Eds.), *Structures of social action* (pp. 152–163). Cambridge, England: Cambridge University Press.

Prabhu, N. S. (1987). *Second-language pedagogy*. Oxford, England: Oxford University Press.

Psathas, G. (1995). *Conversation analysis*. London: Sage.

Richards, K. (1996). *Opening the staffroom door: Aspects of collaborative interaction in a small language school*. Unpublished doctoral dissertation, University of Aston, Aston, England.

Richards, K. (in press). Introduction. In K. Richards and P. Seedhouse (Eds.), *Applying conversation analysis*. Basingstoke, England: Palgrave Macmillan.

Richards, K., & Seedhouse, P. (Eds.). (in press). *Applying conversation analysis*. Basingstoke, England: Palgrave Macmillan.

Riley, P. (Ed.). (1985). *Discourse and learning*. London: Longman.

Roberts, C. (2001). Language acquisition or language socialisation in and through discourse? Towards a redefinition of the domain of SLA. In C. Candlin & N. Mercer (Eds.), *English language teaching in its social context* (pp. 108–121). London: Routledge.

Sacks, H. (1992). *Lectures on conversation* (Vols. 1–2). Malden, MA: Blackwell.

Sacks, H., Schegloff, E., & Jefferson, G. (1974). A simplest systematics for the organisation of turn-taking in conversation. *Language, 50,* 696–735.

Sarangi, S., & Roberts, C. (Eds.). (1999). *Talk, work and institutional order*. Berlin: De Gruyter.

Saville-Troike, M. (1989). *The ethnography of communication: An introduction* (2nd ed.). Malden, MA: Blackwell.

Schegloff, E. A. (1968). Sequencing in conversational openings. *American Anthropologist, 70,* 1075–1095.

Schegloff, E. A. (1979). The relevance of repair in syntax-for-conversation. In T. Givon (Ed.), *Syntax and semantics 12: Discourse and syntax* (pp. 261–286). New York: Academic Press.

Schegloff, E. A. (1987). Between micro and macro: Contexts and other connections. In J. Alexander (Ed.), *The micro-macro link* (pp. 207–234). Berkeley and Los Angeles: University of California Press.

Schegloff, E. A. (1991). Conversation analysis and socially shared cognition. In L. Resnick, J. Levine, & S. Teasley (Eds.), *Perspectives on socially shared cognition* (pp. 150–171). Washington, DC: American Psychological Association.

Schegloff, E. A. (1992). In another context. In A. Duranti & C. Goodwin (Eds.), *Rethinking context: Language as an interactive phenomenon* (pp. 191–228). Cambridge, England: Cambridge University Press.

Schegloff, E. A. (1993). Reflections on quantification in the study of conversation. *Research on Language and Social Interaction, 26*(1), 99–128.

Schegloff, E. A. (1996). Turn organization: One intersection of grammar and interaction. In A. Ochs, E. A. Schegloff, & S. A. Thompson (Eds.), *Interaction and grammar* (pp. 52–133). Cambridge, England: Cambridge University Press.

Schegloff, E. A. (2000a). Overlapping talk and the organization of turn-taking for conversation. *Language in Society, 29*, 1–63.

Schegloff, E. A. (2000b). When "others" initiate repair. *Applied Linguistics, 21*, 205–243.

Schegloff, E. A., Jefferson, G., & Sacks, H. (1977). The preference for self-correction in the organization of repair in conversation. *Language, 53*, 361–382.

Schegloff, E. A., Koshik, I., Jacoby, S., & Olsher, D. (2002). Conversation analysis and applied linguistics. *Annual Review of Applied Linguistics, 22*, 3–31.

Schegloff, E. A., & Sacks, H. (1973). Opening up closings. *Semiotica, 7*, 289–327.

Sebba, M., & Wootton, T. (1998). We, they and identity: Sequential versus identity-related explanation in code-switching. In P. Auer (Ed.), *Code-switching in conversation* (pp. 262–286). London: Routledge.

Seedhouse, P. (1994). Linking pedagogical purposes to linguistic patterns of interaction: The analysis of communication in the language classroom. *International Review of Applied Linguistics, 32*(4), 303–320.

Seedhouse, P. (1995). L2 classroom transcripts: Data in search of a methodology? TESL-EJ, *1*(4), 1–37.

Seedhouse, P. (1996). *Learning talk: A study of the interactional organisation of the L2 classroom from a CA institutional discourse perspective.* Unpublished doctoral dissertation, University of York, York, England.

Seedhouse, P. (1997a). The case of the missing "no": The relationship between pedagogy and interaction. *Language Learning, 47*(3), 547–583.

Seedhouse, P. (1997b). Combining form and meaning. *English Language Teaching Journal, 51*(4), 336–344.

Seedhouse, P. (1998a). CA and the analysis of foreign language interaction: A reply to Wagner. *Journal of Pragmatics, 30*, 85–102.

Seedhouse, P. (1998b). Portraying the complexity of L2 classroom inter-action. In W. Gewehr (Ed.), *Aspects of modern language teaching in Europe* (pp. 108–120). London: Routledge.

Seedhouse, P. (1999a). The relationship between context and the organisation of repair in the L2 classroom. *International Review of Applied Linguistics, 37*(1), 59–80.

Seedhouse, P. (1999b). Task-based interaction. *English Language Teaching Journal, 53*(3), 149–156.

Silverman, D. (1999). Warriors or collaborators: Reworking methodological controversies in the study of institutional interaction. In C. Roberts & S. Sarangi (Eds.), *Talk, work and institutional order* (pp. 401–425). Berlin: De Gruyter.

Sinclair, J., & Coulthard, R. M. (1975). *Toward an analysis of discourse.* Oxford, England: Oxford University Press.

Sorjonen, M. (1996). On repeats and responses in Finnish conversations. In A. Ochs, E. A. Schegloff, & S. A. Thompson (Eds.), *Interaction and grammar* (pp. 277–327). Cambridge, England: Cambridge University Press.

Stroud, C. (1998). Perspectives on cultural variability of discourse and some implications for code-switching. In P. Auer (Ed.), *Code-switching in conversation* (pp. 321–348). London: Routledge.

Sullivan, P. (2000). Spoken artistry: Performance in a foreign language classroom. In J. K. Hall & L. S. Verplaetse (Eds.), *Second and foreign language learning through classroom interaction* (pp. 73–90). Mahwah, NJ: Erlbaum.

Tanaka, H. (1999). *Turn-taking in Japanese conversation: A study in grammar and interaction.* Amsterdam: Benjamins.

Ten Have, P. (1999). *Doing conversation analysis: A practical guide.* London: Sage.

Ten Have, P. (2001). Applied conversation analysis. In A. McHoul & M. Rapley (Eds.), *How to analyse talk in institutional settings: A casebook of methods* (pp. 3–11). London: Continuum.

Torras, M. C. (2002). *Language choice, social identity and the order of service talk-in-interaction: A study of trilingual service encounters in Barcelona.* Unpublished doctoral dissertation, Lancaster University, Lancaster, England.

Torras, M. C. (in press). Social identity and language choice in bilingual service talk. In K. Richards and P. Seedhouse (Eds.), *Applying conversation analysis.* Basingstoke, England: Palgrave Macmillan.

Torras, M. C., & Gafaranga, J. (2002). Social identities and language alternation in non-formal institutional bilingual talk: Trilingual service encounters in Barcelona. *Language in Society, 31*(4), 527–548.

Tsui, A. (1987). An analysis of different types of interaction in ESL classroom discourse. *International Review of Applied Linguistics, 25*(4), 336–353.

Tsui, A. (1995). *Introducing classroom interaction*. London: Penguin.

Ullman, R., & Geva, R. (1984). Approaches to observation in second language classes. In C. Brumfit (Ed.), *Language issues and education policies* (pp. 113–128). Oxford: Pergamon.

Üstünel, E. (2003). Code-switching between English and Turkish: Data from ELT classrooms. Unpublished manuscript, University of Newcastle upon Tyne, Newcastle upon Tyne, England.

Van Lier, L. (1982). *Analyzing interaction in second language classrooms*. Unpublished doctoral dissertation, University of Lancaster, Lancaster, England.

Van Lier, L. (1988a). *The classroom and the language learner*. New York: Longman.

Van Lier, L. (1988b). What's wrong with classroom talk? *Prospect, 3*(3), 267–283.

Van Lier, L. (2000). From input to affordance: Social-interactive learning from an ecological perspective. In J. Lantolf (Ed.), *Sociocultural theory and second language learning* (pp. 245–260). Oxford, England: Oxford University Press.

Vinkhuyzen, E., & Szymanski, M. (in press). The grammar of service requests and their responses. In K. Richards and P. Seedhouse (Eds.), *Applying conversation analysis*. Basingstoke, England: Palgrave Macmillan.

Wagner, J. (1996). Foreign language acquisition through interaction—A critical review of research on conversational adjustments. *Journal of Pragmatics, 26*, 215–236.

Warren, M. (1985). *Discourse analysis and English language teaching*. Unpublished master's thesis, University of Birmingham, Birmingham, England.

Warren, M. (1993). *Towards a description of the features of naturalness in conversation*. Unpublished doctoral dissertation, University of Birmingham, Birmingham, England.

Wei, L. (2002). "What do you want me to say?" On the conversation analysis approach to bilingual interaction. *Language in Society, 31*, 159–180.

Westgate, D., Batey, J., Brownlee, J., & Butler, M. (1985). Some characteristics of interaction in foreign language classrooms. *British Educational Research Journal, 11*, 271–281.

Willis, D. (1990). *The lexical syllabus*. London: Collins.

Willis, J. (1987). *Spoken discourse in the ELT classroom*. Unpublished master's thesis, University of Birmingham, Birmingham, England.

Willis, J. (1992). Inner and outer: Spoken discourse in the language class-room. In M. Coulthard (Ed.), *Advances in spoken discourse analysis* (pp. 161–182). London: Routledge.

Wong, J. (2000a). Delayed next turn repair initiation in native/nonnative speaker English conversation. *Applied Linguistics, 21*, 244–267.

Wong, J. (2000b). The token "yeah" in nonnative speaker English conversation. *Research on Language and Social Interaction, 33*(1), 39–67.

Wong, J. (2002). "Applying" conversation analysis in applied linguistics: Evaluating English as a second language textbook dialogue. *International Review of Applied Linguistics, 40*(1), 37–60.

Wong, J. (in press). Sidestepping grammar. In K. Richards and P. Seedhouse (Eds.), *Applying conversation analysis*. Basingstoke, England: Palgrave Macmillan.

Wong, J., & Olsher, D. (2000). Reflections on conversation analysis and nonnative speaker talk: An interview with Emanuel A. Schegloff. *Issues in Applied Linguistics, 11*(1), 111–128.

Wong-Fillmore, L. (1985). When does teacher talk work as input? In S. Gass & C. Madden (Eds.), *Input in second language acquisition* (pp. 17–50). Rowley, MA: Newbury House.

Woolley, R. (2002, July). Second language classroom conversation and membership categorisations. Paper presented at the British Association for Applied Linguistics (BAAL)/Cambridge University Press (CUP) seminar "Conversation Analysis and Applied Linguistics," University of Newcastle upon Tyne, Newcastle upon Tyne, England.

Wright, T. (1987). Instructional task and discoursal outcome in the L2 classroom. In C. Candlin & D. Murphy (Eds.), *Language learning tasks* (pp. 47–68). Englewood Cliffs, NJ: Prentice Hall.

Yazigi, R. (2001). *A study of sharing time in an L2 second grade classroom.* Unpublished master's thesis, University of Newcastle upon Tyne, Newcastle upon Tyne, England.

Young, R. F., & He, A. (Eds.). (1998). *Talking and testing: Discourse approaches to the assessment of oral proficiency.* Amsterdam: Benjamins.

Young, R. F. (2002). Discourse approaches to oral language assessment. *Annual Review of Applied Linguistics, 22*, 243–262.

INDEX

n after page reference denotes
  endnote

A

Accountability, 10–11, 257
Accuracy, 102–104. *See also*
  Form-and-accuracy context
Action sequences, 40, 41, 44
  adjacency pairs and, 18, 20–21
  intersubjectivity in, 13
  mutual reinforcing, 18
Action templates (norms), 10
Actual pedagogy, 93
Adjacency pairs, 17–22, 40, 51,
  109
  context-free, 45
  intersubjectivity and, 21–22
  linguistic misunderstanding
  of, 22
  question-and-answer, 40, 94,
  170–171
  reflexivity and, 11
Affiliation, 9, 23, 37
Affiliative actions, 24, 26, 29
AL. *See* Applied linguistics
Applied CA, 137–138, 224–226
Applied linguistics (AL)
  conversation analysis and,
  2–3, 223, 224–236
  terms, 138
Asymmetry, in institutional
  discourse, 96, 104–105

B

Background expectancies, 5, 11
Bias, 23

Bilingual and multilingual
  interaction, 233
Bottom-up analysis, 15, 43, 45
Breaching experiments,
  5–6, 7, 9

C

CA. *See* Conversation analysis
CA-for-SLA research agenda,
  252–253
Camouflage, 171
Carrier topic, 60, 62
Change of information state,
  117
Chinese, 44, 231
Choral coproduction, 49–50
Clarification requests, 120, 122,
  128, 157–158, 229
Code-switching, 233
Coding schemes, 57, 65
Cognition, socially distributed,
  240–241
COLT (Communicative
  Orientation of Language
  Teaching), 57
Communicative approach, to L2
  classroom interaction, 66–81
Communicative competence,
  229
Communicative Orientation of
  Language Teaching (COLT),
  57
Competence, communicative,
  229
Complementarity, 208–209
Complex personality,
  208–209

291